C Street

C Street

The Fundamentalist Threat to American Democracy

Jeff Sharlet

LITTLE, BROWN AND COMPANY
NEW YORK BOSTON LONDON

Little, Brown and Company
Hachette Book Group
237 Park Avenue, New York, NY 10017
www.hachettebookgroup.com

First Edition: September 2010

Little, Brown and Company is a division of Hachette Book Group, Inc. The Little, Brown name and logo are trademarks of Hachette Book Group, Inc.

Library of Congress Cataloging-in-Publication Data
Sharlet, Jeff.
   C Street : the fundamentalist threat to American democracy / Jeff Sharlet.—
1st ed.
       p. cm.
   Includes bibliographical references and index.
   ISBN 978-0-316-09107-7 (hc) / 978-0-316-12056-2 (large print)
   1. Fundamentalism—Political aspects—United States.   2. Fellowship Foundation (Washington, D.C.).   3. C Street Center (Washington, D.C.).   I. Title.
   BR526.S52 2010
   322'.10973—dc22   2010028476

10 9 8 7 6 5 4 3 2 1

RRD-IN

Printed in the United States of America

*For Robert Sharlet and
Roxana Ruth*

Contents

C Street

1

THE CONFESSIONS

*"As much as I did talk about going to the Appalachian Trail…
that isn't where I ended up."*
— *South Carolina governor Mark Sanford, at the
June 24, 2009, press conference at which
he confessed to cheating on his wife.*

———————

IN 2008 I published a book called *The Family,* which took as its
main subject a religious movement known to some as the Fellowship and to others as the Family and to most only through
one of the many nonprofit entities created to express the
movement's peculiar approach to religion, politics, and power.
One of these entities is the C Street Center Inc., in Washington, DC, or, simply, C Street, made infamous in the summer of
2009 by the actions of three Family associates: a senator, a

governor, and a congressman, each with his own special C Street connection.

The senator lived there; the governor sought answers there; and the congressman's wife says he rendezvoused with his mistress in his bedroom at the three-story redbrick town house on Capitol Hill, maintained by the Family for a singular goal, in the words of one Family leader: to "assist [congressmen] in better understandings of the teachings of Christ, and applying it to their jobs."

Among the men thus assisted by the Family have been Sen. Tom Coburn and Sen. Jim Inhofe, Oklahoma Republicans racing each other to the far right of the political spectrum (Coburn has proposed the death penalty for abortion providers; Inhofe, who was a defender of the Abu Ghraib torturers, hosts regular foreign policy meetings at C Street); Sen. Jim DeMint of South Carolina, who insists that the Bible teaches we cannot serve both God and government; and Sen. Sam Brownback (R-KS), who says that through meetings of his Family "cell" of like-minded politicians he receives divine instruction on subjects as varied as sex, oil, and Islam. There's also Sen. John Thune (R-SD), Sen. Chuck Grassley (R-IA), and Sen. Mike Enzi (R-WY); Rep. Frank Wolf (R-VA), Rep. Zach Wamp (R-TN), and Rep. Joe Pitts (R-PA). And Democrats, too: among them are Sen. Bill Nelson of Florida; North Carolina's Ten Commandments crusader, Rep. Mike McIntyre; its newest Blue Dog, Rep. Heath Shuler; and Michigan's Rep. Bart Stupak. In 2009 Stupak joined with Rep. Pitts to hold health care reform hostage to what Family leaders, pledging their support for Pitts early in his career, called "God's leadership" in the long war against abortion.

Buried in the 592 boxes of documents dumped by the Family at the Billy Graham Center Archives in Wheaton, Illinois, are five decades' worth of correspondence between members equally illustrious in their day: segregationist Dixiecrats and Southern Republican converts Sen. Absalom Willis Robertson (Pat Robertson's father) and Sen. Strom Thurmond; a Yankee Klansman named Ralph Brewster and a blue-blooded fascist sympathizer named Merwin Hart; a parade of generals, oilmen, bankers, missile manufacturers; little big men of the provinces with fast food fortunes or chains of Piggly Wiggly supermarkets or gravel quarry empires. There was even the occasional liberal—Sen. Mark Hatfield, Republican of Oregon, and Sen. Harold Hughes, Democrat of Iowa—men of good faith and bad judgment who lent their names to the causes of the Family's "brothers" overseas, the Indonesian genocidaire Suharto (Hatfield), the Filipino strongman Ferdinand Marcos (Hughes).

"Christ ministered to a few and did not set out to minister to large throngs of people," says a supporter. The Family differs from more conventional fundamentalist groups in its preference for those whom it calls "key men" over the multitude. "We simply call ourselves the fellowship or a family of friends," declares a document titled "Eight Core Aspects of the vision and methods," distributed to members at the 2010 National Prayer Breakfast, the movement's only public event. One of the Eight Core Aspects is the movement's interpretation of Acts 9:15—"This man is my chosen instrument to take my name...before the Gentiles *and their kings*" (emphasis theirs). The Family's unorthodox reading of this verse is that it is an injunction to work not through public revivals but through private relationships with " 'the king' — or other leaders of our world—who hold enormous influence—for better or worse—over vast numbers of people." The Family sees itself as a ministry for the benefit of the poor, by way of the powerful. The best way to help the weak, it teaches, is to help the strong.

In 2008 and 2009, the Family did so by helping Sen. John Ensign (R-NV), Gov. Mark Sanford (R-SC), and former representative Chip Pickering (R-MS) cover up extramarital affairs, and in Ensign's case secret payments. Not to avoid embarrassment for the Family, an organization that until 2009 denied its own existence, but because the Family believes that its members are placed in power by God; that they are his "new chosen"; that the senator, the governor, and the congressman were "tools" with which to advance his kingdom, an ambition so worthy that beside it all personal failings pale.

On June 16, 2009, Sen. Ensign flew home to Las Vegas to confess his affair. Ensign, fourth-ranking Republican and a man with Iowa and Pennsylvania Avenue on his mind, had made a career of going against the grain of his hometown. He was a moral scold who'd promoted himself as a Promise Keeper—a member of the conservative men's ministry—and a family values man. He'd been a hound once, according to friends, but he'd come to Christ before he came to politics; for Ensign, the two passions were intertwined. He didn't just go to church, he lived in one, the Family's house at 133 C Street, SE, registered as a church for tax purposes.

I'd met Ensign there once, when I was writing an earlier

book on unusual religious communities around the country. I'd seen some strange things: a Pentecostal exorcism in North Carolina; a massive outdoor Pagan dance party in honor of "the Horned One" in rural Kansas; a "cowboy church" in Texas featuring a cross made of horseshoes and, in lieu of a picture of Jesus, a lovely portrait of a seriously horned Texas Longhorn steer.

But C Street was in its own category, simultaneously banal—a prayer meeting of congressmen in which they insisted on calling God "Coach"—and more unsettling than anything I'd witnessed. Doug Coe, the "first brother" of the Family since 1969, used to say that Jesus was not a sissy. That disdain for weakness infuses the movement's theology so completely, so naturally, that it comes across as almost amiable. "I've seen pictures of the young men in the Red Guard," he says in a videotaped sermon, a tall man in a rumpled suit, spreading out his hands like he's setting up a joke. "They would bring in this young man's mother...he would take an axe and cut her head off." Coe makes a chopping motion. That, he says, is dedication to a cause. But there's nothing grim about his presentation; he sounds like he's inviting you to join a team or a fund-raiser. And he is. "A covenant! A pledge!" he exclaims, setting up the punch line. "That's what Jesus said." Such is the C Street style, the most violent metaphors imaginable deployed as maxims for everyday living, from the prayer calendar on the wall that called on the house's congressional tenants to devote a portion of each morning to spiritual war (combat by prayer) against "demonic strongholds" such as Buddhism and Hinduism, to Coe's routine invocation of history's worst villains as models for the muscle he'd rather see applied on Christ's behalf. The first time I met Coe, he was in the midst of a spiritual mentoring session in which he cited "Hitler, Lenin, Ho Chi Minh [and] bin Laden" as models with which to understand the "total Jesus" worshipped by the Family. He sipped hot cocoa while he lectured.

Ensign seemed to fall on the banal end of that spectrum. He missed the prayer meeting, bouncing into the foyer in red jogging shorts and a white T-shirt that made his tan — the most impressive tan in the Technicolor portrait gallery of golf-happy, twenty-first-century political America — glow beneath his equally striking silver hair. Ensign's hair, prematurely gray, is his most senatorial feature; it possesses a gravitas all its own. The man beneath it, though, square-jawed and thick-browed, is something of a giggler. Jogging in place, grinning, bobbing his head back and forth, he boasted to a young female aide who'd been sent to fetch him about the time he'd clocked on his run. "That's great!" she said, then asked him what kind of time he could make showering and getting ready for work. Up popped Ensign's arched black brows: a challenge! "I'm all about setting records today!" he said.

And away he went. When I wrote *The Family*, I devoted only a sentence to him, describing him as a "conservative casino heir elected to the Senate from Nevada, a brightly tanned, hapless figure who uses his Family connections to graft holiness to his gambling-fortune name." After his press conference, a magazine editor, noting Ensign's Washington address and recalling my book, asked me if I wanted to write something about Ensign's apparent hypocrisy. I didn't. The senator's sins were his own.

Next up was Mark Sanford, the weather-beaten governor of South Carolina, *his* tan the result of days spent in the woods, hunting, or on his tractor, planting. He was famous for his frugality. As a congressman, he slept on a futon rolled out across his office rather than coughing up rent, and as governor he turned down $700 million in federal stimulus money because he feared it would lead to "a thing called slavery." In 1995, when Ensign and Sanford were at the vanguard of the right-wing revolution, Ensign quietly continued business as usual, collecting $450,000 from political action committees, more than any other freshman. Mark Sanford refused to take a dime. By 2009, even more than Ensign Sanford was being spoken of as presidential material for the GOP, fabric to be cut, folded, and sewn.

So, when on June 18, 2009, Sanford disappeared, some assumed it was for a good or maybe even a noble reason. For days, there were whispers about where the governor had gone — *gone* being the operative word, because nobody knew where the governor *was*. Not in the governor's mansion in Columbia, not in the airy beach house on Sullivan's Island he shared with his wife, Jenny Sanford, and their four boys, not at Coosaw, the semi-feral, falling-down plantation along the Combahee River that had originally brought the Sanford clan, Floridians, to South Carolina. Calls to his wife, the state's elegantly beautiful First Lady, a *gentlewoman,* in the antique parlance of the state's finest matrons, led reporters to believe the governor was *thinking,* working on a book about the meaning of conservatism. Calls to his staff led seekers to the woods: to the Appalachian Trail, to which the governor was said to have taken in contemplation.

Contemplation of what? Hopes rose, résumés rustled, ambitions flared, as Sanford's circle imagined the governor emerging from the wilderness as a new kind of contender. They didn't see the truth coming. "Mark Sanford literally likes to go his own way," gushed GOP consultant Mark McKinnon, whose clients have included George W. Bush and John McCain. "For this act alone, we're going to move Sanford up at least a notch on our Top 10 GOP contenders for 2012." In the days ahead he'd become a laughingstock: a symbol of all that is pathetic about politics, men, middle age, even romance itself at the tired end of a decade celebrated by no one. But before that, while he was still gone, so long as nobody knew where he was, when the governor for a moment occupied a space in the realm between the possibility of tragedy (was he silent because his broken body lay at the bottom of a gully?) and the transcendent (would he walk out of the woods with the wisdom of one who knows how to quiet the world's noise?), he was almost a folk hero. His supporters—the true believers who loved his Roman nose and his leathery skin and his wry smile, and the Washington slicks who would sell these features as the face of a modern-day Cincinnatus, a reluctant philosopher-king for the common man—asked themselves if this strange departure would herald his arrival. Would the governor return from the wilderness to announce a higher aspiration?

Yes, in a sense: love. On June 24, after a reporter for the *Columbia State* tracked him down in a Georgia airport and discovered he'd returned from Argentina, Sanford called a press conference at which he mused on his genuine affection for the Appalachian Trail, then pledged to "lay out that larger story"—the story of where he'd been the previous week. "Given the immediacy of y'all's wanting to visit," he said, he was forced to intrude private concerns into a public meeting. He began with apologies to Jenny and his four boys, "jewels and blessings," his staff, and an old friend— the memory of whose early support brought the governor close to tears. "I let them down by creating a fiction with regard to where I was going," he said. He had been on an "adventure trip," indeed, but not on the Appalachian Trail. He rubbed his forehead, his eyes glanced off into nowhere, his voice wobbled. "I'm here," he continued, still deferring any concrete explanation of why he actually was there, "because if you were to look at God's laws, they're in every instance designed to protect people from themselves." He warmed to the subject of religion, firmer ground, he knew, for the narrative of public confession. "The biggest self of self is indeed self."

The answer to that riddle was a woman. The "biggest self of self" for Sanford was love; he'd fallen into it, and he wanted us to forgive him.

To that point, I'd been interested only in the convoluted candor with which he was testifying. It was some good church, tension building, a parade of emotions not often on display in political life. I admired him for it. Then came the kicker. In answer to a question about how long his family had known (five months), Sanford paused, as if lost in recollection. Then: "I've been to a lot of—as part of what we called C Street when I was in Washington. It was a, believe it or not, a Christian Bible study—some folks who asked members of Congress hard questions that I think were very, very important. And I've been working with them."

Another spiritual adviser, Warren "Cubby" Culbertson, was at the press conference. Every month, Cubby and two seminary professors invited fifteen well-connected men for a meeting at a downtown office where Cubby, a wealthy entrepreneur, would train them in the use of "spiritual weaponry," with distinctly political implications. "Never underestimate the influence the ungodly have upon the godly," he warned. "The ungodly want to unlord the Lord, but they must first unlord the law." It was a ministry for men who had already achieved financial success and yet wanted more—meaning greater influence. The "up and out," as the Family calls such people. "The ostrich has wings," Cubby taught, "but cannot fly." By which he meant: "The almost saved are totally damned." No half measures. The men Cubby brought to God were instructed to become the "most holy," to "enter God's playing field," to take God's "litmus tests." Ask yourself: Do I keep my eye on "the enemies known as the world"? "The children of the devil are obvious," Cubby advised, citing 1 John 3:9; avoid them or become an "eternal inhabitant of Sodom."

At the press conference, you could almost see Sanford weighing his options, trying to hold on to his ambition, lamenting the loss of the woman he'd already described to Jenny as his "heart connection." Then he made his choice: C Street. "A spiritual giant," Sanford said of Cubby, who was looking on from the back of the room, and finally tears began to fall.

*   *   *

I was stunned. One of the first rules of C Street is that you don't talk about C Street. "We sort of don't talk to the press about the house," C Streeter Bart Stupak, a conservative Democrat, had told a reporter back in 2002. Another C Streeter, Zach Wamp, spoke out against transparency in the wake of the Ensign scandal. "The C Street residents have all agreed they won't talk about their private living arrangements, Wamp said, and he [Wamp] intends to honor that pact," reported the *Knoxville News-Sentinel*, after scandal forced the press to pay attention.

"I hate it that John Ensign lives in the house and this happened because it opens up all of these kinds of questions," Wamp told the paper. "I'm not going to be the guy who goes out and talks."

From the Family's point of view, C Street's code of secrecy is not a conspiracy but a matter of simple efficiency. "The more invisible you can make your organization," Doug Coe observes, "the more influence it will have." True enough; that's why we have lobbying and disclosure laws. It's also part of why we have the Fourth Estate, the press, to hold the powerful accountable. If the press can't comfort the afflicted, as the old saying goes—and even as a onetime employee of a freebie paper used primarily by homeless men for warmth in the winter, I doubt that it can—it may, on occasion, afflict the comfortable.

But most reporters have never shown much interest in C Street or the organization behind it. The exceptions are remarkable for the scrutiny that didn't follow. Not in 1952, when the *Washington Post* noticed that the Secretary of Defense had granted four senators the use of a military plane for international Family meetings; questions were raised, then dropped. No questions at all followed the *New Republic*'s 1965 report on the Family's only public event, the National Prayer Breakfast (then the Presidential Prayer Breakfast), an evangelical ritual of national devotion that politicians skipped at their peril. In 1975 *Playboy* published an exhaustively researched report on how the Family functioned as an off-the-books bank for its congressional members. Then, nothing.

Not even Watergate could goad the press into real action. The *New York Times* noted that President Ford had convened his old all-Republican congressional prayer group—organized by the Family—to consider Nixon's pardon, but asked no questions about what criteria it would use. *Time* did a little better, identifying Doug Coe as the top man of what it described as "almost an underground network," an "intricate web" of Christian activists in the capital, but left it at that. In December 1973, Dan Rather challenged his deputy press secretary to explain why Watergate conspirator Chuck Colson continued to make frequent visits to the White House he'd left in criminal disgrace. "Prayer," came the answer. "Now we all know the way Washington works," Rather replied. "People ingratiate themselves with people in positions of power, and at such things as, yes, a prayer breakfast, they do their business. Isn't someone around here worried at least about the symbolism of this?" Apparently not; the questions that followed were bemused. Nobody seriously wondered why the soon-to-be-convicted Watergate conspirator, a man who had allegedly proposed firebombing the Brookings

Institution, needed to worship in the White House. Not even a few years later, when Colson, never good at keeping his mouth shut, told the story of Doug Coe's collaboration with the CEO of Raytheon, manufacturer of missiles, to bring Colson into the Family fold. "A veritable underground of Christ's men all through government," as Colson called the network that would vouch for his parole after only six months in prison.

Coe himself boasted of what the press *couldn't* see, declaring that the single public event, the Prayer Breakfast, "is only one-tenth of one percent of the iceberg... [and] doesn't give the true picture of what is going on." Ronald Reagan almost dared someone to ask questions in 1985, announcing at the Prayer Breakfast that he wished he could say more about the sponsor of the elite gathering. "But it's working precisely because it's private." By the age of Reagan, much of the press had come to see that as a virtue. "Members of the media know," said Reagan, "but they have, with great understanding and dignity, generally kept it quiet. I've had my moments with the press, but I commend them this day, for the way they've worked to maintain the integrity of this movement." *Time,* for instance, ran a feature on the "Bible Beltway," rife with factual errors and seeming to almost celebrate "the semisecret involvement of so many high-powered names." There was Secretary of State James Baker and his wife, Susan; the Kemps; the Quayles; and a Democrat, Don Bonker of Washington, since departed from Congress to become a free trade lobbyist. The presence of Democrats as well as Republicans, the magazine proposed, proved there could be no politics involved.

The first serious report in decades came in 2002, when Lisa Getter, a Pulitzer Prize–winning reporter for the *Los Angeles Times,* published a major front-page exposé in which she revealed that the Family dispatched congressmen as missionaries to carry the Gospel to Muslim leaders around the world—and did so with a "vow of silence." The media response was—well, there was no response. Several months later, the Associated Press reported on C Street's subsidized housing for the anointed, describing the Family as "a secretive religious organization." Nobody followed up on that story, either. That spring, I published in *Harper's* magazine an account of a month I'd spent living with the Family in Virginia. I included a C Street vignette, a spiritual counseling session between Doug Coe and Rep. Todd Tiahrt, a Kansas Republican. Tiahrt came seeking wisdom on how Christians could win the population "race" with "the Muslim" and left contemplating Coe's advice to consider Christ through the historical lens of Hitler, Lenin, and Osama bin Laden. Like the other stories before it, mine was left to stand alone, giggled over and gossiped about by media colleagues but treated as a true tale of the quirks of the political class that demanded no further investigation.

Or, worse, it fell victim to the rule of *reductio ad Hitlerum,* the sensible Internet adage that holds that the first party in a debate to compare an opponent to Hitler loses. In 2004, a Democratic candidate for the northern Virginia congressional seat held by Republican Frank Wolf noted Wolf's association with Coe. Coe's Hitler talk wasn't limited to the example of power I'd witnessed him offering Rep. Tiahrt at C Street, although it has to be said, immediately and emphatically, that Coe is not a neo-Nazi. He uses Hitler, his defenders declare, as a metaphor. For what? For Jesus. The lion and the lamb are too abstract for Coe. He asks his followers to imagine pure power, as modeled by Hitler and other totalitarians; then, he instructs, imagine that power used for Christ, for good instead of evil.

When the Virginia Democratic candidate pointed to these unorthodox teachings, the *Washington Post* would have none of it, editorializing against this low blow and dispatching a reporter to prove it untrue for good measure. He did so by asking the aggrieved parties and their friends if the accusations were true; they assured him they were not. Case closed—until 2008, when NBC aired videotape given to me by an evangelical critic of the Family's "spiritual abuse," as he put it, depicting Coe rattling on to a group of evangelical leaders about the fellowship model offered by "Hitler, Goebbels, and Himmler." There was more: audio buried deep on the website of the Navigators, a fundamentalist ministry, of Coe going into greater detail on the depth of commitment he thought his disciples should learn from such men: "You say, hey, you know Jesus said, 'You got to put him before mother-father-brother-sister'? Hitler, Lenin, Mao, that's what they taught the kids. Mao even had the kids killing their own mother and father. But it wasn't murder. It was for building the new nation. The new kingdom."

None of this, not even the NBC News video, broke the story beyond a few isolated blips in the news cycle. There was no conspiracy of silence. Rather, all of these reports were lost in the black hole of conventional wisdom. A scoop, for most reporters, isn't actually a new story; it's a twist or a

new variation on a story people already think they understand, a story that reassures the reader that his or her cynicism is justified and yet contained within the known realm
of vice: stuffed in an envelope next to a wad of Ben Frank-
lins or tucked into bed beside a stripper. The parameters
for stories about religion in politics are even narrower: fundamentalism sells, but only if it's low-class, the purview of
sweaty Southern men in too-tight suits pounding pulpits
and thumping Bibles. C Street—a distinguished address, an
upscale clientele, an internationalist perspective—simply
did not register.

Until, that is, sex entered the story. Suddenly, the media
that had ignored C Street for years needed to know all
about it. Or, rather, not *all* about it, not its implications for
democracy and desire; interest was limited to the topic of
hypocrisy, publicly pious Republicans, and their secret lovers. Ensign's affair was at that early stage still mostly limited
to his two-minute press conference and a few grubby, isolated details: that his best friend's wife was the best friend of
Ensign's wife, for instance. Mark Sanford, on the other
hand, offered both sex and schadenfreude, an exotic mistress and love letters exposed, a wife, Jenny Sanford, who
refused to stand by her man, and a man who refused to stop
talking about his lover. And then there was C Street, the
mysterious address linked to both scandals.

I was the only reporter to have written from within its
walls, and suddenly that mattered in a way it hadn't before,
when I'd been bleating on about the Family's support for
murderous regimes in Haiti and Indonesia and Somalia,
machete militias and "kill lists" and rape rooms, all blessed

by the Family's faith and financed by its "leaders led by God" in Washington. Boring! Or, as one young radio producer put it, "What's a Somalia?"

But consensual sex between adults? That could be news. Only by dispensing with the dead, though—"Let's save Somalia for another time!" another producer suggested brightly— and kicking the heartbroken while they were down. That's what Sanford was. The man had fallen in love, and everybody has done stupid things for love, and most of us, at one point or another, have done something awful. That's not really news, it's an Aesop's fable. Evangelicals ritualize this truth with the declaration that we're all sinners; secular folk speak of psychology's contradictions. But such recognitions are reserved for private lives, and Mark Sanford's self-destruction was public spectacle, served up for our satisfaction.

Shortly after the governor's press conference, MSNBC's Rachel Maddow invited me on her evening show. I'd spoken to Maddow several times during her radio days, and I knew she was one of the smartest hosts in broadcast journalism. But I was conflicted about discussing Sanford. Sanford was done. The question that remained was, Do we gloat over his hypocrisy? Or do we welcome him into the human race—where the heart wants what it wants and that's not always a simple or good thing, even when it's a true thing?

I don't think I would have been able to do that in a five-minute television interview, which is why I thank God for the sad intervention of Michael Jackson. I imagine Mark Sanford said much the same thing on June 25, the day the

Sanford scandal started to crest, and also the day Michael
Jackson died. Suddenly, one southern governor's affair was
very small news.

I was buying a new pair of shoes when I heard. When I'd
received the invitation to be on the Maddow show, I was
wearing flip-flops. That seemed too casual for a TV studio,
and besides, I needed a new pair of shoes. I tried Shoe
Mania, in Manhattan's Union Square. The store was abuzz:
He's dead! Who? Michael Jackson! Michael Jackson is dead.
I was stunned. In my grief, I bought a pair of shoes Michael
might have liked, long, polished, and pointy, flashier than
any I'd ever owned.

I walked out onto Broadway, where drivers had opened
their windows and jacked up their radios, "Rock with You"
mingling with the honk and roar of the city at rush hour.
Some people didn't hear it, some didn't care, but sprinkled
up and down the avenue there was immediate mourning. I
saw an old woman crying and three middle-aged white men
with beer guts goofing the moonwalk and girls who hadn't
been born yet in the days of "Billie Jean" gliding backward
up Broadway, smooth as Michael's falsetto. Here was another
spectacle of self-destruction, but the public responded not
with vicious glee, as to a sex scandal, as to so many of Jackson's failings in the past, but with necessary delight; with
the remembrance of transcendence; with the late recognition of something that had been lost long before. Over the
radio and in the faltering and fluid dance steps of the
mourners thumped the beat of pop democracy, Walt Whit-
man you could dance to, songs that mattered more to how
we all imagined and dreamed ourselves than any of

Michael's scandals—much less those of a couple of Republican politicians bent on disowning their own desires. So why the hell was I going on TV to count the sins of the love-struck governor of South Carolina?

I wasn't. I was barely a block away from the shoe store when a call came from MSNBC. I'd been bumped. "Thank you, Michael Jackson," I thought. The King of Pop had saved my soul, prevented me from playing the part of a puritan, scolding Sanford for his confession when his real weakness was not his transgression—seedy, selfish, and human—but his retreat. He'd set out on the road to Damascus but had turned back too early. Instead of becoming an apostle of a love as free as his economic libertarianism, he'd fallen back on "God's law." And that was defined for him by C Street not as liberation but as the sort of freedom that isn't free, that which protects us from ourselves, "this notion," as he put it, "of what it is that I want."

Unless, that is, what we want is power.

And then, King David drew me back to the story. Two days after Sanford's public tears, he seemed back in control of himself. Opening a televised cabinet meeting, he spoke calmly of scripture, as if he were Cubby Culbertson himself, leading a spiritual counseling session. The topic was resignation: Sanford's rejection of his own party's calls for him to do so. As a congressman, he'd called on Bill Clinton to resign after the exposure of his affair. But there was a difference. Clinton was just a president. Mark Sanford, he explained to his cabinet, was like a king. King David, in particular. "What I find interesting is the story of David," he said, all waver and dodge gone from his voice, his tone that of a teacher, not a penitent.

"What I find interesting"—it's an evangelical men's movement phrase, *it is interesting to note, what I find interesting,* the almost casual, seemingly humble approach to a major claim based on a bit of scripture isolated from its text and put to work as a maxim, a law for leaders, an ancient justification for present-day authority. What Sanford found interesting about David was this: "The way in which he fell mightily, he fell in very significant ways."

The governor was speaking of the second book of Samuel, chapter 11. King David, God's chosen leader, is in Jerusalem while his armies are at war, conquering and destroying. All is well; but "all" is not enough for David. One night he wakes in the dark, restless, and goes up to the roof. From his high perch he looks down rather than up, toward the world rather than God, and spies a woman bathing. Lovely. The king snaps his fingers and off his servants go, and when they return they've brought with them the woman David desires, still wet from her bath. Her name is Bathsheba, and David rapes her or perhaps seduces her, offering the prospect of sex with the king in lieu of the loneliness she must feel for her husband, gone fighting the king's wars. And she becomes pregnant.

So David tries to cover it up. He summons Bathsheba's husband, a brave soldier named Uriah, back from the front. Take a break, David tells him, go home, see your wife— sleep with her, that is, so you'll think the child is yours. Uriah refuses to enjoy himself while his comrades are at war. All right, says David, but wait here another night. The next morning, David sends a message to the soldier's commander: "Set Uriah in the forefront of the hottest battle, and retreat from him, that he may be struck down and die."

It works. Uriah, the memory of his good king and his good wife fresh in his mind, presses hard against the enemy, driving them back toward their city until Uriah stands with his sword at the gate, the enemy broken, Uriah and his men strong. Only, there are no men. They've fallen back. Then, an enemy archer rises from the walls and puts an arrow in Uriah's heart.

So David wins his widow. There are consequences—God kills their first child, the one conceived in sin—but their second baby, the one born of marriage, thrives; they name him Solomon.

Yes, says Sanford, David "fell in very, very significant ways. But then picked up the pieces and built from there." The key, Sanford declared, is humility. And he could do humility. He did some right there, apologizing to his cabinet, making clear he wasn't going to resign. Like David, he had a calling. He was chosen. God had put him in office, and God would take him out; until then, Mark Sanford would remain governor of South Carolina.

This logic forms one of the foundations of C Street: the alchemy by which men elected by citizens persuade themselves that they were, in fact, selected by God. That sounds impossibly arrogant but it is, as Sanford said, a kind of humility. The chosen politician does not take credit for his success, he does not suppose that it was his virtue that led the people to elect him. He is just another sinner. But God wants to use him, as He used David. "God appoints specific leaders to fulfill a mission; He doesn't hold a popular vote," writes John C. Maxwell, a management guru on C Street's Prayer Breakfast circuit, in a Bible study titled Leadership: Deliberate Selection vs. Democratic Election.

The other side of such humility is the abdication of responsibility. One chosen for leadership isn't accountable for his own actions. That's not what the rabbis teach when they speak of King David, of course, nor is it the real meaning of Calvinism's doctrine of God's elect. It's American fundamentalism, a response to what one Family leader once lamented as the "substitution of democracy for religion." The bastardization of the King David story reverses the process, replacing democracy with religion. Mark Sanford used that reversal to justify his own power in defiance of the minor sin of adultery. If David got a pass for murder, so, too, should Sanford be excused the contemplation of a beautiful woman's "tan lines," on which he'd rhapsodize in the love letters soon made public.

That calculation seems reasonable enough, if self-serving, until one considers the implications. David Coe, for instance, son of Doug Coe, heir apparent to the leadership of the Family, and Sen. Ensign's C Street moral counselor, puts the application of the King David story in starker terms. The first time I ever heard King David invoked within the Family, in fact, was when David Coe visited the men with whom I was living at Ivanwald, a house I describe in *The Family*. They were a group of young future leadership prospects, and David Coe had come to do some spiritual training. Like his father, David Coe is tall, dark, lanky, and slow-moving, so calmly charismatic one forgets he is teaching; Coe lessons seem like gentle musings. That day, David Coe mused on King David, who "liked to do really, really bad things." Why, then, should we revere him?

The men were stumped. Maybe because I was raised around Judaism, a half-Jew who once celebrated Passover and Easter, I knew the answer. "Because he was chosen," I said.

"Yes," said Coe. "Chosen. Interesting set of rules, isn't it?" Then he turned to another man. "Beau, let's say I hear you raped three little girls. And now here you are at Ivanwald. What would I think of you, Beau?"

Beau, a good-natured jock who loved wrestling, dancing, and long walks in the woods, supposed that Coe wouldn't think well of him at all. But that wasn't so, Coe answered. Beau, he explained, was one of God's tools; that's what it means to be chosen. The normal rules don't apply. Morality—a human construct—doesn't even apply. "Moral orders," he said, "that's for kids. God's will is beyond morals." It wasn't that Coe thought Beau *should* rape three little girls, or that he wouldn't be horrified if Beau did; but such crimes would be beside the point. "We simply obey," Coe said. Genghis Khan, Coe suggested, provided a good example. According to Coe, Genghis Khan had conquered not for greed but because God told him to. When some monks asked him what justified his bloody conquests, Genghis answered, "I don't ask. I submit." Coe applied this logic to contemporary politics: "We elect our leaders," he said, "Jesus elects his."

*   *   *

The first of these leaders, for the Family, was Arthur B. Langlie, who was elected mayor of Seattle in 1938. Three years
earlier, on a night in April, God had come to the founder of
the Family, a Norwegian immigrant named Abraham Vereide. Christianity, God told Abram, as Vereide was known,
had been getting it wrong for nearly two thousand years,
devoting itself to the poor, the weak, the down-and-out. God
told Abram that night that Abram's calling would be the
"up and out," not life's "derelicts, its failures," as a friend
wrote in a hagiography of Abram, *Modern Viking.* Rather, it
should serve "those even more in need, who live danger-
ously in high places." Abram immediately set to work organizing a committee of nineteen wealthy businessmen to
break the spine of organized labor—Satan's legions—in
Seattle. Arthur Langlie, a thirty-five-year-old teetotaling lawyer, was their hammer. "It can be done," he said, at one of
Abram's early prayer meetings. "I am ready to let God
use me."

God—plus the financial backing of that early cadre, a
network of church workers organized by Abram, and a *sieg-
heil*ing, uniformed fraternity called the New Order of
Cincinnatus—used Langlie, indeed, installing him in a city
council seat vacated in fear of Langlie's New Order men.
From there he moved first to the mayor's office—over the
combined opposition of Democrats and Republicans who
accused him of fascism—and then, in 1940, to the governor's mansion, where he set about instituting God's will
as he'd learned it from Abram. It wasn't about church or
vice or soft concerns about pious women: it was about

capitalism—and the invisible hand of the market with which Langlie purged the welfare rolls and ground the unions into corruption or contrition. The defining moment of Abram's early ministry, one to which he'd return again and again over the decades, featured a labor leader named "Jimmy"—Abram rarely remembered union men's last names—giving his teary testimony to a gathering of seventy-five God-led businessmen, apologizing for his rebelliousness in the past and pledging himself to Abram's program, the result of which would be "no need for a labor union." One of the businessmen clapped a hand on the humbled union man's shoulder. "Jimmy," he said, in words Abram would always remember, "on this basis we go on together."

On that basis, Abram took his program—the Idea, he called it—first national and then international. By 1942 he'd organized businessmen's committees in dozens of cities, and relocated himself first to the other Washington, the capital. In the midst of a January snowstorm, he assembled his first meeting of congressmen to hear the Christian testimony of Howard Coonley, the ultraright president of the National Association of Manufacturers. Coonley saw a third front for the war, after Europe and Asia, right there in Washington, against Franklin Roosevelt's socialism and the death of a Christian nation in which God's chosen vessels—the Up and Outers—were free to produce wealth for all to enjoy by way of trickle-down religion. The Up and Outers won their first battle the next year with the passage of the Smith-Connally Act, the beginning of the New Deal's repeal. "It is the age of minority control," prophesied Abram; democracy, he believed, had died back in 1935, no match for communism or fascism. He proposed instead what he called then—and what C Streeters call now—"the Better Way," Up and Outers, guided by God, making the hard decisions behind closed doors.

By war's end those doors belonged to a four-story mansion on Embassy Row in Washington, purchased with the help of a beautiful socialite widow, Marian Aymar Johnson. Abram called this prototype for C Street a "Christian Embassy," headquarters for the movement he'd by then incorporated as International Christian Leadership (ICL). And international it was: in 1946, Abram undertook his first overseas mission with a mandate from the State Department to examine Nazi prisoners for conversion potential. He found more than a few willing to switch out the führer for the American father-god, men such as Hermann Abs, a leader of ICL's German division and the wizard of the West German miracle—until, decades later, he was discovered by Jewish Nazi hunters to have been "Hitler's leading banker." But Abs was an innocent compared to many of the men Abram recruited, men from whom he learned not fascism—a European disease, to which American fundamentalism even at its most authoritarian has always been immune—but the power of forgetting. The blank slate, the sins of the powerful wiped clean—that was an idea, Abram realized, that would flourish in cold war America.

Abram had grasped the cold war before most, declaring at World War II's end the immediate commencement of World War III. In 1955, Sen. Frank Carlson, with whom Abram had launched the annual ritual that would become the National Prayer Breakfast in 1953 by calling in favors from a reluctant Eisenhower, coined the phrase that would serve as the movement's motto: Worldwide Spiritual Offensive. In 1959, Sen. Carlson took the fight to Haiti, where he decreed François "Papa Doc" Duvalier God's man for the island nation and thus worthy of U.S. support, the guns and butter that kept Papa Doc—one of the most lunatic killers of the Western Hemisphere—and then his son, Jean-Claude "Baby Doc," in business for decades. What was in it for ICL? Help the weak by helping the strong. They helped Papa Doc and Papa Doc helped the businessmen who traveled to Haiti with Carlson, and the businessmen helped Carlson and the Republican Party: help all around that somehow never trickled down to the Haitian people. In 1966, ICL moved on to Indonesia, where General Suharto had come to power through what the CIA would later call "one of the worst mass murders of the twentieth century." Abram called the coup a "spiritual revolution," and began sending delegations of congressmen and oil executives who became champions of the genocidal regime. Help the weak by helping the strong: Suharto, ICLers believed, helped the weak of Indonesia resist the temptations of communism, by any means necessary.

Abram's lanky young new lieutenant, Doug Coe, brought a new spirit to the organization. Abram had frowned on publicity as low-class, the currency of the masses, and Coe embraced secrecy as an expression of his religion, a mystic commitment to quiet authority expressed not through a central organization but a proliferation of "cells," as the movement called the building blocks of their power. Each unit "should work behind the scenes," Coe wrote. "It should have no stationery, no publicity." Budgets should be off the books, the official sums nothing more than seed money. "It is important to note what God is doing in terms of finances that is not visible to the casual observer." Each cell, each front, might incorporate separately, Coe wrote, but "in all cases the concept remains the same."

What was the concept? "Men who are picked by God!" Not the many, but the few. Under Coe's guidance, Family politicians embraced the idea that God prefers the services of a dedicated elite to the devotion of the masses. "I have had a great and thrilling experience reading the condensed version of *The Rise and Fall of the Third Reich*," one of Coe's lieutenants wrote him after Coe had given him a reading list for "the Work," as their mission was often called. "Doug, what a lesson in vision and perspective! Nazism started with seven guys around a table in the back of an old German Beer Hall. The world has been shaped so drastically by a few men who really want it such and so. How we need this same kind of stuff as a Hitler or a Lenin." That is, for Jesus, of course.

In 1964, Abram, his leadership dwindling, contributed to the movement a distillation of his Up and Out theology. "The Fellowship"—so ICL had come to be called—"recognizes that no one cometh into the Father and into the family relationship except by Him." That's a paraphrase of Matthew 11:27, the same verse I'd hear former attorney general Ed Meese open a Family prayer meeting with nearly four decades later. "The strength of the wolf is the pack," Abram continued, "but the strength of the pack is the wolf."

Once I asked a young Family leader about the dictators

and thugs and white-collar criminals it seems to specialize in. "I don't worry whether some of them are wolves," he said, "because I'd rather let a wolf in than keep any sheep out." I pointed out that there are no sheep in the Family, since the organization was only interested in leaders. "Yeah," he agreed, "but don't the wolves need Jesus most of all?"

As Coe's authority grew, so did the Fellowship's reach around the globe, with cells in the governments of seventy nations by the late 1960s, more than double that of just a few years earlier. The Catholic generals and colonels who rotated coup by coup through the leadership of Brazil, Guatemala, El Salvador, and other Latin American countries consented to the Protestant ministrations of the Fellowship in return for access to American congressmen. Indonesia's Suharto, ostensibly a Muslim, declared of his Christian prayers in the presence of American oilmen, "In this way we convert ourselves, nobody converts us!" Ethiopia's Emperor Haile Selassie, who believed he was himself God, gladly became a financial backer of the Fellowship in return for the flow of American foreign aid facilitated by its members. It was a pray-to-be-paid scheme, by savvy foreign leaders who could flatter the moral imaginations of American politicians in exchange for military dollars. Sometimes the Family made possible a relationship that might not otherwise have occurred, but mostly it cloaked realpolitik in religion, allowing its politician members to imagine they were doing God's work as they funneled guns and cash and power to dictators such as Generalissimo Francisco Franco in Spain, General Park Chung-hee in South Korea, Ferdinand Marcos in the Philippines.

"Leaders," an early ICL man had written, "cannot afford misinterpretation in the public's eyes." In 1966, Coe took steps to ensure such misinterpretation would not be possible, urging the board of directors toward a reorganization that would, in effect, hide the organization. "Though the background organization would remain the same," went the proposal, "yet to be more effective for the aims *peculiar* to the movement, its administrative operations must be moved underground." Members should not call themselves members; if they were to identify themselves at all, it should only be as "working with" the Prayer Breakfast, never for an organization. "I work with the Prayer Breakfast folks," Sen. Sam Brownback, whose career has been shaped by the Family from college forward, told me, Coe's lingo precisely intact years after its concoction. At the time, Coe offered examples of men doing effective work for the movement without publicizing their connection, among them Secretary of Defense Melvin Laird, the admiral in command of the Seventh Fleet, and the general in charge of the Canal Zone. "The purpose of the changes set forth," Coe wrote, "is to submerge the institutional image of ICL."

The C Street House would become part of that plan. Coe scrapped the name International Christian Leadership and divided its finances between several smaller offshoots, some off-the-books accounting—most of his income would be provided by gifts from supporters—and the Fellowship Foundation, its name chosen to cloak the movement's religious intentions. But even that was too plainly evidence of an institution, so he began referring to the movement as "a family," "our worldwide family," and, eventually, "the Family"—a name that led some within the group to joke about themselves as the Christian Mafia, a label that stuck. He wanted to move the headquarters, too. He first set his eye on a Washington estate called Tregaron, twenty acres of historic gardens surrounding a massive Georgian-style mansion between Woodley Park and Cleveland Park, an address of sufficient status that the Soviet Union tried to purchase it for its embassy. The *Washington Post* reported in 1974 that Sen. Harold Hughes had raised $3.5 million to buy the home for "religious work," and that there was talk of making it the official vice presidential residence—owned by the Fellowship Foundation. "We've asked the Lord to give it to us," Hughes explained, in reference to what he said were his anonymously donated funds.

In fact, Hughes—a bighearted but none-too-bright Democrat seduced by Coe's rhetoric of "reconciliation"—was a front man. Coe had found the money in the pockets of a North Carolina manufacturer and an oilman named Harold McClure, who'd already donated the use of a private plane to fly congressmen on missionary junkets to Africa's newly oil-rich nations. "Tregaron, if handled properly, could on a low profile basis provide the following for our worldwide family," wrote Coe: an "orientation center" to recruit politicians for a "leadership led by God," a communications center for the worldwide work, and housing for members of "the Core," the Family's inner circle.

"Some asked how anything low profile can be done at Tregaron?" Coe continued. "If we have men of national reputation"—Coe proposed making Hughes and several

Republican congressmen the faces of the operation — "it would be easy for the rest of the fellowship to use Tregaron in a manner which would be rather obscure." Coe would be in charge, but not visibly: "My role as well would be done in the background."

But Coe didn't get his mansion. One of the old-timers, a retired marine general named Merwin Silverthorn, responded with fury to what he saw as dirty dealing, railing against Coe's proposal to use "front men" for the work. Coe likely nodded appreciatively; with a voice like a woodchuck out for an amble and a big, dopey smile, Coe seems almost immune to displays of anger. He gave up on Tregaron, but four years later he got his wish, a mansion on a hill across the Potomac River with an even more distinguished pedigree. It was said to have been built by George Mason, though local historians insist it's of a more recent vintage. It certainly looks like a manse fit for a founding father, white-columned and secluded at the end of a cul-de-sac in Arlington. The Family calls it the Cedars, and it's the headquarters of the movement to this day. Across the street from the Cedars is a roomy house valued at $1 million (the Cedars is assessed at close to $8 million) called Potomac Point, used to shelter young women of good breeding who act as unpaid servants across the road. Next up the block is a circle of homes owned by Family associates; then Ivanwald, the house for young men I lived in for a brief period. When I was there, the C. S. Lewis Institute, yet another sister organization, dedicated to fighting the "infection of secularism," was housed next door, and after that came a headquarters for the International Foundation — which is also the Fellowship Foundation.

The Family is as shifty with its properties as it is with its name. Potomac Point, for instance, went from Tim Coe, Doug Coe's son and a leader of the movement, to his parents in 1989 for $580,000. They transferred the property to the C Street Center in 1992, which then transferred it to the Fellowship Foundation in 2002—which, in turn, is the main financial backer of the C Street Center. Tim Coe, meanwhile, sold his house in Annapolis in 2007 for close to $1 million to the Wilberforce Foundation, on the board of which he served, like his brother David, for a salary of $107,000. The Wilberforce Foundation is something of a shell. It employs nobody, is headquartered in David Coe's house, has no conflict-of-interest policy, and exists, according to a board member, "to hold properties"—that is, to protect the assets of the much larger Fellowship Foundation from liability claims. The same year it bought Tim Coe's house, the Wilberforce Foundation turned around and sold Ivanwald—originally purchased in 1987 by Jerome Lewis, an oilman and major donor—to the Fellowship Foundation for $1 million.

Lewis, meanwhile, presides over a related organization in Colorado, the Downing Foundation, which operates an ivy-covered, $6 million estate in Englewood, donated by Lewis in 1997. Downing describes its mission as support of the Family's Fellowship Foundation, to which it sends an average of $88,000 a year. It also supports the Denver Leadership Foundation, which produces the Colorado Prayer Luncheon. The Luncheon's Host Committee—which includes Lewis—describes the annual event as modeled on Washington's, intended to recruit public officials to "renew the dedication of our nation and ourselves to God and His purposes." Where do the funds for such endeavors come from? Downing Partners Inc., an investment firm specializing in oil, gas, and real estate that donates hundreds of thousands of dollars every year to the Downing Foundation — its sole owner. Downing Partners, like Downing Foundation, is led, of course, by Jerome Lewis.

David Coe was one of three incorporators of the Foundation, but the estate's manager says he rarely visits. It is not a sign of disinterest. The Family is linked to so many properties — Downing, Ivanwald, the Cedars, Cedar Point Farm in Maryland, projects across the United States — that it must be hard to keep track of them all. Which is why Richard Carver, a former assistant secretary of the air force who serves as president of the Fellowship Foundation (a post of bureaucratic leadership second to Doug Coe's spiritual authority), told a reporter investigating C Street's tax-exempt status that "it is simply not a part of anything we do" — despite the fact that in 2002, long before the C Street scandals, he boasted of the Fellowship's authority over the property to another reporter. To be fair, Carver has a history of confusion over good housekeeping. At the Department of Defense he was best known for a multimillion-dollar order for fancy china, and his departure for private life and Christian work was clouded by charges of "ethical relativism" related to his decision to moonlight for investment banker Smith Barney while still on the Pentagon's payroll.

The history of C Street as real estate is even murkier. Washington's city tax office listed as its owner until the 2009 scandals a national fundamentalist organization called Youth With a Mission, but YWAM, as the group is known, insists that it sold C Street to the Fellowship Foundation sometime in the late 1980s. Until the C Street scandals brought the Fellowship Foundation under scrutiny, it listed C Street as a "sister organization" on its tax forms, which showed at least $450,000 in operational support for the Capitol Hill town house. But in 2009, the District of Columbia revoked 66 percent of C Street's tax-exempt status, and a group of pastors called Clergy VOICE challenged its federal tax status as a church in 2010—C Street fulfills none of the IRS's criteria for churches, making its exemption an insult to the real thing, said the pastors. The Fellowship Foundation responded by declaring itself entirely separate from its sister. Just in time: Citizens for Responsibility and Ethics in Washington, a good government watchdog, called for a congressional ethics investigation into what they charged was discounted rent for congressmen, which over the years added up to tens or even hundreds of thousands of dollars in subsidies for the Family's political chosen. "It helps them out," says Louis P. Sheldon, chairman of the fundamentalist Traditional Values Coalition, who uses C Street himself for meetings with foreign diplomats. "A lot of men don't have an extra $1,500 to rent an apartment. So the Fellowship house does that for those who are part of the Fellowship."

That's not all it does. Christian college girls provide maid service, turning down the sheets for the congressmen, and young men from Ivanwald are dispatched on occasion for "discipling" by the politicians. There's a chef and a house mother and, in one of the several common areas, a giant-screen TV around which the politicians and their friends—besides Sheldon, Colonel Oliver North is a regular—gather to watch sports and talk policy. The TV replaced a grand piano left behind by former residents, but signs of the building's earlier identity—it was a convent—remain. There is a little-used chapel, and in the formal dining room there is a stained-glass window, two large frames of snowy white bordered in blue, with a medallion of Jesus and a lamb in the middle. But it's not about piety, declared the congressmen, when pressed to explain their residence in a "church" after the scandals broke; it's about relationships—the polite word for politics.

That much seems true: money flows freely from one man's political action committee to another, often across party lines. Stupak, for instance, contributed $2,500 to the gubernatorial campaign of ultra-right Zach Wamp. Rep. Jo Ann Emerson (R-MO), one of the few women to spend time at the house in a capacity other than cleaning or cooking, forged such a happy bond with another visitor, Rep. Emanuel Cleaver (D-MO), that Cleaver refused to support her Democratic challenger. And when two C Streeters—Rep. Jerry Moran (R-KS), a resident, and Rep. Tiahrt, a visitor—squared off in a Republican primary to succeed yet another C Streeter, Sam Brownback, as Kansas's next senator, Moran racked up powerful endorsements and financial support from housemates Ensign, DeMint, Coburn, and Thune, and from former C Streeters Pickering and Rep. Tom Osborne (R-NE)—even though Tiahrt is a closer political match. "The fact that everyone that lived in the same house," said Sen. Inhofe, commenting on the endorsements, "that can't just be a coincidence."

Tiahrt felt double-crossed. A "family values" man, he'd moved his small-f family to Washington rather than spend most of his days away from them in politics and prayer at the C Street house, as Moran did. "My roommate endorsed me," he squeaked. "I've been married to her for thirty-three years."

Tiahrt had misunderstood capital-f Family values. "I'm always third," the wife of a Family man told Ben Daniel, a Presbyterian pastor who as a young man was a member himself until he realized that some "brothers" mattered more than others. "The Fellowship comes first in my husband's life. Then the children. Then me." Anne Ryun, the wife of former representative Jim Ryun of Kansas, kept her husband out of C Street for that very reason. "It appears that the Fellowship discourages congressmen to move their families to DC for the express purpose of keeping the wives out of the loop. It's a very, very separated world."

The Ryuns are hardly liberal critics of C Street; they're conservative Christians, and Anne spoke out only at the request of *World*, a fundamentalist magazine that has come to see C Street as home to the opposite of the family values it espouses. "It's not really about family values," another political wife told me of her own husband's decision to decline an invitation to join. "It's about who you know, your so-called brothers." The point isn't friendship, it's power. "In order for God to do His mighty works," writes Coe, "He doesn't demand the majority, but a committed minority who are absolutely centered on Jesus Christ and the love of one another."

Love—the miracle by which the Family understands itself, religion, politics, and power subsumed into the blurry affection of a "worldwide family of friends." "It's a very wide vision," declares the second of "The Eight Core Aspects," the 2010 draft of the vision first dreamed by Abram amid 1930s labor wars. Wide, but so shallow it can't be said to have depth at all. Rather, the vision is two-dimensional, a screen; a veil; a cloth thrown over religion, politics, and power.

Or, not religion, really, since Suharto was a Muslim, Papa Doc practiced Vodun, Ensign depends on Holy Ghost power, and Sanford is an Episcopalian, a member of God's frozen chosen, as they say.

And not politics, really, not in the sense we speak of politics in America, electoral contests, control of Congress, Democrats versus Republicans. Consider Kansas: heads, the Family wins; tails, they win. Consider C Street, Democrats and Republicans united for the sake of—what?

Power. But even that word is a euphemism, inasmuch as it suggests purpose. At its core, the Family lacks even that: it is conservative by default, the result of its conflation of worldly power with divine will. I asked Tim Kreutter, author of "The Eight Core Aspects," why "the kings" of this world the Family has sought as brothers are so often not just conservative but also corrupt. "Because that's what's there," he answered—an honest man, in his way, seemingly puzzled by the implication of the question: the simple idea that the fact of power is not its justification. Kreutter wasn't interested in "power," he was interested in "love," the Family veil—"the main thing," he wrote in the penultimate Core Aspect, the one that comes before serving kings. *"And the main thing"*—emphasis his— *"[is] to keep the main thing the main thing."* Because that's what's there.

2

THE LOVERS

THE SENATOR, the governor, and the congressman. If John Ensign's was the most banal of the three affairs covered up at C Street during the summer of 2009, and Sanford's the most tragic, the third, that of former congressman Chip Pickering, offers perhaps the perfect distillation of the ethos of C Street. It's not a story so much as a synecdoche, a part that can stand for the whole. Throughout its history, the Family, the Fellowship, ICL—the many incarnations of C Street—has built power not through mass movements or unstoppable voter blocs, not by rallying around a singular demagogue, but by working the margins; lining up the back benchers; recruiting men with the kind of influence that doesn't depend on cameras. Who remembers Sen. Frank Carlson, Eisenhower's "'No Deal' Dealer" from Kansas, the general's behind-the-scenes man? Or Sen. Robert Kerr of

Oklahoma, not so much an oilman as oil's man, recruited by Carlson for the sake of bipartisanship, Carlson's kind of Democrat, "chief of the wheelers-and-dealers," one journalist called him? Who remembers Sen. James B. Allen, a George Wallace Democrat from Alabama who used his mastery of Senate rules to thwart his own party on civil rights; or even Ed Meese, famous once as Reagan's strong-arm attorney general, more quietly influential now as the middleman between big business and religious conservatism, the shepherd who led Supreme Court justices John Roberts and Samuel Alito to their benches?

One of the earliest documents to be found in the Family's archive is a note Abram wrote to himself on a church program in 1935. Imagine the preacher, sitting bored in another minister's pews, preparing to leave the bricks and mortar of church behind. He's a big man with a broad, severely handsome face and ice-blue eyes, wearing one of his fabulous suits, double-breasted with a polka-dot bow tie—he was always a beautifully dressed man, even other men said so. Ignoring the sermon, he scribbles on his program. He's making a list of departments for his new movement, and next to each heading he writes the name of a man who will be responsible for it: for *finances*, for *organization*. Next to his own name, Abram writes *power*. Then he crosses it out. Power, Abram would teach, resides in that which is not seen—politically as well as spiritually. "Our prayer," declared the Prayer Breakfast programs of Abram's successor, Coe, "is 'He shall have dominion from Sea to Sea,'" a statement of ambition matched only by the subtlety with which it's pursued. "We try to be nearly invisible,"

Family leader Rev. Richard Halverson demurred in 1981, the year he assumed the chaplaincy of the U.S. Senate, with no formal recognition of the Family affiliation that made him a pastor to the elite. Dominion, suggests David Coe, Doug's son, is "an invisible Kingdom," won not by conquest but through substitution, the replacement of democratic vistas with "His vision." Not through revival but through relationships, man by man. Such power isn't bold, it's bureaucratic, a machine built of many small parts. We might call these little units "Pickerings."

The actual Pickering is mostly an inoffensive entity, toothy and boyish, with reddish-brown hair and watery blue eyes set a little too close together. Cute, not handsome. Up to the revelation of his C Street affair, Charles "Chip" Pickering was best known outside Mississippi as "that congressman from *Borat*"—and, really, that's how he's been known ever since. In the British comedian Sacha Baron Cohen's 2006 farce of a Kazakh journalist exploring America, *Borat: Cultural Learnings of America for Make Benefit Glorious Nation of Kazakhstan*, Baron Cohen, as the idiot-reporter Borat, makes his way to a revival meeting where Pickering takes to the pulpit to proclaim himself a loyalist of the gathering and its truths: creationism and religious nationalism, America the Christian. Such was his reputation within the Magnolia State, too. "I told Chip often, if he ever wants to stop being a politician he can be a preacher," says Carol Mabry, a Pickering staffer who retired in 2007 after ten years in Chip's service to take care of her grandchildren. "If I get to heaven, I'll see him there."

But Pickering, sadly, is not the hero of even his own

story. Central to every account of the man — "a good-looking boy," says Bill Crawford, an old Mississippi hand who got beat by young Chip for the House in 1996 — is the status, the weight, the influence of his father, Charles Pickering Sr. Originally a segregationist Dixiecrat, he switched parties in 1964. That was the year the Democratic Party began its historic (and incomplete) break with its record of race hatred, the year the long-hidebound political organization agreed to seat two African American delegates of the Mississippi Freedom Democratic Party at its convention in Atlantic City. Pickering declared the people of Mississippi (the white people, that is) "heaped with embarrassment and humiliation." In response he turned his considerable talents over to the GOP. He became one of its chief activists in Mississippi and a man on the national scene, chair of the committee that in 1976 rolled over the party's moderate wing to add an anti-abortion plank to the platform for the first time.

But his fame, even now greater than that of his only son, rests on the racial fault line. The Pickering men, senior and junior, see themselves as progressives on this matter. And indeed, Senior bravely fought the Ku Klux Klan as a young lawyer. In his most famous case as a federal judge in the 1990s, he called the actions of a man who'd helped burn a cross on an interracial couple's front lawn "heinous, reprehensible, despicable, dastardly." He also called it a "drunken prank" and turned down the prosecutor's request for a seven-and-a-half-year sentence, dismissed the federal mandatory five-year sentence, and sent the dastardly fellow to prison for two and a half years, a decision that would lead

Senate Democrats to filibuster his 2003 nomination to the Fifth Circuit Court of Appeals. "Pickering has a prewar mentality," says a legal analyst who has followed Pickering's decisions as a judge. "Pre–Civil War."

Such antebellum attitudes are more complex than they might at first seem. In 1965, Pickering Sr. signed a segregationist declaration in favor of "our Southern way of life," and he bemoaned "racial hatred"—that of civil rights activists. But by all accounts he truly loathes the Klan; hates racial violence; and is proud of his black friends. Is he a racist? That's not a question easily answered. The old ways he clings to are those of the paternalist. The white man or the rich man or simply the powerful man who believes he knows better. The Good Father.

And his son, Chip? If he's something of an afterthought, he's also an embodiment of that paternalism, filtered through modern fundamentalism, dedicated to the new southern order, which is to say the old southern order got up in reconciliation drag; a libertarian with authoritarian tendencies. "He's a glowing example of Mississippi politicians," says the Reverend Eugene Bryant, a Mississippi civil rights activist. "Of what they've always been."

Chip followed his father to Ole Miss and then went to Hungary in the late eighties as a Southern Baptist missionary. Quite an assignment for a boy right out of college; his father, coincidentally, had just completed a term as president of the state Baptist convention. Chip had another advantage not enjoyed by most evangelists. President George H. W. Bush appointed Charles Pickering's son agricultural liaison to Eastern Europe, making him a representative of the U.S. government as well as a missionary. But Pickering's passion wasn't in the soil, it was in the air: telecommunications. Upon his return from the heathen East, Pickering worked as an aide to Mississippi senator Trent Lott, proving himself possessed of a particular talent for the intricacies of telecommunications regulation. Or, more precisely, deregulation, the gutting of laws. It was Pickering, as an aide to Lott, who negotiated into existence the 1996 Telecommunications Act—the culmination of a privatization of the public airwaves begun years before. Once, federal law forbade a single company from owning more than fourteen radio stations. The principle was that any more than that would amount to the transfer of public property—the airwaves—to monopoly power. By the 1990s, that cap had crept up to forty stations. The law Chip helped write removed all limits. Within a month of its passage in 1996, more than a thousand mergers occurred, eventually resulting in the media empire Clear Channel.

That same year, Pickering ran for Congress with more than $1 million in the bank, most of it from out-of-state contributors. Lott's name helped, but Pickering's wasn't too shabby on its own. "I don't support Chip Pickering because of Senator Lott," said Bernard J. Ebbers, the WorldCom CEO who'd be convicted in 2005 of the then-largest accounting fraud in U.S. history. "I support Chip Pickering because of who he is."

Who he really was, Pickering told the people of Mississippi's Third Congressional District, was a missionary. He ran on his record not as a free marketeer in America but as a bearer of the cross to communist lands. That his two vocations amounted to the same thing in his mind hardly needed to be said. He promised Mississippians Christian legislation: the privatization of resources and the public regulation of morality are the twin pillars of American fundamentalism. As a congressman he introduced the Children's Internet Protection Act, requiring schools and libraries to filter computers. When a federal court struck it down as unconstitutional, he declared the court "pornographic-friendly." He tried again with the Protecting Children from Indecent Programming Act, joining forces with two other Family men, Rep. Joe Pitts and Rep. Mike McIntyre, to demand that the federal government cinch its indecency regulations so tight that a broadcaster could be declared a threat to children on the basis of a single naughty word.

The bill didn't pass, but that didn't matter. The truth was that such initiatives were a sideshow. Pickering, by then a Washingtonian and a C Streeter, labored for a different kind of invisible kingdom. Pickering's real work was building on the great sell-off of public airwaves and bandwidth he'd helped orchestrate in 1996. And in this effort he joined forces with Family men, most notably Steve Largent, a fellow C Streeter and another example of C Street's paradoxical politics: authoritarian libertarianism: free-market fundamentalism under God.

Elected from Oklahoma in 1994 after determining that God wanted him in Washington, Largent organized a C Street club that continues to this day. Its members have included Sen. Tom Coburn, Rep. Zach Wamp, Mike Doyle (D-PA), and Bart Stupak. The "M.O." as Largent put it, "is to work behind the scenes." But Largent couldn't resist playing the showman. The press loved him. *People* magazine put the oversized blue-eyed blond with puppy-dog brows on its "Most Beautiful People" list. He was the big man of C Street, literally an NFL Hall of Fame wide receiver for the Seattle Seahawks in the 1980s. And a deeply religious man: when he abandoned his teammates to cross an NFL picket line, he cited the Gospel of Matthew as justification. But he wasn't a scold. A reporter for the *New York Times*, noting his "male model" good looks, gushed that the congressman was "so friendly he might be mistaken for a flirt." Even Largent's unusual living arrangements—C Street—came in for praise, presented to the public as his own special idea, a social club for guys trying to enjoy the capital without straying from their wives. "There are too many people in Congress who don't know how to have fun," said Largent, "and I've taken them on as my responsibility."

He also took responsibility for the so-called Defense of Marriage Act, protecting straight people from the ever-present danger of being forced into gay marriage. He overreached only when he proposed the 1996 Parental Rights and Responsibilities Act, a law so extreme that even some Christian conservatives rallied against its project of tearing down what supporters called "government schools"— public education—piece by piece through parental challenges to any item in the curriculum they found objectionable. Largent denied that tying up school districts in endless losing court battles was intended to destroy them. Rather, he wanted to purify them.

Most of all, Largent was a telecommunications man.

Along with Pickering, Stupak, and Doyle, he served on the House telecommunications subcommittee. After a failed gubernatorial bid in 2002, he took a job with Washington law firm Wiley Rein, joining a longtime Family associate and former congressman named Jim Slattery, head of the firm's public policy branch. Largent left after less than a year to become president of an industry organization called the Cellular Telecommunications and Internet Association, which contracted for $200,000 of Wiley Rein's finesse. Pickering, still sitting on the subcommittee that regulated Largent's new industry, proved an even more valuable friend: while Pickering was in Congress, Largent appealed to him directly and paid for travel by Pickering's staff.

Which brings us to the details of Pickering's affair, with a telecom executive named Elizabeth Creekmore Byrd. But "affair" is too dramatic a term; Pickering seems to have merely substituted one woman for another. Pickering has five young sons, and for that reason he's barely said a word about what happened. His wife, Leisha, is hardly more forthcoming. When Chip filed for divorce in 2008, she resisted, even though by then she knew about his other woman. Perhaps the pain was lessened by the fact that his secret lover was not a stranger, like Sanford's mistress, or her best friend, like Ensign's. What Elizabeth Creekmore Byrd had been, Leisha may have believed, was a closed chapter in her husband's life: an Ole Miss girlfriend with whom he'd broken up before marrying Leisha after graduation. And it was easy to think that the Elizabeth Creekmore of Chip's college years was just a status match. Her family, like Chip's, was one of the wealthiest and most influential in Mississippi.

Their relationship was surely not so much a romance as a merger. And then Chip fell in love with Leisha.

Elizabeth Creekmore Byrd—she married a doctor named Byrd—was "cute," a pixie-like brunette with rosy cheeks and a thin-lipped smile. Leisha was stunning, a blue-eyed blonde with a broad-boned face that seemed like a canvas for powerful emotion. Creekmore was an heiress; Leisha was of more modest means. Creekmore went into the family business—Cellular South. Leisha did church work. Not the C Street kind, but the little-heralded, feed-the-hungry sort of labor. Creekmore went to Washington, cashing in on telecommunications consolidation; Leisha cofounded a nonprofit called HANDS, Helping Americans Needing Disaster Support; after Hurricane Katrina, it became one of the central clearinghouses for Mississippi relief. She wasn't a saint, she was a congressman's wife. If she was far removed from her husband's Washington work, she shared his convictions and his conservatism. But such was the nature of the woman that, when she was in trouble—when Chip tried not just to leave her but to leave her poor—even Democrats rallied to her defense.

The first divorce, though, was Creekmore Byrd's, in 2007. That fall, Chip's old boss, Sen. Lott, abruptly resigned— because, he said, he wanted to spend more time with his family. (As it happened, his brother-in-law Dickie Scruggs was about to be indicted on a charge of trying to bribe a judge, in a case that came perilously close to Lott's name.) According to the lawsuit Leisha would file, Gov. Haley Barbour offered Chip Lott's seat, the one everyone already thought would one day be his. Barbour, who denies such backroom maneuvering, is a great white buffalo of a man, a Washington lobbyist before he became governor. He and Pickering Jr. went way back; Barbour and Pickering Sr. went way, way back. Senior converted to Republicanism; Barbour was one of those rare Mississippians born into the party, political from boyhood and a force in the state GOP since 1968, when he was barely out of high school. He'd run campaigns for Pickering Sr. and Jr.; his nephew Henry had been the strategist who'd walked Chip into Congress with a fat money roll. Getting Chip into the House had been easy enough, but making him senator? Barbour could do it just by signing his name.

But then Chip surprised everyone: he said no. What's more, he announced he wouldn't be running again the next year. Why? Because he wanted to spend more time with his family, of course. But which family? According to Leisha, the one Chip planned on building with Creekmore Byrd. To do that, he needed to get rid of Leisha, and to get rid of Leisha, he needed to be out of the public eye. Leisha says quitting Congress, at least for a while, was Creekmore Byrd's idea—which she presented to Chip along with an ultimatum: give up the Senate seat, since remaining a senator would have required that he stay married, or give up her. It'd be sweet to say Chip chose love over politics, but it's probably more accurate to say that he hoped to have both. He finished out his term, and signed on as a Washington lobbyist, representing Creekmore Byrd's Cellular South, which also happens to be one of the major members of Largent's industry association.

Had it ended there, Pickering might be a happy man

today, collecting big paychecks, married to Creekmore Byrd, biding his time until the retirement of Mississippi's other longtime senator, Thad Cochran. Raised a prince of the New South, his father's word law, every job he'd ever held handed to him, Pickering thought he could play a populist at home while collecting corporate cash in Washington, father five boys by a beautiful woman and then leave her for a rich woman. He left Leisha and rented a house not far down the street from his lover's, on a street called, appropriately, Heritage Hill Drive, and stepped back from power. He waited. He was deregulating, applying the invisible hand, a laissez-faire economy of love and life that would allow him to consolidate, to merge, to grow bigger than his father's name.

And he might have, too, had he let Leisha keep her dignity. Instead, he filed for divorce in a court under the shadow of his powerful family. The judge didn't need to be told what to do: she shut Leisha up, she shut Leisha's lawyer up, she even tried to stop Leisha and her lawyer from talking to one another. "I can't think of a single instance where a client is prohibited from talking to his attorney," says Matt Eichelberger, a Mississippi public defender and legal blogger who's been following the case.

But Leisha had a secret weapon. Mississippi is one of the few states to have retained an arcane statute that allows a spurned wife to sue for alienation of affection, a "tort of outrage." In other words, to sue not her husband, but her husband's mistress, in another court, doubling the legal battleground on which Leisha's lawyers could maneuver. They took advantage of a law from Charles Pickering Sr.'s

Mississippi, an artifact of chivalry and sexism, but Leisha's lawyers turned it around to push the prince of Mississippi out of the court of his home county and into Jackson, Mississippi's closest approximation of a big city. What's more, Leisha claimed to have proof of her husband's sins: a diary. A record of his meetings with his mistress, telling when and *where:* C Street.

Pickering and his old flame; the congressman from Mississippi and his telecom lover.

And there the story stalled. Leisha threatened to release the diary, seven years' worth of records; the divorce court judge ordered it returned to Chip; Leisha had to take out a restraining order against her own lawyer to stop the lawyer from complying with the force of the Pickerings; and then the other judge, the one in Jackson, said, *Wait.* And so it has, locked up from the public in an unusual decision by the divorce judge, the missing link in the seemingly unending case of Pickering versus Pickering.

What Leisha wanted was a decent settlement for her five sons. The C Street diary was what she had to bargain with. What Pickering wanted was what he'd been promised by God, a family and a calling. The C Street religion was his justification. Ensign's and Sanford's hidden affairs, pursued in Vegas and Argentina, had been, by their own accounts, sin. What Pickering had done, under the sanctified and tax-exempt roof of C Street, with the knowledge of at least some of his "brothers," was of God: his love life and his lobbying life converging; a broken marriage, ethics restrictions, and telecom regulations all falling away, Pickering born again,

again. Pickering did not repent, Pickering did not weep for the camera, did not speak of a "heart connection." He sued. He sued the mother of his five sons: the woman he'd betrayed. That's conviction, more powerful than public confession. Belief.

Belief in what? The preposition, *in*, doesn't matter. What matters is the verb, *believe*. Belief covers for business; business covers for belief; they are equal, the yin and yang of an American fundamentalism that mistakes the market for democracy, sex for sin, the dollar for the cross.

"When they say 'Christ,'" a North Carolina businessman named Chip Atkinson says of the Family, with which he broke after decades in 2000, "they're talking about themselves. Two thousand years of history" — the whole of the Christian tradition, its crimes and splendors — "and they don't look at anything but themselves."

*   *   *

When Jenny Sullivan looked, what she saw was a dead man. It was 1984, the days of "greed is good." The future Jenny Sanford was a recent Georgetown grad intent on proving herself as an investment banker at Lazard Frères. One day she was in the company library, high above midtown Manhattan, when she heard a *whoosh*. The corner of her eye caught sight of something falling. "I pressed my face to the window," she'd remember, "...and trembled when I saw a figure imprinted on the roof of a car." A stock trader; a casualty of the life to which she aspired.

She achieved it, becoming a vice president of Lazard before she was twenty-seven. A big-eyed, thin brunette with sharp cheeks and a wide, strained smile, she was near the top of what was then very much a man's world. But it was the dead man who worried her: the corpse on the car. By 1987 she was easing herself out of the career-ladder jobs. She no longer worked deep into the night. She was remembering what it felt like to be human, made of flesh and blood instead of numbers. "I was noticing different things," she'd recall, "or at least I had more time to consider what I was really seeing." She "looked up," as she'd put it, and one day instead of the dead man she saw Mark Sanford.

She was Catholic, from Chicago, a hard-driving woman; he was a Florida "Whiskeypalian" by way of South Carolina, the Episcopal Church filtered through the amber of good bourbon. He was getting a master's in business at the University of Virginia and working for the summer at Goldman Sachs, a bright and earnest but soft-spoken man who drove out to the Hamptons for a vacation in a two-door Honda hatchback. Their romance didn't exactly spark, and it nearly sputtered altogether when seven months later she accepted an invitation to join him at his family's South Carolina plantation, Coosaw, for New Year's Eve. He didn't meet her at the airport. Instead, he left her directions to the hatchback, which he'd left parked outside, and for the fifty-mile drive through fog to Coosaw's long, sandy drive, lined on both sides by moss-covered trees.

When she got there, he practically ignored her. But then nobody had ever accused Mark Sanford of being a flirt. Years later, when he revealed his Argentinean affair, everyone who knew him was stunned. "If I had to name the top ten sins of Mark Sanford, women would not have been one of them," says Gina Smith, a reporter on the Sanford beat.

"I thought he was asexual," says an aide who'd seen women come on to him in no-risk situations. Maybe Jenny Sullivan did, too. The memoir in which she lays out their early romance, *Staying True*, is a chaste book in every sense but one: it is a quietly, effectively vengeful testimony. Even her most cherished moments are recounted with an undercurrent of contempt. And who can blame her? That New Year's Eve at Coosaw, Sanford kissed her at midnight and then deposited her, alone, in a cabin set apart from the main house. Lying in a cold bed, enduring an evening of chill after having won the warmth of one embrace, "the pride I felt from having passed the test fell away a bit and I began to wonder why I had to be tested at all."

A part of Mark Sanford had long felt the same. Why did he need to be tested? As a high school boy and then in college, he watched his father die of Lou Gehrig's disease. The elder Sanford had been given six months and instead he lived six years, which proved to be a blessing and a curse. Imagine a sand castle, and then picture a slow tide, taking it away grain by grain until first a wall and then the whole edifice crumbles. So it was, too, with Coosaw, where Mark had summered as a small boy, and where he'd grown into a young man. The plantation was sold off in pieces until what was left was a wild, filthy farm — but still lovely, not so much hard-won as held on to only through struggle.

It's not surprising that Sanford would come to develop a sense of himself as rooted in these experiences. Or, rather, stuck there, his perspective reaching no further than his feeling of having been victimized by fate: "The tough decisions Mark had to make to save Coosaw," Jenny writes, in one of her rare moments of sympathy, "made him the embodiment of someone who had lived through an experience like the Great Depression." That's what it was like during the Great Depression: many Americans almost lost their vacation farms.

Jenny shared a similarly skewed financial perspective, describing herself as up from modest origins. It was true that her great-grandfather had risen from nothing by inventing the portable circular saw and starting the Skil Corporation, which her grandfather and then father developed into a global concern. "But I never thought of us as wealthy." Her family had owned the Braves when they were in Milwaukee, but, she notes, their home in Winnetka, an affluent Chicago suburb, lacked air-conditioning.

When Sanford first ran for Congress in 1994, by then married to Jenny and building his own small fortune in real estate, he had to struggle again, this time *because* he had money. His Democratic opponent "implied that if you are successful or of means, you are unfit to represent a congressional district," writes Jenny. Not in the staunchly Republican district Sanford ran in; unknown before the campaign, he won with 67 percent of the vote. But the political career that followed was strangely suited to South Carolina, a very poor state with a memory—among the elite, at least—of riches. Sanford, says Chip Felkel, a Republican strategist, "is more libertarian than Republican. But the state of South Carolina is not wealthy enough to be libertarian. South Carolina is a socially conservative state, but not a fiscally conservative one. Everyone has a family member whose job was created by the government. They may claim to want less government, but the only constant in their lives is government."

Sanford should not have been successful: he was serious about much less government, fanatically so. "Mark was an ideologue," declares Jenny, and she means it as a compliment. "You know what he was?" says Kevin Gray, a civil rights activist who ran against Sanford for governor. "An Ayn Rand romantic." Sanford won by making hard-hearted austerity sound like Christian compassion.

Sanford credits the novelist with the development of his own antigovernment philosophy, if his commitment to saving money by slashing services for the poor can be dressed up as that. "He's an old Southern blueblood who's working his hardest to seem like an intellectual," says Felkel. "The kind of person who's got a lot of good books on his shelf but doesn't know what's in them." For Sanford the books that mattered were Rand's novels and the Bible—a seemingly odd collage, given Rand's atheism and the Bible's concern for the poor. It's a fusion that is at the heart of the C Street religion: free-market fundamentalism justified and slightly softened by scripture, "the human needs we have for grace, love, [and] faith," as Sanford would write, in a *Newsweek* essay titled "Atlas Hugged."

Sanford's religion has always been mostly private, and so have his grace and love: matters of personal relations, not policy realities. But as a congressman, he joined C Streeter Steve Largent's Bible-based weekly social gatherings. He may have slept on his office floor, but he'd refresh himself at C Street. He went for Bible studies but hung around for the camaraderie; besides, there was never too much Bible up for discussion, just a verse, or a "thought," as the men would put it, and, on special occasions, leading questions from Doug Coe about what Christ might have to say about Social Security, or building roads, or any other government endeavor. Let go and let God—the popular evangelical catchphrase was transformed at C Street into a mandate for the transfer of public wealth into private hands, for our own good. In lieu of regulation, C Street preaches "reconciliation," a process they put into practice by bringing politicians and business leaders together to declare to one another their earnest desire to do right by God and each other. "Self-interest by proxy" is how an honest free marketeer, Will Wilkinson of the conservative Cato Institute, describes the C Street brand of back-scratching biblical capitalism.

Sanford proved himself effective not so much at the actual details as at the miracle of sales. He thought like a "Randroid," as the author's devotees are known, but talked like a prosperity preacher. "I feel absolutely committed to the cause, to what God wanted me to do with my life," he'd say of himself. "I have got this blessing of being engaged in a fight for liberty, which is constantly being threatened."

"He'd be talking to a crowd of schoolteachers and their spouses and family members about how he stands for efficient government," says a South Carolina Republican consultant, "and they'd be nodding their heads because it sounds good, without realizing that he was actively trying to eliminate their positions." Jenny would put it in saintly terms. "Something he'd learned watching so many poor in India," she writes of a free congressional junket during his last term, was: "'Don't be so attached to things.'" The rich man who can successfully preach this message to the poor man will go far, indeed.

Sanford, one of the brightest stars of the nation-changing Republican class of '94, left Washington to run for governor in 2002. His opponent, Democrat Jim Hodges, had the personality of a desk. But Sanford, says another longtime South Carolina political observer, "governed like a bug lamp. He would hope that his idea was big enough and that others would gravitate toward him." If that sounds like a weak approach, it's because it was. Constitutionally, there are few weaker governorships than that of South Carolina. "Sanford did what no one thought was possible," says Felkel. "He made it weaker." The office was designed that way following the Civil War, in case an African American ever won office. The irony is that the weak governorship has become a foundation for white southern politics, a high-profile position with low commitment cost, power without responsibility. As George W. Bush proved in Texas, another weak governor state, it's a perfect platform for a national posture. Sanford got that; he understood that the next step wasn't reform in South Carolina but ideology, broadcast from South Carolina. Even with a Republican legislature, he got almost nothing passed. But that wasn't what mattered.

The more he failed, the higher his star rose. He invoked the populism of the South without bringing along its baggage. "The Sanfords understood the trap of race southern politicians fall into," says civil rights activist Gray. To be successful, most Republicans and many Democrats make coded appeals to racial antagonism — waving the Confederate flag or railing against "entitlements," and transferring already scarce resources from poor black communities into middle-class white ones. Sanford ducked the flag and avoided racially tainted economic policy by ignoring the needs of the poor of every color. He used religion — "our strategy," says Will Folks, a former press secretary, "was to pay lip service to the social conservative issues" — but only when he had to. "He never mentioned the Bible unless it was to support some kind of frugal measure he wanted passed." He sounded like Reagan, says Gray, but not as scary; like Clinton, but not as Bubba.

But if he possessed the past presidents' ability to connect, he lacked their driving desire to do so. He was ruled by fight or flight. When he wasn't working to demolish government, he was running away from it, on what he called "adventure trips." The disappearance that ended his presidential ambitions wasn't his first. Since the beginning of his political career, Sanford periodically had left Washington and his family behind. Two weeks after his first son was born he took off with friends to climb Mount. Rainier. "Mark's balance," Jenny would write, "is like a gyroscope; he has to keep spinning to feel calm at the center."

And when he spun out of control, C Street was there to cover for him. Sanford never moved into C Street, but the Fellowship became his family in Washington, a bond that increasingly displaced those back home. By the end of his time in Congress, he'd grown so distant from Jenny — "the world Mark lived in illuminated the image, the superficial, the part that was calculated to be unknowable" — that she was beginning to wonder, Why bother? Why should she have to pass another test in her life with Mark Sanford? So Sanford did what any man would do: he asked his C Street "brothers" to talk sense to his wife. Jenny listened. Still Catholic, she'd learned from South Carolina the political uses of evangelicalism, and that private group prayers were the modern equivalent of a backroom cigar.

Staying True is studded with scripture, fundamentalist-style—stripped of context, memorized, and trotted out as proof of one's virtue. Jenny begins before marriage, when Mark first taught her the method with his life verses, Galatians 5:22, a tribute to self-control, and Matthew 5:16: "Let your light so shine before men, that they may see your good works and praise your Father in heaven." Soon, Jenny has her own. Psalm 127, a verse adopted by the self-declared biblical patriarchy movement as guidance for mothers: "Like arrows in the hands of a fighting man are sons born to a man in his youth. Happy is he who has a quiver full." She rolls out Psalm 139, one of the proof-texts of the anti-abortion movement, to take her own measure: "Search me, O God, and know my heart; test me and know my anxious thoughts. See if there is any offensive way in me and lead me in the way everlasting."

She explains the verse thus: "My heart has been pained but it is clean." Maybe, but Psalm 139 isn't. It's venomous. "Oh, that you would slay the wicked, O God!" declares the passage before Jenny's. "And do I not loathe those who rise up against you? I hate them with perfect hatred. I count them my enemies."

That dodge—the Bible's pretty words presented without the rough ones that give them their depth—is the C

Street shuffle, the bait-and-switch exegesis of American fundamentalism. By ignoring the apparent contradictions of scripture, fundamentalism ignores its questions, reducing its complexity to implicit equations. Hate equals love; obedience is freedom.

C Street's instructions for Jenny followed a similar line. When her pride was wounded by Sanford's neglect, C Street advised her to find her dignity in abjection. "A member of the group, whom I'll call Jack"—the only pseudonym Jenny grants in *Staying True*—"advised me that staying angry with Mark was not an option. If I wanted to heal the relationship, I had to open my heart and be kind, even if Mark was in the wrong. *They* would work on Mark." Jack had sexual advice for Jenny, too: "he told me not to withhold it." Jack and his brothers lectured her on the pressures of public life and instructed her in the ways of the good wife, and if Jenny accepted their direction, as she claims she did, she seemed to do so with gritted teeth: "Move on and let go of the anger I did," she says, the Yoda-speak resolution that led her to remain married.

And then Mark met the woman he'd call his soul mate, Maria Belen Chapur, an elegantly handsome brunette with a businesswoman's mind, Jenny without the politics and the Bible verses. The meeting occurred on another adventure trip, this one to South America; he met Chapur at a dance. She spoke four languages, including Chinese, and her idea of a good beach read was a book by Alan Greenspan. She was a fine dancer, and so was Sanford, and that's all it was: economics and dancing.

The beginning of the affair waited until a government

junket to Argentina in early 2008. Sanford's come-on seems to have been the same one that had worked two decades previously with Jenny: he talked about his farm. If that sounds silly, consider the romance of New Year's Day 1988, as recorded by Jenny. The morning after the party, he woke her early and dressed her in hunting gear for an expedition, and as the sun rose he introduced her to the farm's inhabitants, egrets and blue herons, palmettos and oak trees veiled by Spanish moss. It was a "place outside of time," she'd write, a place "where Mark's heart resided."

Maria would feel the same way. "Don't know why you think you bore me with the description of your farm," she wrote Mark, on July 4, 2008. "I am an urban girl but that doesn't inhibit me from loving other things, especially if they are the ones you love. I was able to imagine the place with every single detail."

Much would eventually be made of Sanford's penchant for reciting such details. The media would mock him for writing to his Argentinean lover about his tractor. And yet, Sanford's tractor e-mail—hacked from Chapur's computer, possibly by a jealous ex-lover, and sent to a South Carolina reporter—is the loveliest thing he ever wrote, true romance, the quirky, unpredictable, and deeply personal kind:

> Though I have started every day by 6 this morning woke at 4:30, I guess since my body knew it was the last day, and I went out and ran the excavator with lights until the sun came up. To me, and I suspect no one else on earth, there is something wonderful about listening to country music playing in the cab,

air conditioner running, the hum of a huge diesel engine in the background, the tranquility that comes with being in a virtual wilderness of trees and marsh, the day breaking and vibrant pink coming alive in the morning clouds—and getting to build something with each scoop of dirt. It is admittedly weird but one of my more favorite ways of escaping the norms, constant phone calls and formalities that go with the office—and it probably fits with my weakness in doing rather than being—though you opened up a new chapter last week wherein I was happy and content just being.

*

"I hate to see anybody I love fall," Cubby Culbertson, Sanford's lifeline to Christianity for the elite, would declare. Cubby, Sanford's "spiritual giant," had been thrice-married himself. With such a rich well of experience to draw from, and with money rolling in from court-reporting contracts all over South Carolina, Cubby and wife #3 devoted themselves to conducting relationship boot camps for well-to-do South Carolina couples, including the Sanfords. When the Sanfords' turn at boot camp came (there's a waiting list), Mark and Jenny volunteered the governor's mansion for the sessions of prayer and Bible study on correct relations between man and woman. Cubby taught that as Christ is to his bride, the church, so must the husband be in his wife's eyes: revered and obeyed. In return, he should be to her like Christ, a "suffering servant," ready to die for his sheep— her—and in charge because of that commitment. It's an interpretation of the Christ story based not on the world of the Gospels but on the modern-day fundamentalist romance with the world of chivalry. Women submit to male headship— those are the terms of art—because men sacrifice, or at least make it clear that they'd be *willing* to sacrifice, in defense of womanly virtue. It's an even exchange, goes the thinking; the relationship is "separate but equal," husband and wife each able to claim the title of "servant leader."

That's a revealing label, self-applied in a broader political context not just by C Streeters but also by powerful people across the spectrum. On its surface, it makes no more sense than Sanford's self-annihilating statement that "the biggest self of self is indeed self." But then, reason is not its justification. The paradox of humility as authority that's inherent in the term "servant leader" is the essence of the fundamentalist threat to democracy: not brute force but seduction. It's the promise of support and intimacy in return for power. "The idea of the power," a Family leader named Bob Hunter says of the Family's prayer cells for servant leaders, "is that through the relationships, you can stand before the country and say, 'Look, we love each other. This country can be different.'" "God-led," that is, according to the Family's understanding of Jesus plus nothing. "Maybe it's power, but it's sort of bottomed in love. It's a little tricky."

Tricky, indeed. In *To Serve God and Wal-Mart: The Making of Christian Free Enterprise*, Bethany Moreton, a historian of religion at the University of Georgia, traces "servant leader" back to its origins in a 1968 essay by a New Age management consultant named Robert K. Greenleaf. As a form of management—of control—the logic becomes clear. Employees resent rigid, authoritarian bosses, while study after study has shown that productivity improves when the people in charge humble themselves, rhetorically, at least. Greenleaf's servant leadership wasn't a redistribution of power; it was a revision of its presentation, similar to Doug Coe's decision to "submerge" the institutional identity of International Christian Leadership, rebranding its now-hidden hierarchy as simply "a worldwide family of friends" and pursuing God-led government without recognition.

"Putting aside your ego like Christ," Moreton writes of the concept, "did not mean renouncing your ambitious career goals, but rather furthering them through other people." Remarkably, this is understood as humility, not cynicism. By the same logic, "male headship" is a burden, a selfless choice by a husband to assume authority as a form of sacrifice. It's lonely at the top! Power—the willingness and the ability to define what counts as "sacrifice"—is love.

For C Streeters, though, it really is lonely at the top, since to get there—whether "there" is a corner office in Washington or control of a woman—one must maintain a stubborn denial of what Martin Luther King Jr., outlining a different version of servant leadership, called "the drum major instinct." Everybody wants to be drum major, King taught; everybody wants to lead the parade. That is, everybody wants to be recognized. Ego is real, said King. It's desire. If it's acknowledged and harnessed, desire can make you a drum major for justice. If it's denied, desire will seek other channels—money, status, power. King's Christianity liberated desire and set it to work beating freedom's drum. Fundamentalism hides desire and then monitors its escapes— flashes of joy—and its perversions, desire twisted by repression. Fundamentalism calls both "sin," and trades in them like currency.

Cubby Culbertson's boot camp for the Sanfords culminated in Date Night, spousal counter-interrogations before God and the rest of Cubby's chosen pairs. It was theater for what Abram Vereide used to call "soul surgery," cutting into the self and exposing one's desires in front of a small group of social equals. The price of admission is a controlled confession of one's sins, but those sins, shared in secret, then become a badge of one's belonging. As Abram saw it, they also became a form of control, each "top man" aware of and protecting, if necessary, the weaknesses of the other. "They're into living with what *is*," says the Reverend Rob Schenck, a fundamentalist activist, of C Street's version of private prayer meetings for the elite. That is, preserving "what is," defending the God-given order. Defined by status rather than suffering (as in the case of groups like Alcoholics Anonymous), soul surgery—or C Street, or Cubby's boot camp—substitutes class for accountability.

It's "pretty intense," Cubby told a reporter for the Associated Press. It was the only interview he granted; he was stung, perhaps, that even his evasions would be interpreted as meaningful. "When asked if he had met Maria, Culbertson paused, then looked up, an embarrassed smile creasing his face. 'I'm not going to comment,' he said." The truth was that he had. He'd chaperoned a date between her and Sanford.

In November 2008, the Republican Governors Association made Sanford their chairman. To celebrate, Sanford and some of the governors went to Ireland to shoot birds.

Then, without telling Jenny, he went to Manhattan. He was having some quiet time alone in the city, he explained when she tracked him down. He told her the pressure was building. He said his bald patch was growing. He insisted he wasn't avoiding her. He just needed to be by himself, to consider what was happening. She thought he meant his political ascendancy. But he was with his lover. He was searching, he'd later say, for "the key to [his] heart." The servant leader wanted to be neither for a while.

That January, Jenny was looking for some documents related to a dispute about the farm between Sanford and his siblings. She says she decided to peek in a file labeled "B" because she thought it stood for "Bill," Mark's brother. Instead, she found "Belen," and a collection of their e-mails.

"Sweetest," he begins one of his love letters. He stammers about politics, "the VP talk," the governors association. "There are but 50 governors in my country and outside of the top spot, this is as high as you can go in the area I have invested the last 15 years of my life." That is, his life with Jenny: the career they'd built together. And then, rhetorically, he throws it away — deliberately, rhapsodically:

> I have been specializing in staying focused on deci-
> sions and actions of the head for a long time now —
> and you have my heart. You have oh so many attributes
> that pulls it in this direction. Do you really compre-
> hend how beautiful your smile is? Have you been
> told lately how warm your eyes are and how they
> softly glow with the special nature of your soul. I

remember Jenny, or someone close to me, once com-
menting that while my mom was pleasant and warm
it was sad she had never accomplished anything of
significance. I replied that they were wrong because
she had the ultimate of all gifts—and that was the
ability to love unconditionally. The rarest of all com-
modities in this world is love. It is that thing that we
all yearn for at some level—to be simply loved unconditionally for nothing more than who we are—not
what we can get, give or become....As I mentioned
in our last visit, while I did not need love fifteen years
ago—as the battle scars of life and aging and politics have worn on this has become a real need of
mine. You have a particular grace and calm that I
adore. You have a level of sophistication that is so fit-
ting with your beauty. I could digress and say that
you have the ability to give magnificently gentle kisses,
or that I love your tan lines or that I love the curves
of your hips, the erotic beauty of you holding yourself (or two magnificent parts of yourself) in the
faded glow of night's light...

Tan lines. Following Sanford's confession, he'd be
mocked for those two words almost as relentlessly as for hiking the Appalachian Trail. But there is nothing cheap about
this letter, neither its love nor its lust, and certainly not its
anguish, its need. Later, when he wept before Jenny, the
tears were not for her or for the lover he then thought he
might never see again, but for himself. "He had always been
so *good*, so dutiful," Jenny writes. He had been a servant for

the people, "true to his conservative principles in his political career although doing so meant going against a considerable tide." This was for himself.

It was, for Mark Sanford, the beginning of honesty. Not the service part, the self part. But desire had been down so long that it was stunted. Deep, yes; but narrow. His recognition of himself, and of his lover, did not help him see others. Not Jenny, to begin with, but also not "the people" for whom he thought he had sacrificed himself. By the spring of 2009, under C Street's counsel, he committed himself to falling in love with his wife again — an act not of will but of obedience to God's order. It was a moral austerity plan. At the same time, he was committing South Carolina, a poor state hit harder than most by recession, to something similar, only economically. The weak governor had found his power, and it was to say no: to $700 million in federal funds. Weakness, he preached in an endless succession of appearances, should not be rewarded. Liberty must stand on its own.

Mark Sanford, meanwhile, needed to see his lover. Please? he begged Jenny.

She turned to Cubby. He agreed to escort Mark to Manhattan for one last meeting. "His willingness to help Mark and me discreetly was a tremendously generous and selfless act," writes Jenny. That night, after Cubby, Mark, and Maria had finished dinner, Cubby texted: "Sleep well. He played by the rules."

Sanford had done so well over the years under Cubby's tutelage. He had stayed focused on what mattered: cutting taxes, privatization. If he did not quite speak God's word — he was never a thumper—he paid it lip service whenever required. For fifteen years he had "invested" himself. What had he accomplished? Very little, but that wasn't a problem. The goal wasn't change, it was order. Later he would confess that there had been a "handful" of other women, but that he'd never quite "crossed the ultimate line." Which line was that? Sex, depending on how you define sex. Sanford would say he didn't have any. And if that didn't make him a saint, it meant at least that he was trying.

Slippage wasn't the point, the point was power. Not to change anything; not to build a theocracy; simply to pre-serve what God has already created, a world of privilege and charity, to each according to God's wisdom. The day after Jenny discovered the e-mails, Sanford asked her to call C Street "Jack," the Family man who'd patched their mar-riage together once before. His advice was the same this time, and Jenny meant to follow it. "Jack understood men in power well," writes Jenny. "If Mark said things that hurt or upset me, I was not to respond....I should hand these hurts to Jack, who would confront Mark in a way that my tears would derail. This method would allow me, Jack said, to be like 'the Bride of Christ.'"

She'd later be applauded for *not* standing by her man, but then she dutifully did so until Jack gave her permission to try another strategy. A shock, he decided, was what San-ford needed in order to refocus. Jack arranged for a tempo-rary house for Jenny and the boys in Annapolis, where the Coes lived ("Jack" may well be a Coe, Doug or David or Tim, the men who typically handle the most delicate spiritual situations, angry mistresses, and angry wives). She canceled her plan only when Mark learned of it and declared that he still wanted to go to Argentina. Jack knew what to do. He advised Jenny to put aside her anger, her accusations, and her tears, and to retire to the family's $3.5 million beach house, inviting Mark to join her. No pressure. He could be Christ, and she would play church, the doors always open, waiting for his return.

But that wasn't what Sanford wanted anymore. For fifteen years, he had pursued *service*, by which he meant *power*, but the irony is that he never felt like he had any. He'd been into living with what is. He'd been a gyroscope, and he'd needed something to keep him going: Ayn Rand, then Jenny, then C Street, then Cubby Culbertson. But he was tired of spinning.

So he ran. Someone found surveillance footage of Sanford's last trip to Argentina, and the news broadcast it in a loop, played for laughs and something deeper, too—a warning, because the video itself is a scarlet letter in the image of Sanford in rumpled madras, head down and big beak pointed forward as he hoofs it through a deserted airport alone, dragging his suitcase behind him.

Run, Sanford, run.

One needn't endorse adultery to recognize that this grim-faced man is not a hound but a soul in transit between two worlds. And one needn't be a conservative to forgive him for wanting to flee the political one, the pious one, where "love" is defined as what is, not what could be. He wanted to live in a world where love is a tractor at dawn and glorious tan lines, not a principle but a desire. Which would you choose?

There are, of course, the children. But if conservatives' tolerance for the secret libertinism of their champions is the height of hypocrisy, where on the ladder should we place those liberals who bemoaned the damage done to the sanctity of marriage? They canonized Jenny Sanford—*more* conservative than her husband—and asked why he could not have resisted love "for the sake of the children," the rhetoric used for decades by fundamentalists who'd like to make divorce illegal. " 'Hypocrite!' they didn't quite thunder," wrote JoAnn Wypijewski, a columnist for *The Nation* who enraged liberal readers by defending Sanford. "Christians thunder; liberals sneer, but it amounts to the same thing, counting sins."

The real scandal of Mark Sanford was not his departure but his return. Here was a man walking away from power. Clumsily, selfishly, but headed in the right direction. He wasn't leaving responsibility behind—Gov. Bug Lamp, vetoed into irrelevance within South Carolina by his own party and courted for the national stage precisely for his ability to say nothing a teenage Randroid couldn't imagine, fulfilled no real public responsibility. He was a false front, a prop for American fundamentalism's status quo religion. But now he was leaving C Street behind—letting go of his own empty paternalism.

Instead, he came back. To Jenny, to Cubby, to C Street. He didn't quit power, he praised it. He praised himself: I'm like King David, he said, I'm chosen.

The Republican Party no longer thought so. Sanford's political career is dead, even as newly single mother Jenny's began rising (she has campaigned for Tea Party candidates with Sarah Palin). But what if Mark hadn't slipped past

Cubby to make that last flight to Argentina? What if Jack from C Street and his brothers hadn't been busy handling payoffs for Ensign? What if there had been time for one more round of soul surgery before he made his confession? Perhaps then he would have been chosen the Republican Party's next savior, and the public would be none the wiser. "I can only imagine," laments Jenny, "where I would be this very moment and what our family and future would be like if Mark had listened to and respected the advice of his dear friends instead of following his 'heart.'"

The tragedy of Mark Sanford is that he did listen to the advice of his "dear friends" (a term that surely deserves scare quotes more than "heart" does), only it was too late— C Street couldn't redeem him. Nor could they use him. He wasn't King David, after all. He was unchosen.

But: what if? What if he had kept running? Dropped his suitcase in the airport and sprinted, his loafers pumping, madras flapping, those long legs opening up across the tiles, so fast not even the camera would be able to catch him?

Or: What if he had followed his heart, to Argentina and back again, to call a different press conference?

What if he had said: "I'm sorry, South Carolina, I've learned the hard way that the heart wants what it wants— no, not Woody Allen's stepdaughter, just love and recognition and maybe a living wage—and so I'm going to take that seven hundred million dollars, to start with, and share it among the poorest of us. I'm raising taxes, too, but only on people like me, rich people, and the proceeds are going to go to schools. Sex ed and tango lessons. And then I'm legalizing gay marriage, because I've been thinking about tan lines, and about my mother, and, yeah, that sounds a little complicated, but so is love. It's complicated, but it's not a sin. I love my boys and will always be there for them, but I'm not sorry for loving Maria, here, standing with me today. She's my soul mate. I think. I'm not sure, South Carolina, because the truth is, I don't know a lot about myself. Which, I get it, is ironic, because I'm very, very, very selfish, I'm kind of a creep, or maybe, I don't know, a boy in a man's body. Cut me some slack, y'all, I never really got past *The Fountainhead.*

"Which is why, beloveds, my darlings—is it okay for a guy to say that? Man! I just feel like I can say fucking anything now!—which is why, darling South Carolina, I'm resigning. I have some reading to do. I'm going to start with the Bible, because I'm beginning to think I may have been given some bad information. Solomon, I think, that pretty song"—and here the governor would hiccup, his eyes would go wide, his mouth would begin moving as if by a force not his own, he would be speaking so rapidly we would just barely be able to make out his beautiful words— *"Thy two breasts are like two young roes that are twins, which feed among the lilies, thy two magnificent parts, and the roof of thy mouth is like the best wine for my beloved, that goeth down sweetly, causing the lips of those who are asleep to speak—"* Sanford would stop, awestruck. "Cubby never had us read *that!*" The press corps would realize they had witnessed a miracle, a true gift of tongues. All of South Carolina would forgive him, even as they were glad Gov. Bug Lamp would soon be leaving. Rolling out for Buenos Aires in the tractor at dawn, just Mark and Maria in the vibrant pink, listening to the hum of the huge diesel engine, maybe Toby Keith on the radio singing "You Shouldn't Kiss Me Like This."

*   *   *

Last and least, John Ensign, an ordinary man with extraordinary hair, the only one of the C Street philanderers to remain married. Pickering carried a torch, and Sanford longed for a "heart connection," but Ensign, it seems, really was just messing around. Not because he was a hound—he was a prude, in fact, who called for Clinton's resignation even before Ken Starr—but because he could; because she, the mistress, was there. In the same house as his wife.

His best friend and one of his senior aides, Doug Hampton—a giant, bear-shaped man with a soft voice, who would take his woes to the media before going silent in the face of a Justice Department investigation—lived with his wife, Cindy, in the gated community across from the Ensigns' gated community. In December 2007, their house was burglarized. "We were asked to go over and stay with the Ensigns," Hampton would say. "We're close, really close. Close friends. We've been close friends for a long time. Very close while we live here in Nevada. While living in the house, Cindy and John got together."

The irony is that John and Doug had long been a different sort of couple: Promise Keepers together, C Street brothers. Ensign was a resident of the house on Capitol Hill and Hampton a Family man for many years, appointed by Ensign in 2006 to his staff—with a salary of $160,000, nearly as high as permissible despite Hampton's lack of experience—to help him follow Christ in Washington. "Walk alongside in whatever capacity possible," Hampton would explain. "Same kind of model that Jesus exhibited in the Bible."

What made Ensign betray him? Nobody knows, not even Hampton. Cindy had a history with Darlene Ensign, the same interests, the same style. Both are brunettes, fit, strong-jawed, with nearly identical smiles. They are both devout Christians. Cindy worked for Ensign, and she seemed more excited by Washington than Darlene; but that was likely because it was new to her. If cheating on your wife with a close friend is more awful than dancing in the open air in Argentina, it's also a lot more common. There was nothing unusual about Ensign's transgression except for the way it ended.

"I chose to bring in some really close friends of ours," Hampton told Las Vegas television host Jon Ralston. He decided to go public after an estimate that the damages inflicted by Ensign equaled $8.5 million—so that the Hampton family could be "made whole"—netted only $96,000 (from Ensign's parents, in bundles of $12,000, to avoid tax reporting requirements), and a lobbying job that went nowhere. Hampton turned to the Family. "Men that we've known for a long time, ten plus years. Tim Coe. David Coe. Marty Sherman." And, especially, Sen. Tom Coburn, who, according to Hampton, carried his requests to his fellow C Streeter. (Coburn denied, then acknowledged, then denied having done so.) "They're great men," Hampton said. "They're a part of the men who live at C Street."

But as time wore on, and more details emerged about what appeared to be a blatant violation of congressional lobbying laws by Hampton and Ensign, Hampton grew more critical of his C Street brothers. What was their initial advice, asked *Nightline*'s Cynthia McFadden, in an interview that constituted Hampton's second salvo against Ensign and his first against the Family. "Be cool." "Cover it up?" she asked. "No, no, not initially," Hampton answered. The behind-the-scenes men, the Coes and Sherman, told him they needed "power" to confront Ensign; they decided to make Coburn their "hit man." On Valentine's Day 2008, they confronted Ensign at C Street; they even stood over the senator as he wrote a letter to Cindy at their direction, ending the affair—"God never intended for us to do this," he wrote—and then drove him to the FedEx office to overnight it.

The payment by Ensign's parents to the Hampton family constituted a cover-up, ethically if not legally. But the real trouble for John Ensign is what followed. He fired Hampton and then slotted him into a Nevada lobbying firm with the promise that he'd arrange clients for the lobbying rookie. And he did. (Former staffers say Ensign knew he was breaking the law.) It wasn't enough, financially or emotionally. Hampton was close to losing his house; he was broke; his marriage was a shambles; he'd lost his best friend. He needed more money. Ensign's allies would accuse him of extortion; he'd say he wanted justice, that he understood now the danger to democracy presented by the corruption he'd been victim of and party to. Most people thought he was just out for vengeance; he'd probably try to write a book like Jenny Sanford's. He wasn't a man with a lot of friends left in Las Vegas, and he had almost none in Washington. And then C Street turned against him. They understood the money, and they'd even helped him with his negotiations. That made sense, biblical capitalism. Damage had been done to Hampton's property, his marriage, his headship; compensation must be made. It wasn't the principle but the amount that eventually divided them. Hampton wanted more than they could win him. And when C Street couldn't help him, he broke its cardinal rule: he talked publicly.

If there had been doubts about Ensign, Hampton's betrayal erased them. They doubled down on the senator. "[They] think the consequences don't apply," Hampton charged. "This is about preserving John, preserving the Republican Party, this is about preserving C Street. These men care about themselves and their own political careers, period."

C Street helped destroy the Hampton family. It remains to be seen whether it can save John Ensign. As I write, Justice Department lawyers are in Las Vegas, sitting at a table in a Marriott off the Strip, interviewing potential witnesses in the case against John Ensign. It's a reluctant parade of men whose fortunes depend not on luck or dice or cards but on hedging their bets with money spread around the system; on knowing the right people; on winning contracts, not games. They're not gamblers, they're businessmen; nothing sinister about them. There is nothing sinister, really, in the story of John Ensign, from beginning to end. If it is sleazy and rotten, a story of personal betrayals and democracy subverted for the sake of "relationships," it is considered notable within the Beltway only for the fact that it's playing out in public. That's ironic, given the fact that if

Ensign is indicted (there is more than enough evidence, say legal observers; whether there's the will is another matter), the cover-up executed in part by the Family will come close to the actual definition of "conspiracy," a word routinely misapplied to C Street and its parent organization.

The Family is not a conspiracy. A conspiracy is a secret agreement to break the law. The Family has no intention of breaking the law. It is not interested in law. God-led government is not a specific agenda but rather a perspective through which all decisions, personal as well as political, should be evaluated. That is what the Family aims to provide, that is the gift it sees itself as providing at C Street. Subsidized rent, maid service, mistress management—these are all incidental. Its concerns are of another kingdom. The Family is not a conspiracy but a religious worldview, one that works through the "kings" spoken of in the Acts of the Apostles and in the Family's list of Eight Core Aspects, and those the Family sees as their modern equivalents. The Family believes it values the "least of these," the poor; which is why it must serve the powerful, those blessed by God with the authority to dole out aid to the deserving.

The congressmen and businessmen of American fundamentalism's elite—not just the Family, but the upper crust that funds the entire movement's crusades—are fond of paraphrasing Luke 12:48: "From everyone to whom much has been given, much will be required." A fine sentiment, at first blush; but, stripped of context, divorced from its Gospel and presented as a maxim—the stuff of Dale Carnegie's *How to Win Friends and Influence People,* not scripture—it is disingenuous. The idea that the powerful are powerful

because they have been "given" their rank and position—
that they did not grasp for it, that they did not politick—is
as deceptive as "*noblesse oblige,*" a moral sleight of hand that
exists to preserve social class. So, too, its corollary, that the
poor should be grateful for whatever blessings trickle down
to them.

In 1994, John Ensign, a casino heir working as a veteri-
narian, told his friend Steve Wark that he ran for office
because God called him. *He* didn't want the power; God
wanted him in Washington. Why? Socialism. He'd taken to
watching C-SPAN late into the evening. It made him furious. What he saw was an insult to everything he'd learned
about charity from church and about the market from the
casino. The government, he believed, was playing God. The
government wanted to make us all the same, to take his
money and give it to a poor man, rather than letting Ensign
make the gift himself, as God and his church led him. How
could he be good if government decided for him?

Some are rich, and some are poor, and to each God
gives a calling. Ensign concluded that his was to help the
weak. And the calling of the weak? Well, they were there to
be helped by Ensign. He got to be a good man; they got to
eat. Everybody won. Thus God's economy.

As a representative from 1995 to 1999, and then as a
senator from 2000 to the present, Ensign has been the
Republican Party's faithful servant, a money machine for its
economic royalism. His first year in Congress, he set a
record for fund-raising. It was his simplicity, say his allies in
Nevada: without much of a mind for details, he never muddies issues. Or *the* issue, really: aside from lending aid to

fellow Family men on moral fronts here and there—fighting the distribution of condoms in Uganda, trying to keep *Playboy* out of prisons—Ensign has been a consistent man of principle in Washington for one overriding cause: free markets, under God.

Where do the "gifts" given to Hampton's family by Ensign's parents fit in that market? Charity? Payments for services rendered? What was the exchange? Did the senator, with the help of C Street, try to bribe his way out of a scandal? If he did, it seems doubtful that he had any sense of moral transgression. Certainly the C Street brothers who helped negotiate payments made to Ensign's mistress and her family are not so afflicted. The sin in their eyes was the sex; everything else, the money and the cover-up, was for love, that of brother for brother. Democracy, they believe, pales by comparison.

3

THE CHOSEN

In the wake of the sex scandals, "C Street" entered the American vernacular as shorthand for pious hypocrisy. Liberal bloggers attributed almost any conservative initiative they didn't like—especially those that smacked of self-righteousness or lunacy—to the "C Street band," a pun on Bruce Springsteen's E Street Band. Sen. DeMint's determination to make health-care reform Obama's "Waterloo"? C Street. (Not true.) Birther bill? Total C Street. (Also not true.) Any politician who'd ever strayed beyond his marriage vows, went the thinking, had probably shacked up at what one blogger called "the Prayboy Mansion." Could it really be a coincidence that the DC madam who tended to Sen. David Vitter's diaper fetish called him "David from C Street"? (It was.) Cartoonist Garry Trudeau dedicated a week and a half of *Doonesbury* comic strips to the plight of

"Senator X," led by God to "The House of the Fallen Sons," at 133 C Street, where he learned the leadership lessons of Hitler and Mao. "I have sinned," says the senator, standing on C Street's stoop. "But I'm special." "You've come to the right place," says a faceless voice from within the building.

And yet there was also a certain facelessness to the glee with which liberals mocked C Street's new chosen. To reduce the meaning of a political sex scandal to hypocrisy is another kind of evasion, an escape into euphemism. Not the polite kind; the satirical kind. But satire, like manners, serves the social order. Manners enact it; satire keeps it in line. So it was with C Street. As a hidden establishment, it embodies the arrogance of Washington; as a subject for derision, it reassures us that its excesses were departures from the norm.

The Family's apostates—those who'd belonged and had left it behind—saw it differently. For them, the ethos of C Street is the norm. As insiders, they saw firsthand that for its adherents the elitist fundamentalism exemplified by C Street isn't an aberration but business as usual. That is, for the many politicians within the orbit of C Street, its religion expresses one of the dominant sensibilities of our times. Simply put, it's the idea that what we want is what God wants. That suggests aspiration, but in practice it amounts to stagnation, the preservation of the present order. At the mass-market level, that idea translates into spiritual self-help tomes such as preacher Joel Osteen's ostensibly apolitical bestsellers, *Become a Better You, Your Best Life Now, It's Your Time.* Books like these offer the promise of individual betterment in exchange for obedience. But obedience to what? American fundamentalists, unlike their Puritan ancestors, for the most part lack a vision of what society should be that goes beyond the artificial nostalgia of a mass-produced painting by evangelical artist Thomas Kinkade (a cozy cottage in the woods) or the megahit Christian novel *The Shack* (in which God cooks pancakes for the hero in a cozy cottage in the woods).

But there's an implicit politics to such messages: it's *your* time, not anybody else's. And there's an even more troubling theology: the abandonment of Christianity's prophetic tradition, the call to "contradict what is," in the words of philosopher Cornel West. "To prophesy," he argues, invoking the practice not just as a religious vocation but as a basic form of democratic speech, "is not to predict an outcome but rather to identify concrete evils."

In the life of an ordinary believer, the trade of obedience for peace is harmless enough. But amplified to a national politics, it becomes something more dangerous: the conflation of obedience and peace, the confusion of the status quo and a godly order, under the cover of piety, humble belief.

Following the C Street scandals, a young man who'd been raised in the Family began sending me documents from his youth. The young man's father, an oilman, was a fund-raiser for the group's activities, but the young man had decided to blow the whistle — anonymously, lest he be banished from his own family. "I guess I should also add," he wrote, "that although I grew up within this organization, I do not share their sentiments." What changed? Nothing more dramatic than college, some philosophy courses, the application of logic—the realizations, first, that when the Family speaks about Jesus it is speaking about itself; and, second, that it is projecting that self out onto the world.

The first document to catch my eye was a snapshot of Col. Oliver North, the point man in a scandal of far greater proportions: the 1980s Iran-Contra affair. To fund right-wing Nicaraguan "freedom fighters," which Congress had forbidden, North ran an illegal program of secret arms sales to Iran. North has since become a Christian Right leader and a drum major for spiritual war, actual and literal—see his FOX News series *War Stories*, featuring 2008's *American Heroes: In the Fight Against Radical Islam*—but his involvement with the Family is more benign, if still well armed. Every year, according to correspondence sent to me by the whistle-blower, North organizes a fund-raiser called Godly Guys with Guns. It's a duck hunt. "Ammunition will be needed for ducks (#2 steel), upland birds (#7½ lead) and sporting clays (skeet loads)," wrote North in 2000, announcing the eleventh year of his fund-raiser (the whistle-blower sent me invitations up to 2009). The colonel takes care of the dogs, the luxury accommodations, and servants to clean the kill for those who prefer not to do it themselves. "In the inimitable words of our beloved friend and mentor, the late Senator Harold Hughes"—the Family's liberal beard in the 1970s, a happy, holy fool who believed in the good intentions of any dictator the Family sent him—"'This may be the most expensive duck you ever shot...but it also may be the pearl of great price.'"

The money goes to the Wilberforce Foundation, listed on the Fellowship Foundation's tax forms as a "supportive ministry." What does Wilberforce do? "Aid, train, educate, and encourage young people in the principles of faith and relationship skills [and] provide food and shelter if needed," according to its tax forms. I was one of those "young people" back in 2002 (I was thirty at the time), when I lived for several weeks at Ivanwald, a house then owned by the Wilberforce Foundation. No one mentioned Wilberforce; we spoke only of the Fellowship or the Family, synonymous. The "principles of faith" I encountered and which I've since learned from other alumni include instruction in "biblical capitalism," "faith in foreign policy," and "God-led" political organizing. More often, though, they were abstract: studies in correct gender relations (the brothers shouldn't court women with abuse in their pasts, because they'll only want more); lessons on the nature of loyalty gleaned from history's strongmen (Hitler, Stalin, and Mao owed their achievements to management techniques they copied from Jesus); and the idea that such loyalty, put in the service of a Fellowship of the elite, could change the world. "Talk to the people who rule the world," David Coe told us, "and help them obey. Obey him." Jesus, that is.

But for all the rhetoric, the Wilberforce Foundation also has a more mundane function. Eric Fellman, a Fellowship employee, put it succinctly to *World,* a Christian conservative magazine: the organization was created "to hold properties" for the Fellowship Foundation.

If I left it at that, the Family would sigh, disappointed. They'd say, "You're missing the point. It's not about what you can see. It's about what you can't see." Or, as Tim Coe explained, in a letter to the whistle-blower's father, speaking of the real meaning of the work they'd under-taken together: "Usually these things have to do with some commitment or covenant I have made and are almost always invisible!"

That's a spiritual term, not a conspiratorial one. American fundamentalism resists the idea that it is political because its ambitions, ultimately, are not. Or, at least, not conceived as such. Evangelicalism, from which fundamentalism grows, emphasizes the salvation and transformation of individuals. And on an individual basis, that transformation most often really isn't political. But applied to power as it already exists, the recruitment of elites, it becomes what one Family leader called "benevolent subversion." A means of achieving political transformation without conflict. Inasmuch as the rest of us accede to that seductive idea, inasmuch as we cling to the myth of harmony at the cost of democracy, we become collaborators. Not in the rise of fundamentalism, but in the exchange of democracy for stability.

The fundamentalist threat of this book's subtitle isn't a barbarian at the gate. Nor is it an ideology that erects stat-ues, a theology in jackboots. It's far more practical than that. It's a religion that asks, like Doug Coe does, "What does Jesus have to say about building roads?" And just as important, Who'll get the contract? What's the margin? We've reached a point where piety and corruption aren't at odds but are one and the same. It's a familiar moment to students of history: the late stage of empire, hairline frac-tures shooting through the foundations of society. They're like cracks in the sidewalk; by the time you see them, the damage has already been done.

So consider this chapter a postmortem. I tried to trace the course of the disease, to follow the money and the power out from C Street into the world. The first stop was the Pentagon. Next was Sri Lanka, where the trail ran right up to the edge of a war. I followed it to Lebanon, where the Family's theology of "reconciliation" has been strung like a fuse; and that fuse led me into the schemes of a crooked congressman on the Family payroll, and a senator with a "heart for the poor," as fundamentalists say. It's a phrase that all too often means little more than a paternalistic cover for the predatory instincts of believers who are rich in love, for their own righteousness, and poor in mercy, for the millions who become collateral damage in elite fundamentalism's crusade for the hearts of kings and dictators.

In 1976, Campus Crusade founder Bill Bright, a former candy salesman who'd built up one of the largest evangelical organizations in the world by recruiting students, created a new agency for their guardians. *Our* guardians; Bright, inspired by Family founder Abram Vereide, was moving off campus, up and out to the highest reaches of American power. "Yeast in the capital," an evangelical newsletter called his new ministry. Bright called it Christian Embassy, the same name Vereide had given his original foray into Washington. "There are 435 congressional districts," Bright put it, "and I think Christians can capture many of them by next November." The cofounder of Christian Embassy, John Conlan, a Republican congressman from Arizona obsessed with un-Christlike "income-redistributing policies," was not even that genteel: he got into political evangelism after being forced to suffer a Jewish opponent for his seat, an opponent who, Conlan's supporters deduced, lacked "a clear testimony for Jesus Christ." A vote for Conlan, the congressman told Arizonans, "is a vote for Christianity."

That was 1976. In 2006, I reported on a Christian Embassy video of senior flag officers presenting just such testimonies for Christ, on duty at the Pentagon. I was interested in their language. "We are the aroma of Jesus Christ," bragged Maj. Gen. Robert Caslen. But a watchdog organization called the Military Religious Freedom Foundation (MRFF) was interested in their uniforms, and the fact that they were lending them to a religious cause, a deep breach of military rules and tradition.

MRFF demanded an investigation. In 2007 the Department of Defense issued an inspector general's report finding that seven top officers had violated military regulations; that the Pentagon's senior chaplain had breached security for Christian Embassy's staff; and that one officer, an adviser to the Joint Chiefs of Staff, declared Christian Embassy a "quasi-federal entity," the same status accorded NASA. What should be done? Nothing, concluded the report. "Corrective action" was left to the judgment of some of the same men featured in the video. It was a slap on the wrist. Or maybe not even that—most of the officers who'd crossed the line, singing "Onward, Christian Soldiers," seemed like they'd stepped on a fast track, adding stars to their shoulders and assuming major commands.

So MRFF asked the logical question: Who was the inspector general? Retired Lt. Gen. Claude "Mick" Kicklighter. "Even a cursory look at Kicklighter's track record raises red flags," says MRFF's director of research, Chris Rodda, pointing to his refusal to investigate allegations by a Halliburton/KBR employee in Baghdad that she'd been raped by other defense contractors. But it wasn't until 2009 that Rodda, reviewing old files, noticed that Gen. Kicklighter had served as a board member of the Fellowship Foundation, the Family's main 501(c)(3) organization. It was my turn to review old files. In 2005, I'd interviewed one of the directors of Christian Embassy, Sam McCullough, for a profile of Sen. Sam Brownback. Because I was coming from Brownback's office, McCullough, a dour man who communicates as much through half smiles and long silences as words, assumed I was a "friendly"—a journalist who could be counted on to represent the cause with sympathy.

When I asked him about the Fellowship, he rattled off a list of overlapping members: Rep. Robert Aderholt (R-AL), Rep. John Carter (R-TX), and Sen. Jim Inhofe. "Mike McIntyre from North Carolina"—young, and oddly far-right for a Democrat—"is one you might want to visit with. He lives with a bunch of guys that are believers over in their C Street house."

What was the relationship between the two organizations?

"There's a lot of crossover," said McCullough. "We're really in agreement doctrinally, and cooperative on activities."

"Crossover" should have been enough for Gen. Kicklighter to recuse himself from the investigation. Our curiosity piqued, Rodda and I started digging deeper, and soon we learned that the entire investigation was a closed loop: in 1987, Christian Embassy's Flag Officer Fellowship had been cofounded by—Claude Kicklighter. The inspector general had found himself not guilty. (A call to Kicklighter's civilian office was returned by the current inspector general's chief of public affairs. He argued that Kicklighter hadn't assumed office until April 2007 and thus wasn't responsible, a perplexing point given that the report came out nearly three months later.)

As far as Rodda was concerned, the Kicklighter connection put the Family in MRFF'S jurisdiction. Her first step was to return to the video that had started the trouble. Before, she'd been paying attention to the officers. Now, she looked at the congressmen.

Rep. John Carter, for instance, boasts of a missionary trip to Africa funded by the organization: "We were congressmen goin' over there to represent the Lord," he said. The wall between church and state, he'd discovered, did not extend to the governments of nations dependent on U.S. foreign aid. "Our message was very simple. 'We are here to tell you about Jesus of Nazareth and what he teaches.'"

But there was nothing in his records declaring Christian Embassy funding, a lapse that would likely be illegal under the 2007 OPEN Government Act if Carter took that same trip today. Carter's records did show several trips funded by the International Foundation—a "doing business as" name of the Fellowship Foundation. Did the International Foundation pay for Carter's Christian Embassy mission? Carter's office wouldn't answer. But to the Embassy's Sam McCullough such overlap is natural. "There's some trips we've gone on, they've done with us. We've sent some of the people that we're working with on a trip with them."

The Family usually foots the bill for these missionary expeditions. In 2004, the Family spent $14,980 to send Rep. Carter and Rep. Joe Pitts to Belarus. John Ensign has enjoyed travel to Japan, Jordan, and Israel that cost more than $15,000. The official list of travelers also includes Sen. Jim Inhofe, Sen. Tom Coburn, Rep. Frank Wolf (R-VA), Rep. Pete Hoekstra (R-MI), Rep. Robert Aderholt, and Rep. Mike Doyle, who has done the Lord's work in Aruba and the British Virgin Islands, a popular Family destination. Even the chosen need vacations.

But most of the travel is to foreign policy trouble spots: the Middle East, Eastern Europe, the Balkans, Pakistan, Afghanistan, Iraq, Central America, Africa's oil-rich nations. And even though the political missionaries charge their travel sometimes to the taxpayers, sometimes to the Family, they aren't representing U.S. interests; they're putting the weight of the U.S. Congress behind their private religious crusade. The goal? "Two hundred national and international world leaders bound together relationally by a mutual love for God and the family," according to a document outlining the movement's long-term vision. "The structure is hidden," the document adds. It's a love that walks softly, with the big stick of American power behind it.

The Work—capitalized in Family archives—proceeds under different names. Rep. Robert Aderholt, for instance, a baby-faced Alabaman best known for his crudely theocratic Ten Commandments Defense Act, met with the president of Paraguay in 2004 on behalf of Christian Embassy; he attributes a meeting with the leadership of Ethiopia, which has been fighting a U.S. proxy war in Somalia, to the

Embassy, but didn't report it as such; and the Family sent him to Israel, where the Family's fellowship group in the Knesset is led by Likud Minister of Information Yuli-Yoel Edelstein. The International Foundation paid for seven trips for Aderholt between 2006 and 2010, totaling $62,000. His most recent trip took place in the spring of 2010, when the Family sent him to Greece and the Balkans, for "shopping and sightseeing" and to rendezvous with Family contacts at the Balkan edition of the National Prayer Breakfast, the Southeast European Gathering.

Aderholt's travel records led MRFF's Rodda to the discovery of yet another Family entity, the Ambassadors of Reconciliation Foundation, a nonprofit that lived and died in the space of little more than a year with no publicity, its lifespan like that of a mayfly. It was born, it spawned, and then, its purpose fulfilled, it died.

The Ambassadors came into being in 2004 with a $100,100 grant from an unnamed source, quickly followed by another of $524,107, $100,000 of which came from the Fellowship Foundation—to which it listed its relationship on tax forms as "none." The Fellowship's accountants weren't so coy; they named the Ambassadors a "supportive ministry." The Ambassadors' board of directors said "family" in every way. Along with Doug Coe and another member of the Fellowship Foundation's board of directors, there was a father-son team: William Aramony, the former United Way chief who served six years in prison for looting the charity to pay for his affairs, and Aramony's son, Robert, who had been on the payroll of a United Way spin-off organization.

Its first year, the Ambassadors gave a grant of $10,000 to

the Fellowship Foundation. The next year, it transferred $450,469 to the Fellowship Foundation, a sizable improvement on the Fellowship Foundation's investment, still listing the relationship between them as "none." And then it promptly closed up shop. Its only activity in between seems to have been spending $7,612 to send Aderholt to Sri Lanka, its mission "to expose the U.S. political, business, and spiritual leadership to problems and opportunities in other parts of the world." Aderholt (who wouldn't comment) would have likely met with Sri Lankan government officials linked to a nonprofit called the Grassroots Foundation — granted $148,772 by the Fellowship Foundation that same year. The founder of Grassroots, a Sri Lankan telecom executive named Zarook Marikkar, also founded Sri Lanka's Parliamentary Leadership Group, which he describes as "part of the U.S. Congress Leadership Breakfast Group" — the Family. What did they have in common? The principles of Jesus; also, guns. The American politicians had them, Sri Lanka needed more. One massive killing stroke, the Sri Lankan government believed, could end their decades-long war against the Tamil minority.

Beginning in 2004, the first year Marikkar led his Sri Lankan prayer group to Washington to meet with the mother ship, the money flowed: more than $50 million in military aid over the next three years. (By comparison, from 2000 to 2003, Sri Lanka received a fifth of that amount in military aid.) Also that year, Sri Lanka began receiving money from the State Department's Foreign Military Financing program—$2.5 million, explicitly to buy American-made weapons and pay for the Sri Lankan armed services to receive

American-led military trainings. The money was modest, by American standards, but big in Sri Lanka, a poor island nation of around twenty million people. Really, though, it was the thought that counted: facing international condemnation for its massive human rights abuses, the Sri Lankan government took the infusion as a green light to win its war against the Tamil Tigers by any means necessary.

In February 2008, Zarook Marikkar led another government delegation to the National Prayer Breakfast for meetings with Aderholt, Alabama's Republican senator Jeff Sessions (a member of the Armed Services Committee), and GOP leader Rep. Mike Pence, a member of the Foreign Affairs subcommittee on South Asia. Not long after the Sri Lankans returned home, the Sri Lankan government began its final campaign. Reconciliation? Not exactly. By then, the Tamil Tigers were already beaten. They wanted to negotiate. Three hundred thousand Tamil civilians crowded onto a beach that had been designated a safe zone and waited.

And then the government started shelling. "Intentionally and repeatedly," declares a 2010 report by the International Crisis Group. They targeted "civilians, hospitals, and humanitarian operations." Estimates of the dead are at least in the tens of thousands. Aderholt didn't say a word.

On the day of the 2009 National Prayer Breakfast, a group of fifteen congressmen, including Aderholt, Wolf, and Pitts, delivered a letter to the Sri Lankan ambassador demanding a little payback for their spiritual support: they wanted the nation's Buddhist party to kill a bill that would outlaw the use of "force, fraud, or allurement" in seeking religious conversions.

The Family has good reason to oppose such measures. In Lebanon, a country that has long been violently divided between Christians and Muslims, it has used just such methods to introduce Muslims to its "universal inevitable"— Jesus, American-style. Which brings us back to C Street. At the heart of the effort is Sen. Tom Coburn, the C Street Republican who lied about his efforts to negotiate a financial agreement between Sen. Ensign and his mistress's husband.

Coburn is one of the few members of his class of '94 radical Right coterie to voluntarily honor his commitment to term limits, serving just six years in the House. But he published his book, *Breach of Trust: How Washington Turns Outsiders into Insiders*, in 2003—a year before he returned to Washington, this time as a senator, no term limits in sight. He also returned to C Street. It was Coburn, along with Rep. Steve Largent, who had organized the C Street club that included Zach Wamp and pro-life Democrats Bart Stupak and Mike Doyle. These men were, as Coburn writes, in *Breach of Trust*, "a small band of trusted friends in Congress that gave me the security and confidence I needed to stand up for what I knew was right."

Coburn is the conscience of the Christian Right, the man who never waters down his opinions for the sake of prime time. He took a stand against federal spending based on Psalm 15—scripture he'd framed and hung to face visitors in his office—which is a stretch justifiable only if one sees the federal bonds used to raise funds as a form of "usury."

He railed against "attractive young congressional staffers" oblivious to the wages of sexual sin, and shanghaied them into watching a special slideshow he'd assembled, graphic images of genitals ravaged by sexually transmitted diseases. The "greatest threat to our freedom we face today," he has said, are gays, who've "infiltrated the very centers of power."

In 2005, at the Family's behest, Coburn waded into the politics of possibly the most religiously conflicted nation on earth: Lebanon, a "natural battleground," says a Muslim member of the Lebanese parliament, Misbah Ahdab, who later met Coburn in Tripoli. Coburn listed the purpose of his first $6,500, three-day trip as building the same kind of confidential prayer groups in government he met with back in Washington. The difference is that Lebanon has been bloodied by a civil war between Christians and Muslims for most of the last century. "It's kind of difficult here," said Ahdab, a Sunni Muslim who has taken to calling himself a follower of Jesus when speaking with Americans. He meant the secret Christian meetings inspired by Cohen. "It could be misinterpreted or misunderstood. There are a lot of conspiracy theories around."

There's also a lot of history. In 1958, Eisenhower invaded to protect the divided nation's Christian government, and in the 1970s the U.S. intervened again, this time on behalf of a Christian militia modeled on pre-war European fascism. When that didn't work out, the U.S. gave tacit approval to a Syrian invasion rather than face the prospect of an independent Lebanon. U.S. troops went ashore again in 1982, and left in 1983 after Islamic militants drove two truck bombs into marine barracks, killing 241 American servicemen. There have been lulls in the fighting since, but Lebanon is, in short, one of the most dangerous and fragile countries in the world, a nation that is now just barely balanced between its rival Christian and Muslim communities. It's the worst place imaginable for an American politician to attempt the church-state merger he couldn't get away with at home.

"Coburn could not have demonstrated his stupidity more," says John Esposito, a professor of International Affairs and Islamic Studies at Georgetown University, where he runs a center for Muslim-Christian understanding. "It could affect not just U.S.-Arab relations, but more importantly it could affect the relations within the country itself between Muslims and Christians. This situation is really mindless. Lebanon is a tinderbox. All you gotta do is scratch the surface."

The United States did more than that. Between Coburn's first visit in 2005 and his next, in April 2009, the United States committed to $410 million in new military aid, with a shipment of M60 tanks arriving that spring. But Coburn was bringing something bigger: a new kind of Christ for Lebanon. Upon his return to Beirut, traveling with Rep. Mike Doyle, Tim Coe, and two other Family leaders, Lebanon's Muslim "followers of Jesus" threw him a party. Two hundred members of Beirut's business and political elite, including the U.S. ambassador, turned out. Samir Kreidie, a cigar-chomping entrepreneur who counts on his Family relations to bring in contracts for aid work, hosted the event at his Beirut penthouse, the top two floors of a fifteen-story building, with a wrap-around balcony.

"[Doug Coe] introduces them to me," Kreidie told my colleague Kiera Feldman, a journalist with whom I researched the Family's overseas travels. "[Coe] is like a connector of all these foundations all over the world." Much of Kreidie's work is admirable—for example, eye surgery clinics throughout the Middle East—but it is not without its financial rewards. "For example, with time I go more to the States, and I get introduced to bankers or to franchises and I take their franchises to the Middle East. So we decided that when we do business together, we use fifteen percent of the income to serve the poor, and eighty-five percent to our pocket. Nice formula!" He called the Family, with which he has been working since 1993, "a mafia of good deeds," and had coined a Family motto to express the group's idea of common ground between Christians and Muslims: "Jesus for the world." Another Family man, former congressman Mark Siljander, describes Kreidie as "carrier" for an "infectious agent," his term for Jesus. That's not conversion, argues Siljander, but reconciliation: the submission of Muslims to the true Son of God. Politics, Kreidie says, is only a side effect.

"'I come as a person,'" Kreidie remembers Coburn saying at the reception, "'I didn't come as a politician.'" That wasn't quite true—while Rep. Doyle was on the Family's private tab, Coburn charged taxpayers more than $11,000 for his mission. When traveling domestically, members of Congress must hew to a strict budget; but for overseas travel, there's no limit, and the State Department is responsible for making arrangements. Coburn was on the government's generous tab, he was addressing Lebanese leaders, and he was representing the United States. "Senator Coburn was bringing the spirit of Jesus Christ and the teachings of Jesus Christ," remembers MP Ahdab.

" 'We American people," Coburn continued, according to Kreidie, " 'we love the world, and we want to build democracy. We want to build freedom. And also I came to tell you that I forgive you because not every Muslim or every Lebanese or every Arab is bad.' " Then came the heart of Coburn's message: how to reconcile with Israel, three years after the 2006 July War in which Israeli forces, responding to Hezbollah rocket strikes, attacked Lebanese civilians with "reckless indifference," according to Human Rights Watch. Regardless of one's political perspective, it was a horrendously uneven match, with much of Southern Lebanon reduced to rubble, the ruins seeded with cluster bombs, and more than a thousand Lebanese civilians killed. Forty-three Israeli civilians were killed, as well. But such numbers evidently meant little to Coburn, who prescribed his personal Jesus as a balm for the wounds of a war between Muslims and Jews. The solution was for everybody to become Christian, or "followers of Jesus," as the Family likes to say, imagining that to be more neutral phrasing. Not that Coburn was even-handed. His Christ went well beyond America's already Israel-friendly foreign policy, to instruct the Muslims in their spiritual duties; the burden of reconciliation was on them. "He taught us how to love Israel," Kreidie said, his voice warm with the memory. "Who refuses love?" Kreidie asked. "Who?"

Not Kreidie, Coburn's friend of many years. "When there is a senator who loves me and who prays for me, it affects me a lot," said Kreidie. "He gives me such power. And whenever you need something you can call him."

Next on Coburn's calendar was a trip with Kreidie to the north of Lebanon, to see a Family school called the Development Culture Leadership Center (DCL), in the village of Syr. Traveling with them were Rep. Doyle and Tim Coe. In Syr, they would meet another of the Family's men in Lebanon, Mounzer Fatfat. Kreidie is short and squat, built like a troll; Fatfat is tall and straight-backed and handsome, with an earnest look in his eyes. But both men are natural backslappers, followers of Jesus who keep their eye on the money. Through Doug Coe, Fatfat told a colleague at the leadership center, he met not only Jesus but also George W. Bush. A naturalized American citizen, Fatfat joined the U.S. occupation government in Iraq shortly after the fall of Baghdad and won control of the Ministry of Youth, formerly the lucrative fiefdom controlled by Saddam Hussein's son Uday. "I had to convince them that [he] was not coming back," Fatfat told the *Pittsburgh Tribune-Review* of Uday's death. "People thought it was American Hollywood, a trick." But no: Iraq's 167 youth centers and 350 sports clubs were Fatfat's now. His task? Raising money, helping young potential leaders learn English and computer skills—a mission that Fatfat would soon bring home to Lebanon.

After he left Iraq, Fatfat kept up the relationships that had got him there: with Coe, whom he or his staff in Syr provided with daily updates (the password for the center's computer was "dougcoeleb," for Doug Coe Lebanon), and with the State Department, from which he helped win a $200,000 grant to send five Lebanese students to Christopher

Newport University, a public school in Virginia that provided matching funds. The grant was part of a set-aside arranged by Rep. Frank Wolf, and the president of Christopher Newport is former senator Paul Trible (R-VA), a longtime Family member who, according to a former Family member, Kate Phillips, turned the school's honors program into a recruiting vehicle for the Family. "The expression Trible used to say was, 'I have a small universe, but I'm the king of my universe.'" Christopher Newport's vice president for student services, Maury O'Connell, says that the federally funded scholarships were the result of Trible and Fatfat's "kinship" through the National Prayer Breakfast.

Abir Mariam, a member of the class of 2012 at Christopher Newport, is one of the beneficiaries of that kinship. In 2007, Fatfat contacted the principal of Mariam's high school. There was an opportunity for Syr's best and brightest, and Mariam, the school's top student, was summoned for an interview. Fatfat told her he could help her get a Fulbright to America — but there were more important criteria than grades. She sat for an interview with Fatfat and four others. "They wanted to know how I accept other beliefs." Mariam thought they meant American culture. In a way, they did; the Lebanese Christian community is one of the oldest in the world. One didn't have to travel to America to learn about Christ. But the Jesus Fatfat had in mind? For Mariam, that would require an audience with Doug Coe. An overnight stay at the Cedars was the first stop in America for Mariam and the Fulbright scholars.

Coe told her about Jesus, and about America, and Abir discovered she was very good at accepting other beliefs. She is a follower of Jesus now, she says, and she always was; Muslims love Jesus. "We have to follow the message of Jesus. It's like a message from God. So we have to believe in him." When she graduates, she says, she will take that message back to Lebanon, by starting a branch of the Family's program for young would-be politicians. They'll study the "principle of Jesus," she says, and her mentor, Fatfat, will be there to support her at every step along Christ's path.

"Ahmed"* was an adult student who met Fatfat with Mariam in 2007 as part of the program that would later become known as the DCL Center. But Ahmed didn't get to go to America. He was at the center in 2009 when Coburn came with his Family delegation, expanded by the time they got to Syr to include not just Rep. Doyle and Tim Coe but also a number of American businessmen. "Madam Doria," said Ahmed, speaking of a colleague of Fatfat's named Doria Charmand, "asked me to bring some orphans to the center. But I thought, We don't have orphans in Syr! Then she asked me to bring any children who are poor just to get picture with the politicians." That wasn't the only doctored picture. Fatfat presented Coburn and Doyle with a brochure about the center's future. There was a picture of a Lebanese village with a cross over it. But there are no churches in Syr. Maybe they would build one, Ahmed thought: Fatfat had just bought a piece of land close by, for $1.2 million.

"The families of Syr are thinking our children go to the

---

* The young man I'm calling Ahmed has asked to remain anonymous. He did not wish to be identified as having crossed the Fatfat clan.

DCL just to learn the English language," says Ahmed. "But there are a lot of secrets at the DCL. It's for changing minds and getting students to America to study in the U.S. and maybe come back to Lebanon and they have different ideas about Muslims and Jesus. To abandon our culture and our religion. It's a shame on Mounzer Fatfat, on the American people, especially the politicians that they 'help' us in this way to give money to change our minds."

One of Ahmed's teachers was a man named Toufic Agha. A native of Syr, he'd lived in Canada for thirty years, working as a journalist with Radio Canada International and then developing distance education English-language programs. In 2008, Fatfat invited him to return to Syr to run the center's English-language education. Agha was impressed by Fatfat's government connections, both in the United States and in Lebanon. And Fatfat had a powerful sponsor, he told Agha: an American named Doug Coe. When Agha was barely a month into the job, in early 2009, Fatfat told Agha that Coe wanted to meet him. Agha would be visiting Toronto soon; would he make time to go to Virginia?

"I said, sure, I booked a ticket, I went over there, I met Doug in person," Agha told us. "I spent three days at the mansion." The Cedars. "The one meeting I had with Doug Coe, he asked me a question at the beginning of the meeting: 'What do you think is the problem with the world?' And he answered the question: Curriculum. He meant that people are receiving education all over the world but the real education is the principles of Jesus. We have to educate every citizen on Earth about that and become one community. So it's 'Jesus plus nothing.'"

What bothered Agha most was that some citizens seemed to matter more than others. The center wasn't really about Syr; it was about extracting talented youth from the town and its surroundings. "The ultimate objective is that these are individuals who can be influential later on, occupy certain positions in Lebanon, and their loyalty would be to the Family." And it wasn't happening just in Syr; there are leadership centers like the DCL all over Lebanon, and new projects being launched in Jordan. There is an old and ironic precedent for such a practice in that part of the world: the Ottoman Empire's Janissaries, an elite force composed of poor Christian boys plucked from their families for conversion, education, and privilege—in return for absolute loyalty to the sultan.

When Agha brought his concerns to Fatfat, Fatfat told him to think bigger. Just look at the kind of names they were attracting, "high-caliber persons," he told Agha. Agha sent me pictures of Coburn, Doyle, and wealthy American businessmen. The center, it seemed to him, was for them, the Americans, not the children. Then he read the Twitter feed of an American businessman named Clyde Lear, who was traveling with the congressmen. April 5: "Mounzer showed us an orphan school with 3 room full of kids and its [*sic*] Sunday!"—the center and its students, none of them orphans—"Then an [*sic*] acres of land to build upon." Lear had fallen for the misinformation Fatfat fed him. "Orphans, mostly, being taugh [*sic*] by Toufic Agha and others." Agha decided he was being used as an unwitting front man for Fatfat's fake orphan school, "to raise huge funds" from potential donors such as Lear.

Kiera Feldman and I tried to ask Fatfat if that was true. He's a hard man to track down, so we started with a contact Agha put us in touch with, Rami Majzoub, the DCL's "secretary general," listed as the center's contact person in its United States Agency for International Development (USAID) applications. Were they teaching Muslim children "the principles of Jesus?" "Where appropriate," Majzoub stammered. Call Fatfat, he said, signing off. "He'll know the answers to your questions."

We couldn't call Fatfat; we didn't have his number. But an hour later, Fatfat called us from his American home, near Pittsburgh. Unfortunately, he gave us no answers, only more questions: his. Who had told us about the center? How had we "put the pieces together?" What business was it of ours? Fatfat grew increasingly paranoid, his words running together breathlessly. "How do I know you're who you say you are? I mean I could call you and say I'm President Bush and impersonate his voice."

Interesting idea. When we called Tim Coe to ask him about the Family's work in Lebanon, at a number at which I'd interviewed him before, that was exactly his strategy. He answered to "Mr. Coe," but as soon as Kiera Feldman mentioned Samir Kreidie, he told her she had the wrong number and hung up. When she tried back, he said wrong number again—only this time, he pretended to be a middle-aged Indian woman. Or maybe German. It was hard to guess what accent he was trying to pass off. "Nooo, sorrrrry, you haff wrong num-ber!"

So we tried Coburn and Doyle. We never got past Doyle's press secretary, but one night we managed to get the senator on the line. The only thing he had to say was that he hadn't been to Syr. He hung up before we could offer to send him a picture of himself with the "orphans."

"Senator Coburn, I had the honor of his visit," Misbah Ahdab, the Muslim MP from Tripoli, told us. He was the only one left, it seemed, who'd talk to us. Maybe he hadn't gotten the word to go dark on the Family's work in Lebanon. Through the National Prayer Breakfast, Ahdab had come to see Jesus not as part of his tradition but as the very heart of it. "I can see light around some people. There are very few. Definitely, Doug Coe is one of them." Since Coburn came as an emissary of Coe, Ahdab thought, his mission must be of God. "We had a very interesting discussion. I think that his initiative is a very positive one. I know that there are lots of people trying to move in this direction, trying to listen, and trying to pass a certain message. I know that the contact that I had with him, it's probably a part of a big puzzle that he has."

*　　*　　*

What's the puzzle? A PowerPoint presentation called "Reconciliation" offers an answer. "Reconciliation" is the product of a nonprofit corporation called International Peace Organization, "operating under the name" Bridges to Common Ground. Ostensibly, the double-named outfit is an independent organization, but it has close ties to the Family. At least three of its four directors overlap with the Fellowship Foundation or a related organization: President Eric Fellman; Secretary-Treasurer Robert Aramony, the "Ambassador of Reconciliation" who ran the outfit that his corrupt father—also an Ambassador—quietly spun off from United Way; and Director Nassim Matar, former ministry coordinator for the Fellowship Foundation. The International Peace Organization takes its inspiration, meanwhile, from a 2008 book by another Family man, former congressman Mark Siljander: *A Deadly Misunderstanding: A Congressman's Quest to Bridge the Muslim-Christian Divide.* It's a book that encapsulates the sanctimony and the seediness, the self-declared humility and the barely veiled vanity of the fundamentalist threat to democracy. It may well also be the clearest statement of the C Street ethos available, the most definitive declaration of the Family's worldview—the beliefs that drive men such as Coburn and Fatfat, Sanford and Ensign.

It's true that Siljander was a congressman once, serving six years in the 1980s, but the Michigan Republican found his calling in the "advocacy" business. When Siljander was elected at age twenty-nine, in 1981, he wasn't just a conservative, he was an ideologue so zealous that he made the Reagan White House uneasy. He was red-haired, red-faced, and obnoxious enough to make his extranasal Michiganese heard even as a freshman. His positions made for a long list of antis—equal rights for women, abortion, school busing, and Nelson Mandela—and a short, sharp list of pros: the neutron bomb, MX missiles, and prayer in schools. He claimed to be the boldest voice against homosexuality in Congress, and to prove it the bachelor congressman announced through his pastor that he was seeking a God-fearing woman. Siljander's standards, the pastor warned the ladies, "are very high." His greatest success in Congress was legislation restricting American foreign aid from funding abortions, which should have made him popular in his deeply conservative district. But he went too far: his constituents primaried him out of office in response to his request, in 1986, that they "break the back of Satan" by reelecting Mark Siljander.

After he lost the favor of even his far Right district, he learned the advocacy trade—he's not a registered lobbyist—by flacking against the "homosexual agenda" for an outfit called the Alliance Defense Fund. Then he created his own firm, Global Strategies Inc., to add "value by creating strategic alliances" in the service of "effectively penetrating new overseas markets" and finessing government obstacles. His areas of specialty include oil, telecom, and aerospace. Also, perplexingly, salad bars. He draws on a "list of references" at least half made up of Family men, including Inhofe, Doyle, Aderholt, Wolf, Rep. Tony Hall, Ed Meese, and David Laux, a National Security Council veteran and longtime board member of the Fellowship Foundation. Siljander's "gallery" features a photograph of himself with General Kicklighter.

Siljander has mellowed in the years since he left office, on one issue more than any other: Islam. Credit goes to the Family. "As the humiliating final days of my last term were whimpering to a close," he writes, Doug Coe came to him with a way out of the angry fundamentalism of his past. It doesn't have to be like this, Coe said. Let me show you. In time, Siljander writes, he'd come to realize that this oddly compelling man, otherworldly and yet humble, was a messenger from God. Siljander describes him as one of "the three visiting spirits" God would send him, the three hinges on which the door of Mark Siljander's destiny hung. And his destiny was love. He'd been confused, consumed by hate; Coe taught him love. "Love doesn't mean I like you," Siljander would explain years later, when he had become a visiting spirit himself, traveling the world on behalf of the Family, a Coe protégé bringing the sheep—congressmen, dictators, businessmen—together. Love doesn't equal like; it's more powerful. Like makes friends, hate makes enemies, but love? Love seduces. Look at the world through the lens of love, Coe said. There are no enemies, just opportunities.

Siljander looked, saw, and took. In 2008, the same year he published *A Deadly Misunderstanding*, the Justice Department indicted him on counts of money laundering, conspiracy, and obstruction. The government said that in the pursuit of profit, Siljander helped redirect stolen USAID money toward support of one Gulbuddin Hekmatyar, a "Specially Designated Global Terrorist," on behalf of a banned front organization, the Islamic American Relief Agency (IARA). Siljander's defense? The terrorist allegedly supported by the IARA, a drug-dealing Afghani warlord dubbed Mr. Blowback, was really working for the CIA (which may explain why Hekmatyar dropped out of the case); and the $75,000 that Siljander received from the IARA to try to get the organization off the government's terrorism list didn't constitute payments but "charitable donations" to support the writing of Siljander's *A Deadly Misunderstanding*.

By then, the Family had already led Siljander away from his knee-jerk antagonism to Islam and toward a more sophisticated response. Not ecumenicism; stealth evangelism. The head-on approach of traditional fundamentalism—a crude but honest argument for one faith over another—was a dead end, at least when it came to the "kings," the powerful leaders, whom the Family considers its specialty. For them to convert would be suicide. Besides, Siljander learned, the very term "convert" was a mistranslation of an Aramaic word, *shalem*, better rendered as "submit," or "surrender," or "be restored."

That's what the Family wanted for its Muslim friends: restoration, by way of submission. They could keep the label Muslim so long as they bowed before Jesus. "They make every effort to be as normal as possible and not stand out," writes Siljander, the idea being that these "Messianic Muslims," as he calls them, similar to Jews for Jesus, will be able to pass as Muslim Muslims and thus win the support of their Muslim countrymen. The Family doesn't require public loyalty; it wants back-channel connections. "Anything can happen," reads a planning document for the Prayer Breakfast, which Siljander came to understand in a new light, "the Koran could even be read, but JESUS is there! He is infiltrating the world." In fact, Siljander would conclude, Jesus had already infiltrated Islamic scripture. "Jesus," he declares, "is mentioned in the Qur'an more than 110 times," an irrelevancy he began repeating as he traveled the world for his advocacy business. ("Being an ex-congressman opened all sorts of doors.")

He met with the leaders of a West Saharan independence movement fighting the Moroccans. Give up, Siljander told them; Jesus wanted their surrender. In Beirut, he visited with Samir Kreidie. With Coe, he went to see the Sudanese dictator Omar al-Bashir in Khartoum, later indicted by the International Criminal Court for the genocide he was then carrying out in Darfur. Did they speak truth to power? Offer even a hiccup for human rights? No. They told the dictator they wanted to be friends. "He's my prayer partner, by the way," Siljander boasted on a Trinity Broadcasting Network Christian program. "I love Bashir, his heart was changed, and it sure wasn't by my good looks. The Holy Spirit came into the conversation we had with the king"— he meant the dictator—"and melted his heart."

Siljander claims the dictator was so "flabbergasted" by Siljander's assimilation of Islam into Christianity that, like nearly everyone else whom Siljander meets, al-Bashir said, "This is revolutionary." And that melted Siljander's heart; he became an advocate for lifting sanctions on the oil-rich regime. "They realize it got away from them," Siljander said of the genocide, arguing that business deals with the dictatorship would "incentivize" al-Bashir to stop the killing.

"If Jesus were to have adopted the philosophy of the Family," observes Chuck Warnock, a Baptist pastor critical of the organization, "he would have been working with Herod, and he would have taken Pontius Pilate to lunch."

In 1999, President Mathieu Kérékou' of Benin—a former Marxist military dictator born again to Christ and American sponsorship after the Soviet Union collapsed—set up a meeting for Siljander with Libya's Muammar al-Gaddafi. " 'I told the Colonel he needs to sit down and talk with you, Mark,' " said Kérékou'. Siljander invited Coe, but the U.S. State Department scotched the meeting, so they had to settle for Gaddafi's foreign minister. Writes Siljander: "It has been my experience that the U.S. Department of State…

universally rejects the idea of building personal relationships as a means toward reconciliation." Either that, or it
rejects the idea of surrendering U.S. foreign policy to Christian proselytization and whatever business benefits might
accrue to God's chosen ones on the side.

Benin's President Kérékou', whose government Siljander's
Global Strategies Inc. has advised, is a case in point. "I would
like to run my country the way Jesus would, if he were running it," the president told Siljander and Sen. Inhofe, his
traveling companion on that visit. "Do you any have sugges-
tions for me?" Siljander tells Kérékou' he's doing an amazing job. "Mr. President, from what I can see, I think you
have a pretty good sense of exactly what Jesus would do."
Two years later, Kérékou' stole an election with the help of
$2.1 million secretly funneled in by Titan, an American
defense and telecommunications company. Inhofe, coincidentally, pocketed $2,000 from the company that year, but
there was no other evidence linking him to Titan's interests. Following the reelection, Kérékou' quadrupled Titan's
contracts with his desperately poor African nation. But there
was no evidence linking him to Titan's cash infusion. In
2005, Titan admitted a violation of the U.S. Foreign Corrupt Practices Act and agreed to pay $28.5 million in
penalties.

Siljander's years of experience at Coe's side became the
basis of *A Deadly Misunderstanding*, and the book, in turn,
became the basis for the "Reconciliation" PowerPoint promoted by the International Peace Organization, a summary,
in effect, of the Family's soft-sell evangelism; a distillation of
the C Street approach to religious harmony. "Reconciliation"

warns against so-called Words that Confront, such as *crusade* and *convert*, illustrating the difference between them and *dialogue*—the right approach—by juxtaposing a picture of an enraged Adam Sandler, from his movie *Anger Management*, and a puzzling image seemingly lifted from a warm-up scene for a 1970s porno film: a bearded man with a wedding ring putting the moves on a feathered blonde in gold lamé and pearls, a visualization of the crass seduction the Family calls *reconciliation.*

Then it gets sexier. A section on stereotypes allows non-Muslims to see themselves through Muslim eyes. On one side of the screen, there's an armored knight, swinging his sword from behind a shield emblazoned with a cross, an image of the Christian as brutal conqueror; and on the other, what looks like a film still of two sex bombs behind bars, a blonde and a brunette, both of them stripped down to silver loincloths—evidently meant to be an image of Christians as decadent. Next is a segment, entitled "Jesus in the Qur'an," about "common ground" shared by Muslims and Christians. It consists of screen after screen of quotations from the 110 instances in which Jesus is mentioned in Islamic scripture. But "Reconciliation" is rough on some of the Family's friends. The PowerPoint cites candidly anti-Islamic comments by Franklin Graham and Pat Robertson as "Fuel for the Fire." That won't help. "What do we want?" is the concluding question. "To Convert Muslims to Christianity," reads the screen. That's followed up, *Borat*-style, with "NOT." No, what "we" really want is: "A personal relationship with God through Jesus." And how is it not conversion? The last words of the PowerPoint presentation: "The Qur'an points to Jesus." All of Islam, it turns out, was just a clever scheme to bring Muslims round about the long way, back to the savior.

As this book went to press, Siljander made a deal. He pled guilty to obstruction of justice and to acting as an unregistered agent of a foreign power, in exchange for a pass on the money laundering and conspiracy charges. He faces a sentence of up to fifteen years in prison. Was Siljander a secret agent for jihad? Well, technically, yes; but in spirit, that's no more likely than the notion that he dedicated so many years to "reconciliation" work without believing in his own good intentions. The truth is that he was playing both sides, lobbying for a group linked to Islamic terrorists even as he used his connections to recruit "followers of Jesus" from the leadership of Islamic nations, a strategy that confirms every dark suspicion held by adherents of radicalized Islam. Whether out of greed or naïveté, what Siljander did, with the help of the Family, was to create an almost perfectly antidemocratic strategy.

According to the plea summary, on December 13, 2005, in Arlington, Virginia, Siljander told FBI agents that he hadn't been hired to lobby for the IARA, that he hadn't lobbied for the group, and that the money that had made its way to him from the IARA was in support of the book project. Now, "Siljander admits that when he made each of the statements…, he then well knew and believed that each statement was false." He also confessed that he'd "discussed performing services for IARA, and routing payment for those services through non-profit foundations, on the telephone with Hamed and El-Siddi [*sic*]," both naturalized citizens from Sudan.

"Hamed" is Mubarak Hamed, the director of the IARA. Just weeks before Siljander's guilty plea, Hamed admitted that his group had given Siljander money not to help him write a book about how much Muslims love Jesus, but to lobby to have the group removed from a government list of terrorism supporters. "El-Siddi" is Abdel Azim El-Siddig, a fund-raiser for the organization. On July 7, 2010, El-Siddig pled guilty to conspiracy charges related to the case; he faces a sentence of up to five years and a possible $250,000 fine. His plea agreement is almost as damning as Siljander's. "El-Siddig admits that he entered into a conspiracy with Siljander and Hamed to hire Siljander to act as an agent of a foreign principal." In a 2004 phone call with Hamed, Siljander said, "I think we oughta do this number one through foundations and not professionally." That is, off the books. El-Siddig, by then a personal friend of Siljander's who'd traveled with him on Family junkets, would be the middleman through whom Siljander passed information on how to get the money to him.

But El-Siddig was not just a conspirator with Siljander, he was also a spiritual collaborator; as "Abdel," he has a starring role in *A Deadly Misunderstanding*. El-Siddig and Siljander first met not long after September 11, 2001, at a congressional dining room that Siljander still uses for meetings despite having been out of Congress for more than twenty years. Later, Siljander and El-Siddig would travel together to Khartoum—the headquarters of IARA, a fact the plea agreements say the men agreed to conceal from the United States—to meet President al-Bashir. El-Siddig granted Siljander special status as a "spiritual Muslim," that is, a Muslim in essence even though he does not practice Islam. It was a theological term of political convenience that differed little from the Family's usage of the phrase "follower of Jesus."

And the Family, it turned out, was at the center of the relationship between the two men. They shared not only common ground but also common funds. According to the Justice Department, most of the money Siljander had taken from the IARA, money he'd used to develop his "Reconciliation" program, was funneled through the International Foundation, the "doing business as" name of the Fellowship Foundation. What's more, the IARA had stolen it from a USAID grant for real relief work in the impoverished African nation of Mali.

That is what it means, at the intersection of piety and corruption now known as C Street, to "have a heart for the poor." It's a hungry heart, a heart that consumes. Sometimes it's money; sometimes it's souls.

"I'm guilty of two things," says Sen. Jim Inhofe, Coburn's senior colleague from Oklahoma. "I'm a Jesus guy, and I have a heart for Africa." That heart is linked to a savvy mind with a sharp awareness of Africa's natural resources, chief among them oil; the petroleum industry is his biggest donor, a fact about which he's not shy. "I'm trying to get members of the House and Senate to understand how valuable Africa is," he declares. Inhofe is the most intriguing of the Family's apostles in that he is the most candid. He has covered most of Africa for the Family, bringing its "principles of Jesus," backed by American power. As the second-ranking member of the Senate Armed Services Committee, Inhofe has requisitioned military airplanes, at thousands of dollars an hour in operating costs, for his missionary travel. But he's not robbing the Pentagon; as one of the Senate's archconservatives, he has merged spiritual war with actual war, leading the charge for an American military buildup across the continent.

When Inhofe first ran for Senate, in 1994, he told the voters that he was running on the "3 Gs—God, gays, and guns." Inhofe looks like the state he represents: flat-faced, wide-open, and a little raw. A former navy pilot, he still flies at age seventy-six, fearlessly, according to friends who've taken white-knuckle rides. He has giant, elegant hands, surprisingly gentle in the way they float around his points, which are neither elegant nor gentle—especially when it comes to "biblical" values. His office says it has a policy against hiring homosexuals, to prevent conflict of interest. He once took to the floor of the Senate with a jumbo photograph of his children and grandchildren. "I'm really proud to say that in the recorded history of our family, we've never had a divorce or any kind of homosexual relationship."

Inhofe is just as blunt when it comes to spreading God's word. On December 21, 2008, the *Tulsa Oklahoman* placed on its front page a story that could have become a major scandal, had not the paper's editors run it so close to Christmas. Since 1999, Inhofe had taken twenty international trips, at a cost of at least $187,000 in public money—not including the cost of military transportation—to promote what he called "a Jesus thing." He visited Eastern Europe and the Middle East, but his real focus is Africa, especially Uganda, a country he claims to have adopted as a personal responsibility. He credits the Family, and Doug Coe in particular, with opening his eyes to that duty.

As a young representative, Inhofe attended the Family's weekly House Prayer Breakfast meeting only out of respect for Oklahoma representative Wes Watkins, its chairman at the time. "I assumed I was a Christian," he explained to an Oklahoma evangelical magazine. But that didn't mean much more to him than sitting through a service every Sunday. It was a Christian Embassy missionary, Tom Barrett, who challenged Inhofe to a more zealous faith by suggesting Inhofe was lukewarm toward Jesus. Lukewarm? James Mountain Inhofe—that's his full name—wasn't lukewarm about anything! He was a for-or-against man. "So, right there on September 22, 1988 at 2:30 p.m. in the Members Dining Room, I had an experience I will never forget and came to know Jesus."

He became a Prayer Breakfast loyalist, but it took another challenge to turn him into a missionary. It was Doug Coe who gave it to him. "Doug has always been kind of behind the scenes, very quiet," Inhofe told fundamentalist activist Rev. Rob Schenck, in a video Schenck made to defend Inhofe against the *Oklahoman*. "He talked me into going to Africa," Inhofe said of Coe. "And I had *no* interest in going to Africa." His daughter, a schoolteacher, called him one day to tell him she was going to Africa for school break. "I said, 'Well, guess where Daddy's going? To Africa. And if you go with me, it's free!" It'd also be off the books. Although

Inhofe would go on to charge his missionary travel to tax-payers, that first trip was paid for by a religious organiza-tion, according to a press release. Inhofe never reported it.

What was his mission? "I call it the political philosophy of Jesus, something put together by Doug....It's all scrip-turally based. Acts 9:15"—the last of the Eight Core Aspects outlined in the document distributed at the Prayer Break-fast, which Inhofe paraphrased as "'Take my name, Jesus, to the kings.' And, of course, if you're a member of the United States Senate in Africa, they think you're impor-tant." He chuckled, slapping the arm of his red leather sofa. "You're always going to get in to see the kings!"

His first king? Gen. Sani Abacha, dictator of Nigeria, Africa's largest and most populous nation, not long before Abacha died in bed with three prostitutes in 1998. Abacha was known for two qualities: the greed that led him to steal $3 billion from his country, and the loyalty to the foreign oil companies that made that theft possible. "You can't help who you are," said a Family man, defending the group's outreach to the general. "I mean, can't he have a friend?"

Inhofe would be that friend. "We went in there," Inhofe continues, "not really knowing what we're doing. He started talking about political things." But Inhofe had a greater mission. "'I came all the way across the Atlantic and down to sub-Saharan Africa,'" he said, "'to tell you in the spirit of Jesus that we love you.'"

Siljander says he was there, too. "There was a moment when Abacha sent all his aides out of the room," he recalls, "and I wondered if I was ever going to see Nancy and my four kids again." Abacha wasn't about to murder two American congressmen, but Siljander has to play the moment for the drama it's worth in order to make the "reconciliation" that follows look miraculous.

Inhofe, at least, bought it. "That is probably the first time this man had ever cried, at least in front of other people," he says. And then Inhofe, Siljander, and the dictator— a Muslim in name—prayed to Jesus. "Jesus is the common denominator," Inhofe explained, "because Muslims love Jesus, too.... They sometimes are the first ones to say, 'Yes, let's meet in the spirit of Jesus.'"

Was it Jesus who changed the dictator's heart? The rest of the world might be inclined to say it was oil. Forty-four percent of Nigeria's went to America. The ninth-largest oil producer, Nigeria became a pariah nation under Abacha's rule, officially condemned by Washington since the time of his overthrow of a democratic government, in 1993. But Abacha launched a $10 million lobbying campaign in the capital that won him Democratic as well as Republican allies. He already had four very important American friends: Mobil, Chevron, Ashland, and Texaco. Inhofe, winner of a Lifetime Service Award from a petroleum industry group, was another good friend to have. "Democracy advocates," wrote an analyst for Foreign Policy in Focus in 1997, the year of Inhofe's mission, "worry that Abacha will interpret Washington's willingness to dialogue as a signal that Washington will not follow through on its threats to impose oil sanctions."

None of that mattered to the senator. All he was trying to do was help "millions and millions of poor people," he told Rev. Schenck in the video. And for him, that began with helping General Abacha, one of the kings of Acts 9:15, through his leadership in a successful effort to block sanctions. More recently, in 2008, Inhofe pledged military aid to the government of Nigeria's President Umaru Musa Yar'Adua, who'd stolen his election the previous year.

But it didn't end in Nigeria. Inhofe got involved with a Family initiative called Youth Corps. Endorsed by former secretary of state James Baker and Ugandan president Yoweri Museveni, Youth Corps doesn't lead with Jesus—in fact, its official brochure doesn't mention his name. But a different document I'd been given while I was living with the Family in 2002, "Youth Corps Vision," is more explicit:

> A group of highly dedicated individuals who are united together having a total commitment to use their lives to daily seek to mature into people who talk like Jesus, act like Jesus, think like Jesus. This group will have the responsibility to:
>
> - see that the commitment and action is maintained to the overall vision;
> - see that the finest and best invisible organization is developed and maintained at all levels of the work;
> - even though the structure is hidden, see that the Family atmosphere is maintained, so that all people can feel a part of the Family.

After I published *The Family*, a member responsible for much of the group's Uganda work—including its network of Youth Corps homes and a Leadership Academy to which the Fellowship Foundation has donated several million dollars—dismissed the document I'd quoted as outdated. He didn't volunteer a more recent edition. But, luckily for me, someone else did: the young man who'd grown up in the Family. Inhofe and his staff were all over the documents he sent me, invited to nearly every meeting. But two documents in particular were striking. First, there was an update of the "Vision" of Youth Corps, and it was anything but the ecumenical "principles" the Family proclaims at the Prayer Breakfast:

> Jesus said to his disciples to go to all the nations and tell the inhabitants about Himself (the Gospel).... Youth Corp[s] gives us a simple way of achieving His vision; that is taking 5 men from within a country and training them on how to live like Jesus and share Him with the poor of their country.

The idea was that, as natives known to be close to American power, the five chosen for indoctrination—like Coburn's five from Lebanon—would be more effective than all the missionaries the traditional churches could send. They'd also be cheaper: "For example if we were to send one family over to Russia to live, it might cost $70,000 per year. But 5 men and their families could be supported for $25,000 total if they are already from Russia."

The question was how to choose these key men. "The Execution of the Vision" explains:

> A. A congressman and/or Senator from the United States will befriend the leader of another country

and tell him/her how Jesus and His teachings will help his country and its poor.

B. U.S. leader and foreign leader will select 5 men (mentors) from the foreign country to commit to learn about Jesus and how He will help themselves, their country and the poor.

The five would then be matched with American support teams that would cover their costs, visit them annually, and pray for them as much as possible. The men would not be asked to convert—in fact, the Family believes, it'd be better if they continued to call themselves Muslims, Jews, Hindus, Buddhists, or whatever the customs of the land dictated; that way, they would be spiritual double agents fluent in two faiths, the one required by the politics of their home countries and that of the Family. To those who were ready, however, the true leader, Jesus, would be introduced. A section titled "Training" reads:

> Training for the foreign mentors will be done with strict dependence of [*sic*] Jesus' promise in John 15:26: "The Helper will come—the Spirit, who reveals the truth about God and who comes from the Father. I will send him to you from the Father and He will speak about me."

Actually, it would be the Family that would explain God to the heathen:

> We will teach the mentors to confess their sins (known or unknown) and to ask the Holy Spirit of Christ to

live in them, and to teach them how to live, what to think and what to say. We will teach them to ask the Spirit of Jesus to teach them as they read God's word. They will be asked to think about what did Jesus do, say, and think in relation to the situation.

Kadry reshiut vse, as Stalin liked to say; cadres decide all. Win the leadership, win the nation. The goal, according to the "Vision," was to identify five for each of the 192 countries in the world by the end of 2008. Did they succeed? Not likely. But the "Vision" has gone far and wide with the help of men such as Inhofe, and the Work goes on. The Family apostate sent me a 2004 budget for funds to be raised by businessmen around the country for Inhofe's missionary work. Not his travel—the government would cover that— but that of his protégés, the five men for each country he was to select with the help of a local leader. The budget covered eleven African nations (Inhofe has since said he stepped it up to twelve): Benin, Burundi, Congo-Brazzaville, Côte d'Ivoire, the Democratic Republic of Congo, the site of the worst war on the planet at the moment, Equatorial Guinea, Ethiopia, Ghana, Mauritius, Rwanda, and Uganda. For each country, the local liaison is listed. In all but Ethiopia and Mauritius, it is the president. Then the U.S. leader: Inhofe, down the line. The sums that follow are small, but that's the point: power, not cash, is the Family's currency. Costs for 2003 were mostly covered; for 2004, the budget projected between $20,000 and $40,000 for each country, except one, Uganda, for which $70,000 was to be raised.

"We know Senator Inhofe," David Bahati, a Ugandan

member of Parliament and a rising star in the country's ruling party, told me. "We respect him. We know him." I repeated Inhofe's comments about bringing to Africa the "political philosophy of Jesus, something put together by Doug." Bahati knew Doug Coe, too. I wondered if he'd be insulted by what sounded to me like "The White Man's Burden." Bahati didn't hear it like that. "I think when he says 'political philosophy of Jesus,' I think he's responding to politics as the management of society, according to Jesus, how he brings Jesus to the issues of society."

Bahati was doing just that when I spoke to him: bringing Inhofe's Jesus to his society. So that, I decided, was where the story would take me next: Uganda.

4

THE KINGDOM

SEVERAL MONTHS after the C Street scandals, a radio producer called to talk about Uganda; was I aware of what was happening in the East African nation? I was—inspired by missionaries, Uganda had declared a war on homosexuality—but it hadn't struck me at the time as a story that would interest Americans. Not much in Africa does. The systemic destruction of Somalia was a footnote to the deaths of a handful of Americans in a Hollywood movie, *Black Hawk Down*. Uganda? They'd already had their movie, *The Last King of Scotland*, starring Forrest Whitaker as the 1970s dictator Idi Amin. He won an Oscar. What more was there to say?

We might start with the phrase "never again"—the pledge to prevent genocide that has been reduced to an ad campaign for the business of inspirational Holocaust movies, *Defiance, Triumph of the Spirit, The Boy in the Striped Paja-mas*, its meaning in the world off the screen, meanwhile, made moot many times over in Cambodia, East Timor, Rwanda.

The radio producer was calling because, in Uganda, the idea of genocide had once again been set on a simmer. And the men responsible were those the Family calls its Ugan-dan brothers.

On October 14, 2009, the Ugandan MP David Bahati introduced legislation called the Anti-Homosexuality Bill. Among its provisions:

- three years in prison for failure to report a homo-sexual within twenty-four hours of learning of his or her crime;
- seven years in prison for "promotion," which would include not only advocacy but also even simple acknowledgment of the reality of homosexuality;
- life imprisonment for one homosexual act;
- and, for "aggravated homosexuality" (which includes sex while HIV-positive, sex with a disabled person, or simply sex, more than once, marking the criminal as a "serial offender"), death.

Bahati, the secretary of the Family's Ugandan branch, called his bill traditional, Ugandan "family values." Both the disease — homosexuality, that is — and its diagnosis had been exported from the West, said Dr. James Nsaba Buturo, Uganda's minister of ethics and integrity and the chair of the weekly Family meeting in Parliament. But the solution, he added proudly, was Ugandan, an idea that came from the people.

"Is the death penalty a good idea?" I asked a pretty girl named Sharon, at a weekly abstinence rally on the campus of Makerere, Uganda's top university.

"Yeah!" She smiled, a flash of neat little teeth, and leaned in close to be heard over the music, hip-hop thumping. The rally doubles as the school's big Saturday night party.

"Have you ever met a homosexual?" I asked.

"I have never!"

"If you met one, would you kill him?"

"It's hard for me to kill." That smile. Those teeth. "It is hard for me to do it alone."

"But together?" She giggled and nodded.

Winston Churchill called Uganda "the pearl of Africa." The Family thinks it is, too. In the last ten years, it has poured millions into "leadership development" there, more than it has invested in any other foreign country. A Family leader takes credit for turning on the tap of U.S. foreign aid through which billions have flowed into Ugandan coffers. Or private bank accounts, as the case may be. The government of Yoweri Museveni, hailed by the United States as a democracy since the general marched into Kampala twenty-four years ago, in 1986, is ranked 130th on the most reliable corruption index—better than Belarus but just behind Lebanon. "Corruption is not just an element of [the] system," observes Ugandan journalist Andrew Mwenda, "it is 'the system.'"

Every year, right before Uganda's Independence Day, the government holds a National Prayer Breakfast, modeled on the Family's event in Washington. It's organized, with Washington's help, by Bahati's Parliament prayer group, called the Fellowship—also modeled on the group in Washington. Americans, among them Sen. Jim Inhofe and former attorney general John Ashcroft, both longtime Family men, and Pastor Rick Warren, are a frequent attraction at the weekly meetings of the Parliament group. Inhofe and Ashcroft are nearly defined by their vocal anti-gay beliefs, but Warren presents himself as a moderate. "I'm no homophobic guy," he says, even as he equates homosexuality with incest. But in Africa, he doesn't parse words. "He said that homosexuality is a sin and that we should fight it," Bahati recalled of Warren's visits. "He was making a strong point that we should not accept it."

The question isn't whether American fundamentalists support the death penalty for gay people. Most don't. The real question is one of ideological transmission, the transfer of ideas. If Inhofe and Warren, for instance, eventually caved to public pressure and came out in muted opposition to Uganda's gay death penalty, it isn't because they dispute the motive behind it, which is the eradication of queer people. They may disagree on the means, favoring a "cure" rather than killing, but not the ends.

For years, American fundamentalists have looked on Uganda as a kind of laboratory. They sent not just money but also ideas. If the money disappeared, the ideas took hold. Ugandan evangelicals sing American songs and listen to sermons about American problems, often from American preachers. Ugandan politicians attend prayer breakfasts in America and cut deals with American businessmen. But it's not a one-way exchange. American evangelicals cite

Ugandan churches as models for their own, and point to Ugandan AIDS policy—from which American politicians nearly stripped condoms—as proof that public health is a matter of morality. It's a classic fundamentalist maneuver: move a fight you can't win in the center to the margins, and then broadcast the results back home.

David Bahati denies any direct American influence on his bill. That's not how it works, he told me. It's about a shared passion, he said, not orders; a common desire for a government by God. That desire might be centered in Washington, but it had grown just as strong, maybe even stronger, in Kampala. When I asked if there was any connection between the Fellowship in Uganda and his legislation, he seemed puzzled by the question. "I do not know what you mean, 'connection,'" he said. "There is no 'connection.' They are the same thing. The bill is the Fellowship. It was our idea."

A young man who called himself Blessed had agreed to meet me in front of the Speke Hotel, the oldest in Kampala, but he was late, very late, and I had no way to contact him. E-mailing me from a café, he'd said he didn't have a phone; calling from a pay phone, he'd said he didn't have a watch. The friends who'd put me in touch with him said he didn't have an address. I'd seen a picture of him: he had a long neck and a tall, narrow head, a broad smile that made him look both kind and a little sly. I wanted to talk to him precisely because he was hard to find, because he was gay and because he was on the run. His pastor had outed him; his parents could not bear the shame. "Am being hunted by my family at the moment," he'd written, by way of apology for his difficulty making dinner plans. "Am moving place to place now." Then, in case I didn't understand: "They want to kill me." He suggested that I bring a magazine to read while I waited in the lobby.

The Speke Hotel is nothing grand, just a succession of stucco arches, but smartly located halfway up the hill from the business district to the seat of presidential power, with the gated gardens of the luxury Sheraton in between. Late at night, *muzungus*, white men — missionaries on the down low, aid workers, oilmen — come to shop for twenty-dollar prostitutes at the outdoor bar. Earlier in the evening, little clusters of gay men — mostly foreigners these days — mingle at the garden restaurant. Throughout the day, the Ugandan elite meet at the sidewalk tables. They ignore the whores and their giant madam, regal women sipping colas while they wait for the night, and have no idea that the hotel also serves as one of the city's few havens for gays and lesbians.

Certainly Miria Matembe didn't know. I'd been looking for her, too. Then one night, there she was, pointed out to me by my friend Robert, a Ugandan radio journalist I'd hired to show me around town. "That is Honorable right there," said Robert. Uganda's first minister of ethics and integrity, she retained the honorific though she was out of government and working as a private lawyer. A small woman in a brown power suit, with short hair cut upward, she charged through the café's tables with two cell phones simultaneously in action.

"Honorable!" I called, and ran after her. She trapped one phone between her shoulder and her ear, stared at me, and held up a finger. Stop. She crooked it: follow. She pointed: speak. I whispered beneath her two conversations, telling her that I'd heard she'd been at a planning meeting for the Anti-Homosexuality Bill; that I was writing about the Fellowship; that I wanted to understand the connection.

"Wait!" Matembe said into her phones. Then, to me: "You are funny!" She chortled, held up five fingers, and walked away. Half an hour later she and two friends plopped down at my table. Night had come and the air was cooling, the whores were rustling, and the guards, skinny men with wide-mouthed shotguns, were guiding the white-and-silver SUVs of Uganda's elite in and out of the drop-off zone a few feet from our table. "The funny guy," said Matembe, her East African accent hard on the consonants and sharp on the vowels. "You wanna talk about homos?" She drew the word out for comic effect, mimicking my homely American accent. Honorable — the names of all politicians could be shortened this way — had a booming voice that rose above the *boda-boda* bikes, the careening motorcycle taxis that rule Kampala's cratered streets. Her eyes were glowing wrath-of-God beacons as she stage-whispered a list of practices she knew to be common to homos — boy-rape, blasphemy, "golden showers" — and then they became ball bearings rolling around in their sockets as she threw back her head and cackled at the obscenity of it all, the "piss-piss" of the homosexuals and our top-volume conversation about their secret ways.

"I was the first person to fight homosexuality!" she shouted. She meant during the late 1990s. American missionaries were rushing in, a revival sweeping the land, Ugandan Catholics and Anglicans caught up in the power of evangelicalism and all its concerns—including homosexuality. Matembe, one of the original members of Uganda's parliamentary Fellowship group, was among the first to grasp the new creed.

"I used to come here and catch them!" She mimed sneaking up and pouncing with hands like claws. "Catch these people!" Her eyes watered. "Eh?" she said to her friend, a woman named Joy, who didn't need the prompt to giggle. "Eh?" Honorable stopped, choked by laughter, and then grew serious. "People used to tell me where they were hiding. This Italian thing here—what is it?" The hotel restaurant, called Mama Mia. For a brief period, gay life had almost flourished in Kampala. Gay men cruised straight men on the street, and parties at the restaurant began to take on the political cast of an identity in formation. "Mama Mia!" Matembe shrieked, throwing her hands in the air. She'd put a stop to that. "Ha!" She'd march through the café, leading her troops herself. "And did I find them here?" Joy and the other friend—a shy older man in a sport shirt whom she introduced as Uncle Ben—nodded. "You see Matembe walk into a place," said Matembe, "and you disappear!" Matembe took a sip of beer and ate some groundnuts. "Eventually, of course, people went underground."

That was all right with her. The closet, she believed, was a fine African tradition. That made her a liberal; unlike her successor at the ethics ministry, the current chairman of the Family's Ugandan outpost, she didn't want to kill gays. "First of all, I am a human rights activist," she said. To prove it, she dispatched Joy to her car to retrieve a copy of a book she had written, a feminist memoir called *A Woman in the Eyes of God.* "I think you should buy," she said. "Ten dollars."

"No, twenty!" said Joy, turned out for the evening ahead in a plunging red dress.

"I said ten," declared Honorable. Then she instructed me to buy them a round of drinks. "My activism is guided by godly principles," she continued. "Therefore, I don't support homosexuality as a human right. I don't! Why? Because my beautiful—my godly conviction is that homosexuality is not a sin but a curse! Looking at homosexuality as a curse by God, I do not prescribe the death sentence for such people."

The bill's most draconian clause would add "aggravated homosexuality" to Uganda's short list of capital crimes. But that wasn't what really brought Matembe out in opposition. The problem, she said, "is it makes us all potential criminals." She was referring to a provision of the law designed to make every Ugandan a soldier in the war against the gays. "Like, if I am speaking with you, and if I find you are a homosexual..." If that turned out to be the case, she'd have twenty-four hours to report me or face a prison sentence of up to three years. This, she thought, was unfair. To her.

"But that is a good purpose," Uncle Ben interjected. "It will lead to prevention. It is necessary. We must use all means to stop this!"

Matembe scowled and said something in Lugandan, central Uganda's native tongue; Ben answered likewise, bickering. Then he switched back to English. "We have no choice," he said, turning to me. "They"—the gays—"are trying to end the human race."

Before we could discuss this apocalypse, Matembe brought the subject back to her. She wanted to make it clear that she bore no responsibility for the bill. "The Prayer Breakfast continues, but I no longer go to it. They were corrupted. It is the Americans! Confused as usual, exploiting." She sighed, depleted. Then she rallied, remembering the good old days, returning to the beginning of her monologue. "But I was the first! I fought the homos!"

The owner of the hotel swooped down on the table, cutting her off. "Honorable Matembe," he cried. He took her gently by her arm and lifted her from us, petting her and flattering her, quieting her. She was scaring away the trade.

The lobby was empty when Blessed arrived, an hour late. He wore crisp black slacks and a lime green long-sleeved shirt underneath a black sweater vest, too warm for the weather. Blessed was twenty-one, but he tried to carry himself like an older, courtlier man. He apologized for his impeccable appearance with what he hoped sounded like a joke. "I am a bit homeless at the moment," he said, and then chuckled, as if this was merely an inconvenience. As we walked up the hill to the Sheraton for dinner—Blessed's choice, and who could deny him a good meal when every one might be his last—he began to tell me his story.

He was the oldest child and only son of an educated family, his father a lawyer and his mother a bureaucrat. He had a happy childhood, "normal," he said, in every way. His parents loved him, and he loved them. They sent him to an elite boys' school in his father's hometown, and Blessed loved that, too. He was an affectionate boy, and he liked to touch people, to hug, to kiss. By the time he was twelve, he knew that his hugs and his kisses with other boys—not unusual in Uganda, where straight men sometimes hold hands—felt different from those with girls. And this didn't bother him, either. He was a bright boy, a good student, but his teachers told him his head was in the clouds. He thought that sounded nice. Up there, he didn't see conflict. Instead, he saw love. By the time he was fourteen he'd found six other boys in the school who felt as he did, and he loved them.

All of them?

"Of course I loved them. Because God loves me."

His family was Catholic but not very religious. Neither was Blessed; he said he felt spiritual. Not in the vaguely agnostic American sense. More like a holy fool, a boy for whom everything was sacred: church and his friendships, and the rainbows over Lake Victoria, the white egrets in the trees, and also his studies, his books, his romances—his first love was an older boy named John—and his pleasures, the touches, the caresses. The orgasms? Of course. Everything sweet, he believed, everything he'd been given by God, was holy. He began calling himself "Blessed," for instance, not long after he and his group of friends were turned in to their headmaster. Blessed said the headmaster beat them, expelled them, and then sent them to the police, where they spent forty-eight hours in prison before a lawyer for Amnesty International managed to get them freed. "It was so much fun!" Blessed exclaimed. Just imagine, he said— he held my eyes, his voice low. "Remember when you were sixteen?" Sixteen, forty-eight hours, the six sexiest people in the world, as far as you were concerned, all in one cell. "I call myself 'Blessed,'" he explained, "because that's what I am, so fortunate to be born like this."

Like this: gay, and so in love with the world that even in jail he forgot about the bars.

We'd taken an outdoor table, as far as possible from other people. Dinner was a buffet, and Blessed had heaped his plate high. He was built like a willow sapling, but the hillock of food disappeared and he went back for seconds. "I think you need to eat more, too," he told me, even though I'm no sapling—more like a baobab tree. "I like white men," he added quickly, reassurance in case he'd accidentally insulted me. "Are you gay?" he asked. "Well, no," I said, embarrassed, a straight man in a country ruled by would-be gay killers. But Blessed didn't see it like that. "Oh!" he said. "Then you have children?" That's how it is in Uganda. "Let me see!" said Blessed. He spent the next ten minutes cooing over pictures of my daughter.

After Blessed was expelled, he moved back to Kampala and began attending a new school. His parents wouldn't pay; Blessed washed cars. Now his love took a more political form: he began organizing youth clubs to talk about sex. Not just gay sex but straight sex, too, and all the shades in between. He knew he was an unusual kid, straight or gay. He'd never experienced sex as anything but a gift. But he understood that most teenagers are as terrified of sex as they are drawn to it. He wanted them to know about the precautions, condoms; about HIV and abortion; and also about the good parts. He wanted them to believe that the good parts were good parts, "good news," in fact, just like their pastors said of Christ. "I don't think Jesus is against us," he said, waving the absurd thought away with such a fey gesture I looked over my shoulder to make sure the waiter hadn't seen.

Around the time Blessed became Blessed, he began attending Pentecostal churches, "spirit-filled" places where you sang and danced and maybe experienced the gift of tongues, babbling in languages granted to you by God. The songs were American as often as African, the churches were sprinkled with handsome *muzungus*, and there was a lot of laying on of hands. It felt cosmopolitan, international, modern. Blessed's favorite pastor was a man named Martin Ssempa, who appeared in music videos in Uganda and in pulpits in America, where he was a favorite of Pastor Rick Warren's. Every Saturday night Ssempa led a service — a party, really — called Primetime, held at Makerere University's outdoor pool. It's fun, even though, technically, it's anti-fun, an abstinence rally. But Blessed, and plenty of straight kids, were there to cruise. It was hard not to — there were usually at least a thousand students, girls in their Saturday best, hot-pink dresses tight around the hips and clinging baby T's, boys dressed in American hip-hop, their pants low and their shirts giant and their young faces lean. Ssempa was beautiful too, golden-skinned, the handsomest bald man you ever saw, a smooth man beckoning them from the stage across the pool that glowed in the night. The band thumped and Ssempa called, as if the kids might actually walk on the water. The story he told was almost always the same: sex, "the greatest sex" (it's going to be awesome!), sex (it'll be wonderful *someday*), sex (wait...), sex (just a little bit longer now...). And then everybody would jump. A thousand, sometimes two thousand young Ugandans hopping in time as high as they could, holding on to one another lest they fall in the pool, giggling. "Holy laughter," some called it. It was a gift they believed came from the Holy Ghost, just like tongues; and some had heard about "holy kissing," too, another gift—not carnal!—the Spirit in the flesh. There were gay boys there, and drag kings, and straight kids who might peer around the bend, all of them waiting, of course, abstaining, all of them not having sex together, except when they were. "It was so hot!" said Blessed.

Then came the day Blessed had to choose a side. It was 2007, and he was in court, as spectator and supporter. The case being heard was called *Victor Mukasa and Yvonne Oyoo v. Attorney General.* Victor Mukasa, a transman, born female, living male, interested in girls, taught Blessed, the sweet, femme boy, to be a man—a gay man—without ever meeting him.

Like Blessed, as a child Juliet Mukasa knew she was attracted to children of the same sex. And like Blessed, she'd been raised Catholic but had joined an American-style Pentecostal church, hoping that in the music and the dancing and the Holy Ghost—the ecstasy—she would find the resolution of her desires. But Juliet Mukasa was not as skilled as Blessed at leading two lives. She dressed as Victor; she couldn't think dressed like a girl. A pastor determined that she was possessed by a "male spirit" and asked his flock to help him heal her. The exorcism took place at the altar, in front of a thousand Christians, boys and men from the church's healing ministry laying on hands and speaking in tongues as women in the pews swayed and sang for Mukasa's liberation, as the pastor called it: her freedom. They took her arms, gently then firmly, and then they held her, and stripped her. Slowly, garment by garment, praying over each piece of demonically infused cloth. She'd bound her breasts. They bared them. "I cried, and every time I cried they would call it liberation." They slapped her, but it was holy slapping, and when she stood before them completely naked, the men's hands roaming over her body and then inside, they said that was holy, too.

Then they locked her in a room and raped her. For a week. This is known as a corrective; a medical procedure, really; a cure.

When it was all over, the pastor declared that the church had freed Mukasa. Maybe, in a sense, it had. Victor Mukasa no longer believed there was a demon inside him. The demons were in the church.

Mukasa became a man and an activist, determined to prevent what had happened to him from happening again. In 2003, he cofounded Freedom and Roam Uganda, an organization for lesbian, bisexual, transgender, and inter-sex human rights. In 2005, Ugandan police, led by government officials, raided his house. They didn't find Mukasa. But a friend, Yvonne Oyoo, was there. They took her down to the station. They stripped her. You look like a man, they said. We're going to prove you're a woman.

It happened again.

Mukasa fled. But in hiding and then in exile, he planned. The plan wasn't lesbian, it wasn't gay, it was... human, Blessed would say. It was a citizen's plan: Mukasa sued, and never was a lawsuit more like a gift of the spirit, the romance of the rule of law.

Blessed, of course, was a romantic boy. He thought the trial was exciting! He wanted to be there, and so did his friends. They would swish for dignity, drag for democracy, be themselves for God and Victor Mukasa. Blessed could hardly wait.

What he didn't know was that his golden-skinned pastor, Martin Ssempa, was gathering an opposing force. Blessed, with his head in the clouds! He hadn't paid attention. When he walked into the courtroom — late, as always — he could not have faced a starker choice. The two halves of his life sat on opposite sides of the aisle. "Blessed!" called his church friends. Pastor Ssempa himself saw him and smiled. Blessed looked down at the T-shirt he'd chosen for the occasion: a rainbow. He looked to the other side of the room. His gay friends looked back. Some of them sighed. They knew how it was. If, with a sly, earnest smile, he chose Ssempa today, they would forgive him tomorrow. If he didn't — the truth was, he didn't know. All that would follow, all that he would lose, was beyond the seventeen-year-old's imagination.

"I don't know if I have a very strong heart," he told me. "I do not know if I am a tough man."

"How did you make your choice, Blessed?"

He gave me the smile, a mask for all he had lost. "I had a breakthrough."

"Breakthrough," in the Ugandan church, is a spiritual term. A gift from the Holy Ghost. Grace, in whatever shape it's needed.

"I got courage."

Blessed sat down with the homos.

*   *   *

And then something like a miracle occurred: Victor Mukasa and Yvonne Oyoo won. The court ruled that the state had transgressed. Yes, homosexuality is illegal in Uganda, but officially there is still due process, even for homos, and the police had violated it. Without warrants, you cannot kick in doors, you cannot take prisoners, you cannot strip them, you cannot do what had been done to Victor Mukasa and Yvonne Oyoo.

Unless, that is, you change the law. Which is what a small coalition of Ugandans, inspired by American fundamentalism—its activist hatred of homosexuality, a politics based on sex without precedent in East Africa—set out to do. In the beginning, they weren't shy about their American influences. They invited American anti-gay speakers, most notably Scott Lively—the coauthor, with Kevin Abrams, of a book, attributing the Holocaust to homosexuality, called *The Pink Swastika*—to address Parliament. "I can't say this in America, but I can say it in Africa," Lively declared during a 2009 visit to Uganda. That's hard to imagine, since in *The Pink Swastika* Lively writes that "from the ashes of Nazi Germany, the homo-fascist phoenix has risen again—this time in the United States." But in Uganda, he went into greater detail, with a chart outlining different types of gay men, ranging from "monster" to "super-macho" (that's worse) to "butcher." "This is the kind of person it takes to run a gas chamber," he said, and then brought it home for the Ugandans: "The Rwandan stuff probably involved these guys."

Lively has much less influence in the United States than he does overseas. The leadership of the Family dismiss him as the representative *par excellence* of the vulgar fundamentalism to which they see themselves as offering an alternative. But the Ugandans aren't so concerned about the finer points of the American class system. They look at a fanatic such as Lively, or a politician such as Inhofe, and they see the same thing: a smiling white man come to preach moral "purity" as the path out of poverty.

"In Africa," observes Rev. Kapya Kaoma, an Anglican priest from Zambia, "the Christian Right...operates under the banner of 'evangelicalism.'" That is, he argues, most Africans don't distinguish between the varieties of American fundamentalism, so long as they all come bearing gifts in the form of support for African churches and, sometimes, African politicians. They are only too happy to return the favor, providing for their American allies examples of the policies too extreme to be implemented in the United States. In the past, American politicians used Uganda's anti-condom campaign as a justification for abstinence-only sex education in the United States. So it is now, with Uganda's anti-gay campaign an inspiration for American fundamentalists to hold the line here. The first draft of the Anti-Homosexuality Bill, for instance, seems to have been written with the concerns of Bahati's American friends in mind. It singled out same-sex marriage as a threat to Ugandan heterosexuality, and in an opening clause declared the bill a model for other nations—such as those where same-sex marriage is actually a possibility.

Human rights activists saw the bill as the direct result of a March 2009 conference in Kampala featuring Lively and

American "ex-gay" activists. The truth is, however, Lively and his friends were not so much the cause of the bill as a catalyst for a process that had already been set in motion. Some Ugandans date the roots of Uganda's anti-gay witch hunt to a 1996 race for the mayoralty of Kampala, in which one candidate successfully gay-baited the other. Ugandan lesbian, gay, bisexual, and transgender (LGBT) activists point to 2003, when a coalition of semi-legal groups called Sexual Minorities of Uganda formed. The politicians who hate them tend to agree, only they look back to the early 2000s as the period when "neo-colonialists," foreign human rights activists, began "recruiting" straight Ugandans into homo-sexuality under the cover of anti-AIDS work.

One camp within the anti-gay movement, led by Pastor Michael Kyazze, of the Omega Healing Centre, a compound of sports fields, a giant pavilion, and an even bigger sanctu-ary under construction, argues that Ugandans must admit that homosexuality is an internal Ugandan problem. By contemporary Ugandan standards, this point of view marks Kyazze as a progressive, since he acknowledges the univer-sality of homosexuality, albeit as the worst of all plagues. "Let's be honest," one of Kyazze's allies explained the pas-tor's position to me. "'Pedophilia' is really just a euphe-mism for homosexuality."

But Kyazze's friend Martin Ssempa had a different per-spective, Kyazze told me, when I went to see him at his church. "Now Martin, he believes it is *you*."

"Me?" I had worn a suit and tie to our meeting, a terrible choice on a sweltering day. I began to sweat.

Kyazze, a tall, broad, bald man with a slight stoop and a

warm, gentle rasp, laughed and patted my hand. "No, not you, Jeff. You Americans." He signaled for an assistant to bring me a small glass bottle of Coke. Kyazze, a pastor named Moses Solomon Male, and I were sitting around a café table by a window in Kyazze's office. Outside the window, a cow stared at us, chewing grass. Omega was a small church by Ugandan standards, almost pastoral—just 2,500 regulars and a full-time school for 400 students, a humble spread of one-story classrooms arrayed around a garden spiked with signs reminding students of the righteous path. Say No to Homosexuality; Avoid Sex Before Marriage. A young teacher, Joanna, took my photograph beside the most ambitious proverb of all: Always Say No to Sex. Behind it, a mural of the human digestive system added extra force to that injunction.

"What Martin means," Kyazze continued, "is that the Americans, the Europeans, the Dutch, are under the control of the homo." That was an ironic stand for Ssempa, since he'd received significant support from the United States, most notably at least $90,000 for his church, through the federal PEPFAR (President's Emergency Plan for AIDS Relief) anti-AIDS program. In 2004, he testified before Congress, and in 2005 and 2006 he appeared at Rick Warren's massive Orange County, California, church. "You are my brother, Martin, and I love you," Warren's wife declared from the stage, her eyes watering.

Kyazze, with a more modest network of American supporters, worried that his friend Martin was too close to the West. "The homosexuals can use your organizations to spread their ways. To recruit, you see. There are many methods, you know."

I did; David Bahati had listed several by phone before I came to Uganda. Among the most insidious, irresistible to kids: iPods. Also, laptops and cell phones. Gay recruiters are said to offer them the way pedophiles entice with lollipops in the park. "But it is technology. So much more seductive," Bahati had explained. "Always the new thing."

"The iPad?" I'd asked.

"Yes, this could happen."

"To me?" One could hope.

Kyazze had bigger trouble in mind. "The homos use a UNICEF—this is true!—to attempt to colonize Uganda." He meant a United Nations Children's Fund "Teenagers Toolkit," distributed to schools in 2002, that had referred to homosexuality as natural. "And, my friend, they begin with the children. That is what we want the world to understand. Now." He clapped his hands together. "This is absolutely correct, what I am informing you. But. It is only one half of the story!"

"Yes," murmured Kyazze's sidekick, Pastor Male. He was a graying, fine-boned man, given to stroking a stiff, blue-striped tie that looked like it might be permanently knotted. "Is it possible that one nationality would have homosexuality and another would not? No. You see, this is an area where we disagree with Pastor Ssempa. We have democracy, and we have science. We have these two powerful weapons and—with God!—we can fight homosexuality. And we know it is here. It is in *us*." Pastor Male patted his tie. "In us. Yes. Not me! But in Uganda. It is even"—he paused—"in the church."

Then he stopped. I waited. Finally I said, "No," mustering a little shock to keep the story going.

"Yes," Pastor Male said, smiling gently at my naïveté. He produced from his briefcase a thick blue spiral-bound document, a report on homosexual infiltration of the church he had prepared for the Ugandan parliament, urging them to take action. "Mob justice," he read from it, "is not a deliberate attempt to flout the law, but an inner compulsion due to people's lack of trust in the judicial and entire law enforcement system based on any previous attempts to get justice in vain."

It was true that, despite anti-gay laws dating from colonial times (they were a British import), there had been very few convictions for homosexuality. There were, however, plenty of arrests. Most of the gay men I spoke with in Kampala had been through the routine. Someone they thought was a friend or someone who was a lover would turn them in, and the police, working with the blackmailer, would offer the gay man a choice: prison or money. The art of it, one of Kampala's few out gay men, Long Jones, told me, was for the blackmailer to spend enough time with his mark to determine how much he could be bled for.

What was different about Male and Kyazze, along with Ssempa and their other allies, was that they were attempting the trick on a much bigger scale. "Our number-one problem," Kyazze said, "is Kayanja." Bishop Robert Kayanja, that is, the Billy Graham of East Africa, a church leader with a bigger following than all the gay-haters combined. Part of their problem with Kayanja was that he took no position on the bill, but the real issue was money, especially American money. He had it, they wanted it. He sold uplift; they had on offer something newer, more exciting: death to the enemy.

Kayanja is a miracle healer—he claims he can make the lame walk, the blind see, and exorcise AIDS—and a prosperity gospel preacher, practicing an old variation on a new con. God's promise, Kayanja preaches, is wealth and health, and his flock could hasten their realization by making "love offerings" to his 80,000-member Miracle Centre Cathedral or his 1,216 satellite churches. He says his "spiritual father" is Tulsa, Oklahoma, faith healer Dr. T. L. Osborn. American star pastors such as Benny Hinn, T. D. Jakes, and the aptly named Creflo Dollar make pilgrimages to Kayanja. The Americans get to show off their compassion for Africa in special broadcasts for their American followers, and Kayanja gets screen time in the wonderful and lucrative world of American televangelism. He's now one of the richest men in Uganda.

Compared to the product on offer from Kyazze and Ssempa—the idea that you could make a lame nation walk by eradicating an internal population of five hundred thousand homosexuals—what Kayanja practices might be considered honest graft. But Kyazze and his allies decided to call it something worse, by Ugandan standards: homosexuality. Most of the documents in Male's blue binder were police reports related to the claims made by young men Male brought to the authorities to accuse Kayanja of rape. Kayanja certainly wouldn't be the first televangelist to abuse his flock. According to the *Los Angeles Times*, one of his biggest American supporters, Paul Crouch, paid an employee

$425,000 in 2004 to silence the employee's claims that he'd been forced into sex. But the police ruled Kyazze's alleged victims not credible. Kyazze, in turn, pointed to an order of new toilets purchased for Kampala police by Kayanja as a bribe. The truth, inasmuch as it can be discerned, is that Kayanja *is* untouchable; and that he didn't rape the men in question, unless the passport stamps and travel receipts one of his lawyers showed me to prove that he had been out of the country at the time of the alleged crimes are evidence that U.S. and UK customs and British Airways are part of the international gay conspiracy.

Kyazze and his allies wouldn't put it past them. Gays, he believes, control unimaginable wealth, which they use to fund decadence in weak nations. They also secretly run the media. I thought I'd heard this story before. "What about hooked noses?" I asked.

Kyazze rumbled with laughter. "You are from America! You should know! Gays can disguise themselves as anybody." Indeed. An alleged rape victim of one of Kayanja's associate pastors told me that beneath his suit the handsome preacher had breasts as "big as Dolly Parton's."

Kyazze and Pastor Male are nothing if not ambitious. Their only critique of the bill is that it is actually too soft on homosexuality. They see a clause forbidding the media from exposing victims of gay rape as evidence that there's a gay infiltrator within their ranks. Even Buturo, the minister of ethics and integrity and chairman of the Fellowship group from which the bill emerged, is suspect in their eyes. They don't think he's gay, but they wonder whether he's protecting powerful homosexuals. Like many Ugandans, both pastors believe the bill's timing has much to do with a massive corruption inquiry that has brushed closer to the dictator than any other.

"First," said Male, "Buturo does nothing. Then, all of a sudden, we must act right away! We said to him, 'Please, Honorable, let us be scientific about this. The government must provide funds for a proper study of the scope of the problem. We must know how many homosexuals there are, where they are, who can be cured, and who cannot. We must be modern in our approach.' But Buturo said to us, 'We're going to kill them, so we don't have to have this inquiry.' You see, he is afraid of the inquiry, because he insists homosexuality is a Western problem. He knows that if we study it, we will find it here. We will find it in the government! And then we will be able to do nothing. 'If we kill them,' he says, 'we don't have to count them. If we have an inquiry, we are shooting ourselves in the foot!' "

"What about Bahati?" I asked. Both men sighed.

"Honorable is a good boy," said Kyazze, who, at forty-nine, is thirteen years Bahati's senior. "But he is too eager. He says, 'Forget about the inquiry! We must stop them right now.' He sees the danger. He feels the evil wind of the homosexual. But the eye of the storm and the whirlwind are two different things. What we are dealing with is a moral problem." That didn't mean it couldn't be defeated, but it would take a war, not a battle, and a force greater than law: Christ, transcendent, purifier of nations.

There was a hint of sectarian rivalry in their critique. Bahati, like Buturo, is an Anglican, their pastor the American-educated Archbishop Luke Orombi. Orombi travels back and forth to the United States with ease; in America, he stays in a room with his name on it in an elegant home across from the Cedars. Kyazze and Male are Pentecostals; when Kyazze goes to America, it's to preach in working-class churches. Bahati prays quietly, his eyes closed and his hands folded in front of him. Male in prayer looks like the bride of Frankenstein, his head tipped back, his hands rigid, his eyes jolted wide by the Spirit. Kyazze roars, his hands above him.

There are ethnic differences to consider as well, and those matter in Uganda, though Ugandans are careful when speaking of them, now more than ever. On September 11, 2009, the Ugandan military opened fire on a crowd of rioters, killing at least forty. They were members of the Baganda, Uganda's largest ethnic group, furious that Museveni—a member of the Banyankole people—had attempted to stop their king from visiting a section of Kampala traditionally under his rule. Even more frightening to many Ugandans than the killing was a government ban on four Lugandan-language radio stations—on the grounds that their live coverage of the state murder of their tribesmen constituted incitement to genocide.

Genocide, in Uganda, is not an abstraction but a living memory and a neighbor, always close at hand. In the 1970s, Idi Amin murdered hundreds of thousands of his countrymen. In the '80s, a war between dictator Milton Obote and Museveni's bush army killed hundreds of thousands more, the country fracturing down ethnic lines. But Museveni in power was different. He disposed of his enemies through "accidents" and frame-ups, not massacres. He depended on the press to show similar restraint in its coverage of corruption. He wasn't a kleptocrat, but he surrounded himself with thieves—on the theory, apparently, that rich men are peaceful men. Better to steal than to kill, so long as you can persuade your people that there are no other options.

That may be changing. He still holds the peace, but now less through the balancing act of his younger days than through brute force. He is a dictator, and dictators need enemies. For years, the enemy was a vicious rebel group called the Lord's Resistance Army, but the LRA has been reduced to a few hundred child fighters at best. Enter the homosexual. Singular; an archetype, for the monster that has grabbed hold of the Ugandan imagination is a bogeyman. If genocide comes, it will have as much to do with actual queer people as Kyazze's caricature of shape-shifting millionaires buying sex with technology. If genocide comes, it will come to the tribes, recast as a crusade for family values against one group or another said to have fallen, like the Americans, on decadent ways.

A few days later at the Speke Hotel, I spent an hour with a *boda-boda* driver named Andrew Maira, a gaunt, earnest man with gallows eyes who carried with him a well-worn envelope of documents creased almost to tearing—proof, he said, that he had been framed for homosexuality. One day, he said, he received a call from a childhood friend. "A homo," said Maira. "We all knew this, he dressed as a lady." It was George Oundo, who, as head of an organization called Ex-Gay Uganda, had become a useful ally for Ssempa, providing "inside" information on the homosexual conspiracy. Oundo invited Maira to come meet his new friend

Ssempa at Makerere University, a posh address for a poor man like Maira, who spoke little English. He didn't have the money for the trip across town, but Oundo told him he would cover the cost. When Maira got there, Ssempa had only one question: Did Maira worship with a certain Catholic priest, Father Anthony Musaala? Maira did. Musaala was a bigger star than Ssempa, an award-winning gospel singer. So Maira wasn't surprised when Ssempa introduced him to another man who wanted to know all about Musaala. He did wonder why the man took his picture.

Two days later, as Maira set out to work, a news vendor called to him. "This is you?" He showed Maira a copy of *Red Pepper*, the national tabloid. "I SODOMISED CATHOLIC PRIEST," blared the headline, next to a photograph of Maira. He'd been nothing more than a stone for Ssempa to throw at a rival.

At work a driver smashed the paper into his face and his friends surrounded him, shouting, "Homo!" He fled to his family, but they wouldn't speak to him. When he got home, his wife and kids were gone.

"And are you gay?" I asked.

"No," he said. "But—"

He waved at the newspaper, which he'd unfolded before me. In the shadow of the Bahati bill, its principles already set in motion, it didn't matter. Homosexuality was just another name for the enemy. Anybody might be one.

A few days later, I went to meet David Bahati at his office, on the fourth floor of the Parliament building. But he wasn't there, and when I called his cell phone, I couldn't get an answer; nobody in Uganda uses voicemail. I waited in the hall, skipping my meeting with another member of Parliament, who'd made headlines boasting that he'd kill his son if he confessed to homosexuality, but Bahati never showed. Which was strange, since I was in Uganda because he'd invited me. He wanted to talk about the Family.

As the Anti-Homosexuality Bill was becoming a story, I began giving interviews on the Family's Ugandan connection. A "God-led" government of men with secret alliances, a nation caught up in a witch-hunting frenzy, the hateful far reaches of fundamentalism made law—Uganda was what ordinary Americans feared C Street could lead to. Only, it wasn't happening in the United States; we were too busy giggling over the Appalachian Trail. It was happening in Uganda: landlocked, poorer than the hard red dirt of its roads, as spent as oxygen-starved Lake Victoria, and cursed by the new discovery of oil, which most Ugandans outside of government view as simply one more thing to be stolen from them.

Uganda's renewable resource is souls. There's the happy version of that thought—so much potential! And there is the fundamentalist variation—a "harvest," as though souls were a crop to be measured by the bushel. The week after I left Kampala, the parliament Fellowship group hosted Pastor Tom Anderson of Oklahoma, who'd come to lead a five-day crusade. Such crusades are expensive, but they can pay for themselves. Not through the "love offerings" of African attendees but through the fund-raising potential, back home, of a "mission to Africa." Pastor Tom had written a bestselling book, *Becoming a Millionaire God's Way*, and his son had written a sequel, about how to become a billion-aire. Both men were going to instruct the Ugandans on how to get wealthy by getting godly. Pastor Tom brought them four gospels, a Ugandan reporter was told by a leader of the anti-gay movement called Pastor Queen.

1. The Gospel of Punctuality. Ugandans are poor, he said, because they don't look at their watches. Make the trains run on time. Wealth will follow.
2. The Gospel of Work. Ugandans are poor, he said, because they're lazy.
3. The Gospel of God-Fearing. Self-explanatory.
4. The Gospel of Purity. Ugandans, he said, have a special opportunity: They can stop the homosexuals before they get started.

The Family's view was subtler. "I know of no one involved in Uganda with the Fellowship here in America, including the most conservative among them, that supports such things as killing homosexuals or draconian reporting requirements," declared a spokesman, Bob Hunter. The statement contained a fine distinction. Nobody "here in America" supported the worst elements of that legislation, but Ugandan members of the Fellowship certainly do. Hunter seemed to be suggesting that, for all the rhetoric of a "world-wide family of friends," some brothers counted less than others. He wouldn't see it that way, but there was no clear way out for him: either the rhetoric is real, in which case the Ugandan members represent the Family as much as Hunter does; or Washington's in charge—"the world's Christian capital," as an early Family leader put it.

The kill-the-gays bill wasn't conceived at C Street or the Cedars. The Uganda Fellowship that launched the bill was. The Family didn't pull the trigger; they provided the gun. The weapon was an idea: "God-led government" in lieu of democracy, scripture in place of law, and the structure of a special anointed through which to achieve it, with high priests of the American religion—politicians—to consecrate it. The bill is a bullet, and whether or not it's made law, it's already been fired. What's left for the Family is damage control.

After the sex scandals, the Family called in media allies to advise them, including conservative columnist Cal Thomas and one of Rick Warren's top PR men. Some within the ranks thought it was time to surface. Former representative Tony Hall proposed a website, but Doug Coe held the line. They would stay quiet and wait for the storm to pass. The irony is that the origin of the Family's relationship with the current Ugandan regime is the only piece of "our worldwide family" that's been public all along. Public, that is, as a parable that Doug Coe has repeated so often that it turns up in evangelical books and magazines and sermons across the country, stripped of the particulars and recast as a story about the power of prayer and the fate of a nation.

Doug Coe made a bet with a skeptical friend, the story goes: pray for something every day for forty-five days, and if God didn't grant it, Coe would give him five hundred dollars. What to pray for? They settled randomly on Uganda.

And it worked! Through divine intervention, Coe's friend met a woman who worked with a Ugandan orphanage, traveled to Uganda, and met the president of Uganda. According to Coe, the American said to the president, " 'Why don't you come and pray with me in America? I have a good group of friends—senators, congressmen—who I like to pray with, and they'd like to pray with you.' " The president said yes, continues Coe, and he came to the Cedars, where he met Jesus. "And his name is Yoweri Museveni, and he is now president of all the presidents in Africa. And he is a good friend of the Family."

Documents in the Family's archive tell a different story. The skeptical friend was Hunter, a former government official who has lived across the street from the Cedars since the early 1980s. He did indeed travel to Uganda, many times, and he met the last dictator and the current one, who became a close friend. He submitted two memos about his travels to Coe, whom he calls "the prime source of what's happening all over the world," a prophetic figure with the power "to replicate Christ (i.e. put part of the Spirit) in a few who can go on to take the delegation from Christ." Who are the few? In "A Trip to East Africa—Fall 1986" and "Re: Organizing the Invisible," he cites a distinctly political cast of characters. Not just Ugandan officials but American ones, too, Sen. Chuck Grassley, "friends on the Hill," and Reagan's assistant secretary of state for African affairs, Chester Crocker. Grassley was by then an old Family hand. Crocker wasn't, but he thought like one. An advocate of "reconciliation" rather than confrontation with South Africa's white supremacist government, he oversaw the U.S. abandonment of the United Nations arms embargo against South Africa during Reagan's first term; a tenfold increase in arms shipments to the apartheid regime followed.

The purpose of Hunter's trips was a different kind of reconciliation. When Museveni came to power, Hunter says now, he was seen as a "left-wing fanatic." The memos seemed to suggest that part of Hunter's mission was to bring Museveni into a religious relationship with American politicians. In "A Trip to East Africa," Hunter conveyed the prayer request of a Ugandan politician, for whom he recommended financial support, "that the most Christian country in Africa not take the wrong ideological direction"; shared plans for a prayer cell with the minister of state, who, Hunter notes approvingly, "witnesses at every opportunity, including at political meetings with the President"; and investigated Museveni's faith directly. He found it in need of repair, the sort of spiritual "discipling" that is the Family's specialty. "Particularly at this time of crossroads in the life of the country—with Kadaffi and Korea beckoning," he concluded, "Jesus Christ is the key man in Uganda's immediate future."

Today, Hunter insists it was simply a humanitarian mission—and it's true that he raised millions for two hospitals in Uganda at a time when few Americans cared about Africa at all. (He was especially pleased by a missionary administrator who'd called a meeting of four hundred staff members to announce "that no corruption or sin would be tolerated [and] that a pregnant, non-married nurse would be fired.") It's also true that Museveni came to Washington the following year for meetings with Reagan, Bush, Crocker, and World Bank officials, and that he soon forgot all about socialism, shelved his human rights commission, and made Christianity a regular part of his speeches, stoking the fires of what became a world-famous evangelical revival. Uganda, meanwhile, became America's proxy in the region. Coincidence, Hunter says. "That was not my goal."

The goal, as spelled out in "Organizing the Invisible," was much grander, the formation of an expanded "core group" that would coordinate the efforts of Hunter and figures such as Crocker and Grassley to bring Christ to Africa. Of course, Africans already had Christ, if they wanted him. Hunter meant governments, a leadership led by God. Coe had assigned him the task of studying Exodus 18:17–21, a passage on the delegation of authority at all levels, "officials over thousands, hundreds, fifties, and tens." Hunter interpreted it as Coe's call for "key men" to represent Coe "in Kartoom [*sic*] or Bombay or on the Hill." Citing Marshall McLuhan, Hunter proposed digitalizing the network: databases of embassy contacts in every country, State Department briefings, "key men" loyal to the Family throughout Africa. He wanted limbs, organs, blood, the Body of Christ as an international network of influential people, all "led by the head, which gives it its purpose and direction."

If the Family is understood as the Body of Christ, he argued, then it suffered from a learning disability; a failure to fully exploit "opportunity nations" such as Uganda. "I know that this family is at work on this question already, but are we succeeding?" What was needed, he argued, was greater organization. "I am convinced that the Lord's headship must be linked to the body of Himself by an invisible central nervous system and that it is a servant's role, behind the scenes, supporting the visible in quiet efficiency."

After I told both versions of the story, Coe's and that of the documents, on NPR's *Fresh Air*, Hunter wrote to host Terry Gross. He was angry that I'd described him as a former Ford administration official — he'd been federal insurance administrator under both Ford and Carter, a consumer advocate fighting insurance companies since, and considers himself a liberal — and that I'd inaccurately dated the Uganda National Prayer Breakfast, which he had helped found, to the late 1990s (I'd trusted an account in a book by evangelist Luis Palau; it began in 1991, a few years after Museveni took power.) And he took serious issue with my characterization of the Family as conservative, faulting me for failing to mention "key left wing Democrats in 'The Family' like Tony Hall and Jim Slattery."

It was true that I'd left them out of the story; but then they're not exactly on the left. Hall, for instance, is anti-abortion and anti-gay, although he was first elected as a liberal. He attributes his changes of position to his Family-guided conversion. "I think I was getting fed from the Fellowship. I was getting fed, and I was growing as a believer," he told an evangelical interviewer. As for Jim Slattery, politics seems to be about the money. Moderately liberal on social issues, he's a big-business conservative when it comes to government oversight. His clients at Wiley Rein include the wireless industry association represented by C Streeters Chip Pickering and Steve Largent, and steel giant Nucor, a major donor to his Senate campaign for which he testified to Congress against climate change regulations.

But Hunter's greatest grievance was my statement that he had gone to Uganda at the behest of the U.S. government. He didn't go at the government's behest, he'd declare; "they"—the American politicians he took to Uganda—"came with me at my behest." He didn't work for politicians; they worked for him.

My copy of Hunter's letter to NPR came to me by a circuitous route—via Uganda. Hunter had e-mailed not just Terry Gross but also Tim Kreutter, the author of the Family's Eight Core Aspects and its permanent American point man in Kampala. Kreutter had shared Hunter's letter with someone who shared it with me. Hunter's phone number was at the bottom, so I called him. His anger was intense enough to make him speechless for a moment when I explained why I was calling. I made my pitch fast: If the Family could forgive Suharto—Indonesia, a million dead—and the Somali dictator Siad Barre, then one American writer shouldn't be a problem. Right? There was a long pause. "Reconciliation?" I said, asking for a meeting. And then, to my surprise, Hunter agreed.

We met at his house across the cul-de-sac from the Cedars. He is a tall, broad-shouldered man with a thatch of white hair, an imposing figure gone genially soft with age. But there was something about his voice, an oddly confident stammer, that suggested the formidably handsome man I guessed he'd once been. His memory fails him sometimes, he said, but he could be quick-witted when he wanted to, and sharp as well. He'd prepared for our meeting with a notepad full of questions and a tape recorder (he'd have our conversation professionally transcribed). Whether he normally wears as dour a face as he did to meet me, I can't say; he twitched up a smile when we shook hands, but it vanished inside. His house was dark, but his office, with windows nearly all the way around, was a brilliantly lit shambles. There was a picture of him with Museveni by the phone.

Coe's account of Hunter's relationship with Museveni wasn't true, he said. "The essence is the same, but the facts aren't the same." First of all, there was no bet—only prayer. He chose Uganda "because Idi Amin was in the papers." There was a woman, Gwen Whitaker, but no orphanage. It was a hospital, and she was a missionary. Hunter decided to visit. And that's all it was, to begin with, one Christian helping another Christian help some very poor people.

Hunter had been a Presbyterian, he said, until 1978, when "I became a believer." Not just a Christian but "first-century," searching for a faith as raw and immediate as that of the first disciples. Doug Coe, a friend of a friend, offered it to him. " 'If you guys' "—Hunter had joined a small group of men connected to his church—" 'really stick together for twenty-five years and pray for Africa, you'll begin to see Africa's problems solved on the backstroke.' "

"He's a golfer," Hunter explained, "so he uses those kinds of analogies."

Hunter, meanwhile, is an actuary, a human calculator of variables not easily quantified. He presented me with a careful case study of the Family's modus operandi as seen through his eyes.

On Hunter's second trip, in the midst of the Ugandan civil war, "I said, 'This is crazy. We're pumping money into here. The whole country's falling apart. I've got to start working on

finding ways to bridge gaps.'" He went to see the speaker of
the Parliament. "Thousands of people trying to get in to see
him. They parted like the Red Sea because I was white."

"They would see you as a missionary?"

"Yeah, which I was, in a way. And I said, 'Basically, all I'm
trying to do is find some people who might sit down together
and talk about ways to end this. Do you want to keep doing
this? Do you want your children doing this and your grandchildren? It doesn't make sense.'"

He discovered he could get in the door, but he couldn't
get anything done. The Ugandans weren't willing to act on
his advice. He needed a bigger name, he thought, "a rock
star"—someone whose presence was such a draw that he
could provide cover for Hunter's Ugandan friends to meet
and plan. "I called Andrew Young." At the time, Young was
mayor of Atlanta. Once, he'd been Martin Luther King Jr.'s
right hand—King's cautious lieutenant, the one who said,
"Go slow." Over the years, that caution turned into conservatism. These days he's a lobbyist, selling Walmart and the
interests of big oil to Africa, and African dictators to
Washington.

But back then, he served a different purpose. "I said, 'I
want to be able to tell people we're going to have a meeting
for ministers and top-type-level people. It will be one meeting, and you've got to come with all the other guys there,
too, or you don't get to meet Andrew Young.' That was
pretty powerful."

Powerful enough to win Hunter an audience with Milton Obote, the dictator at the time. "It didn't necessarily get
exactly anywhere yet." Where Hunter wanted to get was

unclear, even to him. He doesn't like to think of himself as a peacemaker or a negotiator—those terms strike him as too political. His mission was spiritual—if Obote would accept the principles of Jesus, as Hunter understood him, then maybe he'd stop the killing.

Soft-sell evangelism? I asked.

"It's so soft you don't even notice it."

Obote, responsible for the deaths of hundreds of thousands, really didn't. So Hunter turned up the volume. Not on the Gospel, but on the power Hunter could marshal to promote it. His next guest was Chuck Grassley.

I was confused. On the one hand, Hunter said he went without a political agenda; on the other, he recruited the most influential politicians he could wrangle to go with him. What were they there for? I asked.

"They were bait."

Oh.

"They wouldn't like to hear me say that, but that's what they were." Big names to attract big men to Hunter's meetings. But Grassley was strange bait for Africa, a freshly minted senator who'd campaigned just years before on a platform of preventing integrationist busing. Hunter said he didn't know anything about that. To the Ugandans, the name didn't matter. It was the title that got them into the room.

For good measure, Hunter also brought three members of the West German Bundestag and a German businessman named Rudolf Decker, a European counterpart to Hunter. "I purposely try to give an illusion of—I was like the Wizard of Oz, because I kept coming with guys." The German ambassador, Gunter Held, met them at the airport. "Why are you here?" he demanded of the German delegation when they'd gathered at his residence, with the American ambassador on hand. "You shouldn't be here. You're giving them cover. You're making Obote look better."

"I don't know why we're here," Decker told his ambassador. "Grassley wanted us to come." Decker had collaborated with Grassley in the Family's Somalia intervention — a disastrous project that devolved into a pay-to-pray scheme on behalf of the Somali ruler, Siad Barre. A Family document prepared in the early '80s, marked "Confidential," declares Barre ready to switch his loyalties from the Soviet Union to the United States in return for guns. "The Pentagon has the list of priorities of the most needed military equipment in Somalia." Barre was honest, at least, about the cost of his prayers: access to the American players who could — and did — open the spigot of military aid.

The ambassador turned to Grassley. "Same question for you, Senator. Why are you here?"

"I don't know," said Grassley. "Hunter wanted me to come."

"Why are you here, Hunter? Why did you bring all these people here?"

"I said, 'Well, we'd like to build a bridge of reconciliation across some divided people.'" Obote and Museveni, who was marching his children's army ever closer to Kampala.

"And who," asked the ambassador, "are the pillars upon which you are going to build this bridge of reconciliation?" It was a fair question. Obote would tell him that Museveni was a murderer. Hunter chuckled at the memory. The funny thing about that, he'd tell Obote, is that Museveni said the same thing about him!

"I don't know," Hunter told the ambassador. "But God does."

If Hunter's stories ended like Coe's fables, a beam of light would illuminate the ambassador at that very moment and lead him to join the happy group, off to see Obote. But Hunter was more candid. "He says, 'That's the most ridiculous thing I've ever heard.'"

Hunter didn't really have an answer. He still doesn't. Obote *was* a killer, and so was Museveni. He knew them both, Obote in office and Museveni in the bush. "You can't fight a war without killing people," Hunter observed. "The reason we went to see Obote was basically to give some cover to the guys we were trying to meet with and bring together." But Obote didn't have much time left.

I thought of one of Coe's maxims: "We work with power where we can, build new power where we can't." I thought of Hunter's 1986 proposal to Coe to formalize the Family's research on "the transfer of power" in African nations "so that the opportunities they present are not lost."

When Museveni and his child soldiers took Kampala in 1986, Hunter offered his new friend the same prescription he'd given Obote: reconciliation. What did that mean to Museveni? One of the first things he did was to establish a human rights commission to investigate the recent past. Not just Obote, but Idi Amin before him. And then he let it languish. The commission soldiered on, though, and recommended prosecutions. Museveni said no. Veterans of the former regimes were filtering into his government, and

Museveni calculated that peace at the price of justice was a fair trade. Reconciliation.

"Love forgets," preached one of the Family's leaders, in a sermon reproduced for congressional leaders. "That's what God does with your sin and mine when it's under the Blood. He forgets all about it."

Today, most of Amin's men are gone, but those of Obote's who were willing to switch their allegiance from the old dictator's pseudo-Marxist regime to Museveni's pseudo-Christian one are thriving. Museveni's ethics minister, Buturo, the chairman of Uganda's Fellowship group, is one of them. He'd been one of the many little magicians of the Obote years, famed for his ability to make enemies of the state disappear, but he had been born again since then, he told me, though he couldn't quite remember the details. Now, he said, he is a "spirit-filled Anglican"—Pentecostal and High Church at the same time—who worships under Archbishop Luke Orombi, the American-educated priest who always has a bed in Hunter's home, called "the bishop's room." Orombi wants the gays out of Uganda, but he fears a witch hunt. "Go slow," he tells Buturo.

Buturo listens; reconciles. If it was true that he once strong-armed for the dictator, he now hunts gays "democratically." The kill-the-gays bill, he said, was evidence of his commitment to the rule of law. It was a kindness to its victims; better the firing squad than the fists and feet and clawing fingernails of a mob. "It is in the interest of those who are homosexuals because people will start lynching them. Take the law into their own hands."

People already had taken the law into their hands,

acting on the evidence of hints and rumors, the turn of a wrist or a baseball hat worn by a woman, "kill lists"—names, photographs, and addresses—in *Red Pepper*. And this was democracy, too, Buturo said. Free speech, free media, the freedom of religion.

Freedom was all Hunter had ever wanted for Uganda. What they did with it—that was democracy. The Family gave them the principles of Jesus: "Seek God, discover His laws, and obey them," the same message they brought to all the world's leaders, great and small. What they did with the message was their religion, not his.

"I wasn't sent to recruit Museveni for anybody," he said. "I've never asked Museveni to do anything."

"One doesn't need to ask, do you?"

"No. Well, that's true."

But Hunter had asked. "He came to Washington to go to a Prayer Breakfast, and I insisted that the embassy give me a day and a half of his time....I said to him, 'I want you to go and have lunch on Capitol Hill with the staffers of the two House committees, two African committees.'"

Museveni's advisers wanted the president to meet with congressmen instead, but Hunter knew their staffers would actually write the legislation that set foreign aid for countries like Uganda. "I said, 'You got to humble yourself.' You know how it says in the scripture, 'Humble yourself and you will be raised up.' And he did. He said, 'The hell with you guys. I'm going to do what Hunter says.'"

While Coe cultivates top men, Hunter practices what he calls the nail-on-the-wall approach to politicians. You want to get something done? Ignore the man in the presidential portrait and look for the nail that's holding it up. "My vision, it's different from some of the others who like to meet with leaders. I don't care about meeting with leaders. I care about meeting with the guys — and women — in the various groups that are working behind the scenes."

Like the staffers who actually write the legislation that determines U.S. foreign aid. "When the budgets came he had this big jump in the budgets." Had Museveni gone through official channels, Hunter believes, he might have gotten nothing. "So, there was one time I tried to maybe influence American policy."

And what about Grassley, Inhofe, the Family's long list of conservative politicians? Conservatives comprised 80 percent of its membership, estimated Hunter. What was their goal? Why had they taken such an interest in Uganda? Was it Jesus? Or proxy politics in a little-noticed region of the world?

Grassley, to his credit, had challenged Obote, an American enemy, demanding that he account for the dead of Uganda's civil war. But he didn't challenge Museveni, an American ally with nearly as many bodies behind him. Inhofe, flying in on military planes, mixed his missionary work with efforts on behalf of AFRICOM, the United States African Command. The United States isn't fighting any wars in Africa, but Uganda is, its troops dispatched to combat a popular insurgency in Somalia. It's a mission no Ugandan I spoke with saw as anything other than a favor for the Americans, Museveni's deal with the empire.

"I think one of the points you make [that] is valid," Hunter said, "is the tension between accessibility and accountability.

There is a tension." That is, there's a politics, a calculation. If you hold a dictator accountable—if you speak truth to his power—you might not get back in the door. And if you're not in the circle of power, what good are you? It'd be a catch-22 if it weren't for the fact that, so often throughout the Family's history, the contradiction resolved itself on the side of access to power over holding power accountable.

Hunter was more concerned with the other side of the equation. "If you do what Grassley did to Obote and confront him directly, in front of other people, you can easily not get back. Now, he did that. I'm glad he did it, but *he* did it. There are people who don't build a relationship close enough—and what's the point of building a relationship if it isn't close?—to actually talk to people about issues. And there are some people who basically come here to social climb. And they're never going to confront anybody, because they are here for access. Some of them are actually here to make money. But, you know, I see that.

"There is tension. I'll give you another example. There's a picture of me with Museveni right there. I remember that day because I had the Bible in my hand, because I was taking him through part of David." King David, that is. Hunter led Museveni through a study of 2 Samuel 8:15–18. It's just a list of David's governmental appointees: Joab the general; Adoniram, "in charge of forced labor." But to a dictator who already ruled as if by divine right, the passage meant that his anointing from God trickled down to his functionaries. It wasn't just one man who was blessed but the entire system through which he ruled. The system was a sacred machine.

There was one more office to be filled, Hunter told Museveni. Not elective, not officially appointed. "You need a friend," Hunter told him. "It doesn't even have to be public."

"Surely Museveni had some friends," I said.

"He has lots of friends," said Hunter. But that wasn't what he meant. More like an adviser. Someone to help the ruler stay true to God. David, said Hunter, appointed a friend. At first I thought Hunter meant Nathan the prophet, who holds King David accountable for his seduction of Bathsheba and the murder of her husband. But it was a bad analogy, since David didn't appoint Nathan: "And the Lord sent Nathan unto David." David didn't choose. That's the distinction between the Family's religion and the prophetic tradition. The prophets were outsiders, speaking truth to power, usually in public, often with more than a touch of fever in their words. The Family shifts the job within the ruler's circle of power and replaces the prophet with the courtier. Instead of a Martin Luther King Jr., a Henry Kissinger. Instead of Nathan, "a friend." Someone who keeps your secrets, even when you're wrong.

That would be Hushai, the "king's friend" in the story of David. "Friend" was a formal title, and it meant not a relationship of affection but an adviser and a spy. When David's son Absalom rose up against him in rebellion, David sent Hushai the friend to pose as an adviser to Absalom and his army. "Just as I have served your father, so I will serve you," he told the rebel. Absalom thought Hushai had pledged loyalty to him; he didn't understand that Hushai had subtly declared himself a double agent. The friend a king, or a dictator, needs, according to scripture, is the one who serves through deception.

"There are times when you have to have secrecy," Hunter explained. "I was trying to get an accessibility—I mean an accountability component built right in, right there." It didn't work. The friend would have to be Ugandan, and Ugandans were scared of Museveni. One man volunteered, but Museveni rejected his counsel. From his perspective, he had friends: the Americans. And the Americans shared their friend, Jesus.

"At least I tried," said Hunter. No accountability, then. Both sides agreed access would have to do.

"At what point are you building relationships and at what point are you giving—"

He was good at finishing my sentences. "Cover," he said, nodding. Then he shrugged, his palms open. He saw the implications of his actions, but he preferred to think about his intentions.

"Maybe you're a saint," I offered at one point.

Hunter liked that. He reminded me of it when I pressed him on the lies told by his brothers in the Family. "You're being completely open," I said, hoping he would be. "Maybe this is an issue of, here's a—"

I wanted to say something about the structure of the Family, the self-assurances in which it traffics, but Hunter had a better idea for the end of my sentence.

"A saint!" He laughed.

"A saint amongst the wolves."

That made him laugh even harder.

*   *   *

When I finally met Bahati, we spoke at first not about homosexuality but about Bob Hunter.

"You know, Bob was here," said Bahati. We were eating lunch at the Serena, an international hotel in Kampala where the buffet, with bananas for dessert, costs a week's wages. In Ugandan shillings, that is. Most of the trade was in dollars.

Bahati gestured to a table behind us. The restaurant was white, Scandinavian, windows halfway around. Outside, sculpted greenery around a pond, lily pads and spiky trees, tall grasses, like Africa on TV.

"We sat right at that table."

The purpose of the meeting had been reconciliation: "to mend fences," Bahati said, since a conflict around the 2010 National Prayer Breakfast in February. Bahati was expected—Hunter himself had arranged housing for him at a past Breakfast—but after gay rights groups asked Obama not to attend, Hunter had first told the American press that Bahati hadn't been invited, then that he had been but had declined. Bahati said neither statement was true.

My relationship with Bahati began when he'd reached out to me. I would tell the Americans the real story, he'd hoped. "When Bob talked to me he was talking about the pressure the gay community is exerting on the Fellowship," Bahati had told me by phone in February. "He communicated his fear that this might cause the destruction of the National Prayer Breakfast. He was trying to control the damage. To do damage control. He has never said, 'David,

what you are doing is a problem.' What he has said is to discuss the pressure from the gays."

And now?

"We talked about you!" He said Hunter had told him I
was not to be trusted, that I was interested in the story just
for money. (Hunter denies this part of the conversation
took place.)

Bahati giggled, displaying a spray of teeth. A scar down
the middle of his forehead gives him the appearance of having a permanently furrowed brow, but he sounded like a
boy when he laughed. It was the most reassuring thing
about him. Then he clamped his mouth shut, the right side
of his jaw pulsing as he waited for my reaction.

Bahati had skipped our morning meeting, so I'd gone
to talk with Buturo instead. "He already knows you're here,"
my Ugandan colleague, Robert, had told me. Uganda is a
soft police state, the surveillance of journalists taken for
granted. "I guarantee it. You might as well go and see him."
So we did. We had to bribe a soldier to get into the parking
garage, where we found a spot for Robert's beat-up little
hatchback amid the vehicles of high government officials,
Mercedes-Benzes and BMW SUVs. Inside the ministry flickering fluorescent bulbs, a fuzzy TV in the closet-sized waiting room. Then, the brightly lit order of Buturo's office. He
was a studiously formal man, his accent as British as it was
Ugandan, his talking points a metronome of contradictions. The Bible demands death for all homosexuals, he'd
said, but the bill did not; this was not a conflict, because all
things would be reconciled in time. There was no need to

discuss genocide, he'd said, but then he'd done so himself, because homosexuality is worse than murder, "a threat to our existence"; the gays are attempting genocide, not Buturo. The bill had begun in the Parliament Fellowship, he'd said, through the democratic process. "Was there a debate?" I'd asked. "No," he'd said, "there is no debate, because it"—the Bahati bill—"is the best thing that ever happened."

After we'd left Buturo, we tried Bahati again. Still no answer.

So we'd called Pastor Ssempa. "Yes, I know about you," he'd said. His wife, an American, monitored U.S. media; Ssempa had heard the same interviews Bob Hunter had. "I think you may be a homo," he said. "I will not talk to you." Later, though, he'd called Robert after I'd left Kampala, thinking to find me still there. "I have a piece of land I want to sell to Jeff," he'd told Robert. "We need to meet so I can show it to him."

Two hours after we'd left Buturo, Bahati called. "Jeff!" he said. "I hear that you are in Kampala. We must meet!" So we did, with no mention of the fact that he was supposed to have met me that morning. Robert drove me to the Serena Hotel. "Should I be worried?" I asked. As an American, I was nearly immune to government reprisals, but Bahati was a special case, a man determined to redefine crime and punishment for his nation. "Oh, no, I don't think so," said Robert. He was thirty, compact and gracious in style, a news director for a radio station, freelancing as my fixer. He carried himself like a man holding a microphone for someone else to speak into. He had twenty brothers and sisters and one little daughter, for whom he was building a school because the government wouldn't bother. He planned on entering politics himself one day. "Honorable will find you useful, I am sure," he said.

The soldiers at the gate were top-shelf, no bribes necessary. Just a little frisking. Up a hill, then, away from the red dust and into the green of the Serena's manicured grounds. Robert dropped me at the lower parking lot. "There he is," Robert said—Bahati riding up the hill in the backseat of a silver SUV. He nodded through the window. And then, a few minutes later: Bahati, cool and calm in the lobby.

Bahati was dapper, not a dandy but a man with a style. He wore a dove-gray suit, a tie of chocolate brown stripes, and an ivory shirt. He'd chosen our table carefully; it was on an elevated platform, in the middle of the restaurant but with a high wall behind him. He could take the corner but still be the center of attention. The maître d' knew him; the other politicians in the room—identifiable because they *were* in the room, one of the most expensive in Kampala— wanted to talk to him. He offered them little flutters of his fingers. But for the waitstaff, or an occasional businessman, he'd rise up out of his seat and twist around over the wall behind him, clasping hands with controlled explosions of giggles followed by terse exchanges. People liked him. They were afraid of him. He wasn't what I'd imagined: a bumpkin, a Tom Coburn, a country mouse come to the city and crying "gay!" at everything that offended him. He was something more compact, tougher: a Pickering with juice: a cannier George Wallace for Uganda.

"David," I said, "you're a player."

He smiled, half-shy, half-pleased, and summoned a waiter with the same flutter he used on his colleagues, ordering for both of us in Lugandan, one of his three languages along with English and his native Rukiga, the language of Uganda's Bakiga minority.

He was a man of many influences. Thirty-six years old, he'd been educated in Uganda, the University of Cardiff in Wales, and the Wharton School at the University of Pennsylvania, with financial support from a foundation in Norway. He was an orphan. His mother had died in childbirth. His father, he says, was poisoned by a business associate when Bahati was three years old. He was sent to his grandmother; she died when he was in elementary school. He lived off the streets of Kabale, a market town of forty thousand in southwestern Uganda. "I sold things you cannot understand," he told me. That sounded dramatic, but what he meant was bananas.

He won one scholarship after another and he became an accountant. But he felt God wanted more from him. In 2004, on the advice of two friends who'd studied in the United States at the fundamentalist Family Research Council, he went to America to learn the art of political campaigning at the Leadership Institute, a well-funded school of "political technology" for conservative activists. Lesson number one: a black African conservative will always have friends in a Republican Party eager to prove itself past racism. The institute, in Arlington, Virginia, made Bahati a star of its fund-raisers, and soon, he said, he was on a first-name basis with men like "Mitch" (McConnell, Senate Republican leader) and "John" (Ensign). Young man, one of the politicians told him—he won't say whom—you need to visit the Cedars. There he met John Ashcroft and a philanthropist-lawyer heavily involved in Uganda. When he won his seat in 2006, the first thing he did was look for the Ugandan Fellowship he'd learned about in America.

"God uses instruments to make his purpose be fulfilled," Bahati said after we'd filled our plates. "He uses voters." He chewed as he spoke. "He uses voters to lift somebody up to bring them where you are. Eh?" Eh—that was his all-purpose word, good for acknowledgment, dismissal, or coercion. I nodded despite myself, confirming his self-anointing. "God puts people in place," he continued, satisfied. "The Bible says in Romans 13 that all authority comes from God." He pointed his fork at me. "All authority comes from God. Eh?" Nod. "Yes," he said, smiling, as though I were an apt pupil.

There was a sense in which his conflict with Hunter was a result of his belief that he himself was no longer a student of the Family's, but rather, as the acting head of the Ugandan branch (after Museveni), an elder in his own right. He remembered his excitement at his first discovery of the Family. "To know that you have leaders who trust in God. And you are a part of a global movement like that, that family, that global family. You can travel from here to Ukraine and know you have a brother or a sister." *We are alike*, the Family tells its foreign relations. *We are all the same, Christian and Muslim, the weak and the strong.* It's a way of dealing with differences—the haves and the have-nots, on a global scale—by denying difference. We are the same, he said to the Americans, to Hunter, to Coe: you are like me. "They want to distance themselves from a Bahati," he'd said in one of our first conversations. He spoke of himself like that, in the third person, when he wanted to make a point about his own universalism. "But they cannot. Because we are a family! Doug Coe has gone into a very high level of thinking on these issues. It is about a sense of belonging."

Not in a personal sense, but in terms of what evangelicals refer to as discernment, one of the gifts of the spirit interpreted from the Acts of the Apostles, like speaking in tongues. Discernment means more, or maybe less, than being perceptive. It means opening yourself up to the *gift* of discernment, God's revelation direct from Him to you. "For example, I didn't champion this issue, homosexuality, for the whole world. I did it for Uganda. That was me. But God!" Bahati pointed up. "God made it bigger. We are going to get the bill through, now or later. And when we do, we will *close* the door to homosex, and *open* society to something larger."

That was the crux of the matter for Bahati. To him, homosexuality is only a symbol for what he learned from the Family is a greater plague: government by people, not by God. "The original sin," according to "Jesus Transcends All," a sermon distributed to international guests at the National Prayer Breakfast (Bahati had been twice, in 2007 and 2009), "was not murder, adultery, or any other action we call sin. The original sin was, and still is, the human choice to be one's own god, to control one's own life, to be in charge."

"Homosexuals have won the battle in America," Bahati said. He believes they have seduced straight Americans, tricked them into believing they could make their own choices. The empire was rotting from within. *The burden is on you, David,* his American friends told him. Inhofe's people had sent word, Bahati said. "I have spoken to his assistant, Mark Powers," he explained. (Powers is an Assemblies of God missionary on Inhofe's Senate staff. He's also well represented in the Family's Africa documents.) In total, Bahati said, about half a dozen leaders had sent their support. He couldn't name them, though, because the gays would destroy them. That's what they told Bahati. *You must fight the battle.* "We have talked to a number of conservatives in America who believe what we are doing is right, and that if we do not close the door to homosexuality at this time, it would be too late for us to breathe," he told me. "They wish that homosexuality was confronted and fought severely in America."

There was still hope for Africa. God would use the weak to teach the strong, a Bahati to send a message to America. God had given him a Word, divine insight. Six years before, on the eve of his first journey to America. Five words, actually, Isaiah 6:8, illuminated for Bahati by Jesus: "Here am I; send me." The words of the prophet Isaiah to the Lord, the words of the Lord for Bahati, his ticket to America and his calling in Uganda; in 2006, his "prayer team" had used it as a campaign slogan. Smartly divorced, that is, from what follows, just two verses below:

> *Then I said, Lord, how long? And he answered,*
> *Until the cities be wasted without inhabitant,*
> *And the houses without man,*

And the land be utterly desolate,
And the Lord have removed men far away,
And there be a great forsaking in the midst of the land.

Prophecy isn't kind, but Bahati was brave. He knew his bill, if passed—and in Uganda, voters wanted it passed— would lead to a great forsaking, indeed: of foreign aid, the lifeblood of what passes for an economy in a country where job seekers outnumber jobs fifty to one. People would starve. There would be no medicine for AIDS. And it might be worse than that. The dictator was old, his grip was weakening, and war might be coming. It was hard to conceive, after at least three hundred thousand dead under Amin and as many as half a million lost in the fight that brought Museveni to power, that Uganda would ever return to slaughter. But they would do what God asked of them, Bahati believed. They would be a God-led nation, a light unto the world.

Even as the American brothers of the Family shied away from controversy, Bahati's African brothers in reconciliation gravitated toward him. He was in demand; Bahati and a pastor ally whom he'd put on the government payroll said Fellowship groups in the governments of countries across the continent—Rwanda, Burundi, Tanzania, Zambia, Congo—had requested copies of his bill or, better yet, a personal appearance. The message was spreading, with Bahati as its apostle, suddenly the most famous Ugandan since Idi Amin.

Bahati wanted to bring the message back to the source. "If I came to America, what do you think would happen?"

"I think there would be protests," I said. In 2010, there'd been protests at the Prayer Breakfast for the first time in five decades based just on the possibility that Bahati *might* show.

"I want to come one of these days and see. What do you think is the best way to come in? Eh?"

"I wouldn't make it public."

"Ah! So the best way would be to sneak in?"

"Just go as a regular traveler."

"But they wouldn't hurt me?" He claimed to have survived several gay poisoning attempts already. "I will be coming to America very soon. To do something very private. I will not announce it to the world. I will just come. To our friends in Washington. I will tell private people, whom I'll visit. There are people willing to host me."

Not Hunter, he added. He no longer trusted Hunter, though he didn't blame him for what he saw as cowardice. The Family, he'd been told, was also under gay attack. In Uganda the gays used poison; in America, "blackmail." How did that work? He couldn't explain. The gays, he said, have secret ways.

"Spiritual warfare?" I asked.

"Mm-mmm." Bahati smiled, pleased that I had invoked the dark side of reconciliation, the invisible work of the spirit that selects between right and wrong, men of God and those outside His circle. Spiritual warfare is a concept as old as the Bible, but, through the literalist filter of twentieth-century American fundamentalism, it has taken on magical meaning, imbuing the actions of its believers with supernatural power. "Imagine a small bill in a small country like

Uganda," he said. "Sponsored by a Bahati. An ordinary member of Parliament. And—"

He gestured toward me, my presence in Uganda, and the dining room of the Serena, Kampala's international stage. I saw where he was going.

"You think something must be going on here."

"Yes. Something..." He paused. "Invisible." Spiritual warfare, that is, the amplification of angels and their worldly counterparts, American allies. With that power came enemies.

"You believe in the reality of demons?" I asked.

"Demons, yes."

"Do you think homosexuality is a form of demonic possession?"

He giggled, like Pastor Kyazze rejecting my simpleminded suggestion that, according to his logic, gays might have hooked noses to go along with their financial wizardry and control of the media. "It is *modern* witchcraft," Bahati clarified. Modern witchcraft isn't a matter of chicken heads or curses, he explained; it's about information, the suppression or selective release of truths. "It is manipulation for control and dominance."

And what about the lies he claimed that his American friends had told about him, about his role in the organization and his visits to Washington? Was that "modern witchcraft"?

No.

But he thought Hunter had lied?

Yes.

What was the distinction?

Perspective, thought Bahati. Take a lie and turn it upside down. What do you see?

The truth?

Bahati giggled. No. "*Unnecessary* truth." Truths, that is, that are too subtle for the public to understand.

The following afternoon, Bahati called me. "Jeff," he said, "I think we must meet again." He didn't explain why, but my guess was that it had something to do with Tim Kreutter, the author of the Family's Eight Core Aspects.

Robert and I were driving back from a three-hour conversation with Kreutter when Bahati called. Kreutter, an American, runs a Family-funded project of youth homes and schools centered around a "Leadership Academy," created to train a new political and professional elite instilled with the principles of Jesus from childhood forward.

Kreutter is, in Uganda, what Hunter calls "the nail on the wall," one of the men behind the face of power. When Hunter had explained to me his theory of advocacy—reaching out to "the little group around the president" instead of the big man himself—I'd thought he'd meant Bahati's Parliament Fellowship group, which meets on Thursdays. No, Hunter had said; "the Friday group is really the power group." Kreutter's group, that is. "They are the ones we'd go to if we really needed something done," he'd explained. It was Kreutter, a senior finance ministry official named Paulo Kyama, and a former MP who'd cofounded the Parliament group. "They're the ones who decide who to recommend to Congress for the Ugandan delegation. They have great connections, if you need to get something done. Plus, they have the added advantage of being almost—well, Tim *is* an American. Paulo, for all intents and purposes, is. In terms of, you tell him to do something, he'll do it. They know how to get through to the First Lady, the president. I mean, Doug Coe could pick up the phone and call. I suppose I probably could." But they hadn't, he said, not in a long time. They hadn't asked Museveni to fight the anti-gay crusade. They'd left that matter to the "nail," Kreutter.

Kreutter had been raised in Africa, the child of missionaries. He'd lived under a succession of dictators, and now counted the dictator Museveni, and especially his wife, Janet, as personal friends. While I was with him, two missionaries came by requesting help from the First Lady, through Kreutter. The missionaries were worried, though; they'd heard rumors that Janet Museveni could be a dangerous woman in her own right. Kreutter had seen power from every side, a 360-degree perspective that had taught him to be forgiving. Americans are arrogant, he warned; Africa and her leaders need a greater understanding. That's what he gave his students.

That, plus connections: the Musevenis are patrons, Kreutter guides the annual Prayer Breakfast delegation to Washington and helps organize its Kampala counterpart, Sen. Inhofe parachutes in, and then there's Hunter, himself one of the most influential Americans in Uganda. A senior aide to Bahati works with one of Kreutter's programs, African Youth Leadership, and Kreutter, a tall, thin man so mild-mannered as to be nearly invisible, had been a mentor to Bahati. Bahati said that from Kreutter he had learned that, in the end, he had no enemies, only opportunities.

But Kreutter was displeased with his protégé's new initiative. Bahati had brought his idea for the Anti-Homosexuality
Bill to a Fellowship dinner attended by Kreutter and several
other international members a week before he'd introduced
it the previous October. When the bill had become a political issue in the United States, Hunter had declared that the
Family's men in Kampala had cautioned their junior brother
Bahati against proceeding. Bahati was emphatic in denying
this: "No one opposed. Not one." He'd taken the meeting
as a green light to proceed with the biblical agenda he
thought they shared. Kreutter sighed when I told him Bahati's interpretation. "I know David's heart is good," he said.
"But." He shook his head. Bahati wasn't revealing "unnecessary truths" in speaking of his intimacy with the Family so
much as unnecessary complications. Kreutter didn't like
strong language: truth, lies, right, wrong. "Complex": that's
what he called Bahati's legislation, which he neither fully
condemned nor supported. "Essentially I am against it," he
later told me, but he did not want to use language that
would hurt Bahati's feelings.

Bahati and I agreed to meet for dinner again the next
night. "Why?" Robert asked, puzzled. "I guess he likes me,"
I said. This time, we had the Serena's white room to ourselves. It was early evening; I wanted to leave time for Ssempa's Saturday night abstinence party at Makerere. The clientele
were in one of two theme bars, sophistication or safari, or at
a fabulous wedding being held on the grounds. Bahati was
upset that he hadn't been invited. We took the same power
table on the platform, but this time there was nobody to
admire him. Just the waitstaff, with whom he was no longer

so kind. "Okay," he said, once we had our food, "let us pray."

He had two items on his agenda. The first was a book: he wanted to write one. He had learned so much in his war with the homosexuals, he wanted to "give back." To America, that is; he wanted my help finding an American publisher.

I tried to make a trade. "Tell me first who the American politicians are who say they're supporting you," I said. "The ones who tell you the gays control the media."

Bahati chuckled. "I can't tell you this!"

"You're protecting them?"

"No, I am not protecting them. I am *defending* them." He saw himself as a martyr to the cause, taking the heat for his American friends. There were times in our conversations when he seemed tempted to name those for whom he suffered, but every time he'd rally by reminding himself of the meaning of love between brothers: "We must protect each other's secrets, eh? That is what the Fellowship is, men we can trust, take our sins to."

He called this idea the context of lying. For him, he said, it was African, but the context was like Christ, universal. He told me a story about the East African revival of 1935. "The same year," he said, tapping his plate with his fork, "Abraham Vereide began the Fellowship in America, eh?" He smiled. He liked showing off his knowledge of the Family's history. The East African revival began in similar fashion: a roomful of foreign-educated Ugandan elites in Bahati's hometown, Kabale, singing foreign songs and declaring themselves the *balokole*, the saved ones, responsible for the

future of their nation. But they made a mistake: they confessed their sins in public. That might be all right for the
masses, but not for men to whom God had entrusted power.
If a leader revealed his secret lovers, the rabble might take
his confession as license; if he admitted he had stolen, even
less scrupulous men would use that information against
him. Better to let like handle like, leaders tending to each
other's sins behind closed doors. "The best way to kill a
snake in the house is not to destroy the house. Eh?"

The second item on Bahati's agenda was an invitation.
"I think, Jeff, that we cannot keep meeting like this." He
waved at the empty Serena. "You have come so far to see
me. I must, therefore, let you know me. You must come to
my house."

This did not seem like a good idea.

"Well, tomorrow is my last day here."

Bahati threw his hands in the air. "Perfect, then! I am
just in time."

We cut dinner short. I was headed for my abstinence
rally date with Sharon, the Makerere college girl who wanted
my help killing homosexuals. I invited Bahati. "No," he said,
"I cannot go to church tonight. I have some arrangements I
must make. Eh? For our brunch tomorrow!" He patted my
shoulder. "Who will drive you?"

"Robert," I said.

"Ah, good. He is a nice boy. I'm glad you two will come
together."

"David," I said.

"Yes, Jeff?"

"I have your guarantee of safety, right?"

Bahati wasn't in the least offended. "Of course! I am a Christian. Am I not?"

Later that night, after the abstinence rally, Robert and I went driving. Up along a ridge through a park of tall grass overlooking the city's skyline, not illuminated but merely spotted with light, like a horizon of stars, and then down along avenues of street fires and mud-hut discos and night-watch churches, Pentecostal services that went through to dawn. And finally out to a street party amid office buildings and warehouses, shiny sheets of corrugated steel slicing the road off from traffic, men with guns, soldiers and cops and for-hires, leaning against a maze of fencing thrown up to slow down the entering crowd. Inside there was a stage and a light show and Uganda's biggest hip-hop musicians, a solid brick of a crowd not really dancing, just throbbing, except for the gay men around whom circles formed like they were prom stars in a high school movie. There they'd be joined by the girls who wanted more movement than the stiff-legged weeble-wobble straight boys would offer. We did, too; we'd had enough of Bahati and Buturo and Kreutter. We found two girls and I bought us all awful sweet-ened bottles of vodka and we took refuge in a tiny gay king-dom ruled by two men who seemed brilliantly, secretly, obviously queer. Or so I thought. When we left, at around 2:00, Robert refused to believe me when I told him he'd just danced alongside gays. "At the street jam?" he asked, incredulous. "Those boys?" I'd thought their lipstick might give them away.

Robert was devout on Sundays, more forgiving the night

before, anti-gay like nearly every Ugandan but also a libertarian, troubled by what we'd learned of the Family's presence in Uganda. "I think they are trying to steal my country," he'd said. Tim Kreutter and his Leadership Academy in particular had disturbed him. The calm with which the American had described his academy's quiet construction of a new elite class. "What Tim is doing is owning people, training them and owning them. Even if he wants them to do good things, the principle is corrupting. It is the seduction principle."

That was the irony of Bahati's anti-gay fantasies, his vision of gay men from Europe and America trolling the streets of Kampala, trading iPods for blow jobs. It was Bahati who had been seduced, recruited for a foreign agenda, reconciled. "Now he is caught in the middle," Robert had said. "They gave him a structure, but they disown him. Let me tell you one thing. When you go to make love to a girl, you buy chocolate, buy flowers, you entice her—in order to use that thing." To use her, that is. "That's exactly what's happening." Robert thought of Bahati like a ruined woman in a Victorian novel. He no longer belonged to himself, but he was no longer wanted, either. He could neither drop the bill nor carry it forward. But there was one play left, a powerful one. The bill he was holding—just the idea of it—was a bomb, and he'd already lit the fuse.

"I don't know if it's wise to go see him tomorrow," Robert said, as we left the party. Before we could consider the question, the risks, Robert spotted a photographer he knew, and then another and another, a herd of journalists rushing toward the sheet metal walls. "Look!" the photographer shouted. We turned and saw a circle of soldiers, in their midst a man down. He was shirtless, perfectly muscled, his skin almost liquid, red and shiny. He was lying on his back, half curled, rolling left then right as soldiers on either side planted their boots in him. Not in a fury; more like a simple rhythm. Tick, tock. Every time a boot hit him he made a noise that sounded like a question. "Eh? Eh?" Like Bahati. "It is sick justice, man," said the photographer. He took some pictures. "This boy, though, he brought it on himself." Robert asked in Lugandan what had happened. "Acid attack," the photographer answered in English, like it was a sad but everyday crime. The bloody man had thrown acid at somebody, supposedly one of the stars. The word was that the attack had been some kind of message. Nobody knew what it'd been meant to say, and it didn't really matter. Tick, tock went the boots. "They say this boy, he was paid," said the photographer. He crouched to hear the beat from the bloody man's perspective. "Disgusting," he said, rising to leave. "Well, I got what I need."

It's a month later. Blessed has left Kampala to hide. Tim Kreutter e-mailed me a phrase he found meaningful, sourced to a forgotten writer from the Thirty Years' War: "IN ESSEN-TIALS UNITY, IN NON-ESSENTIALS LIBERTY, IN ALL THINGS CHARITY." Pastor Ssempa has some land he wants to show me. But I'm home, in America, and tonight I'm working late, listening to my recordings of Bahati and thinking about what I owe him. Literally, that is: his two boys, David Jr. and Daniel, had decided to make movies of themselves with my iPhone while their father and I were talking at his house, and I had said I'd e-mail them when I got home.

Bahati's house was a redbrick villa high up a hill outside Kampala. Robert's car barely made it. You needed a heavier vehicle to handle the rutted, red dirt roads. There were no *boda-boda* drivers in those hills, just big cars with chauffeurs to drive them and houses with servants inside to crank open the great iron doors that guarded each plot, small maps of close-cropped grass in the suburban style within walls topped by razor wire and seeded with shards of broken glass. Bahati's was an especially lovely compound. "There are so many right ways to get here," he told us on the phone as we discovered many wrong ones, grinding the underbelly of Robert's hatchback and rocking ourselves gently out of little canyons, not so much driving as rock climbing. So many ways, but Bahati could not name them; the roads weren't like that in Bahati's hills. Named, that is. And the servants we saw weren't talking. So we found it by trial and error, or maybe the gift of discernment, because when we made our guess it was the right one: a hobbit-sized door within the iron gates opened and a servant woman peeped out, clanged it shut, and then swung both shrieking doors open and we were in.

Bahati stood above us on a terrace, unsmiling. "Hello, Robert," he called. We hiked up the hill and the stairs and joined him. "Eh?" he said, gesturing to the view without pride: the red tile roofs of his neighbors interlocking down the hill below him, steely rain clouds over Lake Victoria, Africa's biggest, beyond. And in the yard, evidence of family: a miniature army Jeep on the grass, a BMX bike ridden into a hedgerow. The bike, I believe, belonged to David Jr., six years old; the Jeep was just right for his Daniel, a four-year-old cross between General Patton and Cecil B. De-Mille. "He is already stronger than his older brother," Bahati boasted. It was Daniel's idea to use my phone to shoot movies. "Make a movie of me dancing!" he shouted; it was an order. David Jr., a joyfully bucktoothed boy, introduced himself to us not long after our arrival by presenting to his father one of my notebooks, lifted from my briefcase while we were in another room. He'd flipped the page on which I'd written a remark of Bahati's — "all acknowledgement of homosexuality is defilement" — and had added commentary of his own in a script of looping flourishes, remarkably neat for a six-year-old: "You are not enabled to view this channel or your account has been suspended." He'd copied it from the screen of his father's big-screen TV. "Ah no," Bahati told his son, "this belongs to Uncle Jeff." And so I was made a member of the Bahati family.

We sat in one of the living rooms, modeled, it seemed, on the Serena: minimalist white with bright red Scandinavian-style furniture. We took one corner, Bahati far across the room with his back to a wall-sized window, a small round glass table between us on which a servant placed a glass pitcher of sticky-sweet orange juice. Bahati wore a black soccer shirt with red panels and long black shorts. Today, it seemed, there was nothing on his agenda. He leaned back and tugged up his shirt, distractedly rubbing his belly, just going to paunch, watching international news out of the corner of his eye. He sifted through a small heap of cell phones beside him to take calls, short, clipped, or murmuring, receiving news from his supporters.

"I do not understand you Americans," he said, sighing. "Look at a woman like Hillary Clinton, supporting the killing of babies, and then you say no, you should not threaten to punish somebody with death." He was beginning to come to terms with the possibility that the threat of losing foreign aid—Sweden said they'd cut it; Germany would offer Museveni $148 million to muzzle him—would force him to cut a deal: no death penalty. He'd have to settle for prison and purges, an outcome Western governments, eager to do business with the newly oil-rich country, would call a human rights victory.

Bahati was disillusioned by such half measures. "Leviticus is very clear. If a man sleeps with a man—punishable by death. If a woman sleeps with a woman—punishable." He meant Leviticus 18:22, not clear at all and subject to great debate among serious Bible scholars: *Thou shalt not lie with mankind, as with womankind; it is abomination.* "But if the majority say this clause of death is not necessary," Bahati continued. "Well." He gave me a sad smile, no teeth. The majority had at first said it was necessary, and it had quickly become the most popular political idea in Uganda. Even those known to be secretly gay themselves, when presented with a choice— vote for death or mark themselves candidates for it—were willing to choose death, for other people. Now, under the direction of the dictator and possibly pressure from Hunter— "even Jesus was betrayed," observed Bahati—the majority was tiptoeing away from the killing clause, waiting for signs from above. But Museveni was no clearer than scripture. Go slow, he said to one. Stop the homos! he ordered another. "It's a democracy," said Bahati. "Eh?"

He could live with that. He was already adjusting his stance, narrowing his position. His new line was that his bill would not deliver death to adults engaging in consensual sex, but life: in prison, where they'd be protected from themselves and cured, if possible, using the latest scientific techniques developed in the churches of America. He had never intended to kill anyone but child rapers, he claimed. "But David," I said, "the big clause, 'aggravated homosexuality,' only three of the seven varieties punishable by death involve minors." Death, also, for HIV-positive homosexuals who have sex, regardless of precautions; for sex with a disabled person; and, most alarmingly, for "serial offenders."

Bahati started laughing, rubbing his belly faster. Not one of his little giggles, but sustained laughter. Robert and I glanced at each other, waiting for the joke. It never came. Instead, this, between guffaws: "A serial offender. A serial! Like, like, a serial *killer!*" That was even more of a knee-slapper. "It's a guy who does not kill for *good* causes. But he is like a, a fun—"

Laughter cut off the last word. He tried to calm down. "No, you see, the law, it's for adult / minor. If you are a boss. Or a guardian. Or you are a known"—this one cracked him up—"just to be molesting kids, you know?"

"That clarifies it," I said.

But "serial" was just too funny to let go. "No, no," he said, leaning forward and holding up a hand. "If I have a boyfriend"—that was too rich, he had to fall back and

laugh—"and I go and have *another* boyfriend"—snort—
"do I become a serial?"

"No?" I guessed.

"No," said Bahati. "So what I want to call it—"

He stopped, shaking his head, the corner of his eyes
watering. "A 'Safe Family Bill.' 'Save Children Bill.'"

"Better branding?"

"Too late!" said Bahati, and that was a hoot, too. "No.
No. That was actually what many wanted, many thought
'Anti-Homosexuality' would be a little stigma, stigma—"
He looked to Robert for help.

"Stigmatizing, Honorable."

"Yes. But I still believe the title of the bill is what we need.
We must confront it."

"But you're not, are you?"

"Mmm?"

"Your law is not biblical."

"The law *is* biblical—"

"But you're letting some homosexuals get away, aren't
you?"

The question was a trap, and he knew it. Or rather, more
like a fault line, between the idea of "God-led government"
and the bloody prospect of "biblical law."

"You just quoted Leviticus," I said. "You said that if a
man lies with a man, he should die." All of them, that is, no
qualifiers. "But your law doesn't provide for that."

Bahati chuckled. "Well, Jeff. I was not writing a Bible! I
was writing a law. Eh?" He laughed, and Robert and I
laughed with him. Our response was an instinct, I think, to

provide an embarrassed man cover. "The principles of the Bible only guide you," he said, nodding at his own explanation. "The fundamental issue is homosexuality is sin. And if it is sin, it must be punished. Now. We live in the world, so we must see how best we can punish these people. Yeah?"

"Yeah. But if you thought there was the political support to follow the law of Leviticus, would that be a good idea?"

Bahati was silent a moment, leaning back into the breeze of the window behind him, the red and green hills of Kampala, a sweep of gray rain falling farther off over Lake Victoria. He looked at the ceiling, then at me, holding my eye even as he giggled without humor; it was, I realized, like a cough for him. "If it was a political possibility?" he said.

"If you proposed a law that said kill *all* the gays, on sight."

"It wouldn't pass."

"Would it be a good idea?"

His hand dropped to his belly, tugging his shirt up again and making circles beneath his sternum. "I mean," he said quietly, "if we had an opportunity to implement what is in the Bible, that would be a perfect position." He paused. "But we don't live in a perfect world."

No, just something like a democracy. The Kingdom is yet to come.

But the story doesn't quite end there, with the promise of murder. Because what I owe Bahati, I realized, is recognition—of that which is obscured by the slogan *never again*, words that suppose that murder begins with hate, ugly and easily identifiable, something other, outside, far off in Africa. But Bahati began with love.

"The Fellowship teaches us that we all come together," he said, explaining that to him the perfect world would not be a theocracy, a word he despised, or a regime of one religion over another. Once, he might have thought that; but Kreutter had showed him something better. "God does not know whether you're a Christian or not. He just knows you. And we just need to develop a relationship with him." This was open to anybody, Muslim or Jew or Christian. Even a homosexual? Even a homo.

"Through Jesus?

"Yes," said Bahati, his smile now warm and sincere.

"That's reconciliation?

"Yes! And *love*. The Fellowship. We call it Fellowship. It's part of the world Family."

That's what he had learned from the Family, he said. Begin with love, end with love. In between, civilization and its laws. That's what I owe: the recognition that the killer is a civilized man.

That recognition requires that I confess that when Bahati told me he was writing not a Bible but just a law— it's not a perfect world!—I laughed with him because, I think, we were being civil. He had promised me that, if I returned after his law is passed, he would have me arrested for promotion of homosexuality; and he understood I was there to tell a story about him that would hurt him; but despite it all we had found common ground: civility. We were within the circle of reconciliation.

Better that I'd been the criminal of the night before, within the circle of boots.

But I lacked that courage. I thought of my conversation

with Hunter. At what point, I'd asked him, are you giving cover? At what point was I?

Bahati had taken up another matter. This was a friendly lunch, and we should not limit ourselves to the problem of homosexuality; we should all get to know one another, exchange views. Our new topic was a media regulation bill being considered in Parliament that would require Ugandan media organizations to be evaluated for "values" and licensed anew on a yearly basis. We discussed it civilly, debating its pros and cons.

Robert was opposed. He saw it as one more vestige of democracy slipping away from Uganda, the end of a semi-free press. Semi-free? That meant the kind where the worst he had feared for our visit this afternoon was perhaps a brief detention, some bribes required for policemen, and even that had not transpired—we had been welcomed. But the bill, Robert thought, would end all that because if it passed he would never get to be a journalist at all. The Bahatis of Uganda would make that decision for him.

Bahati saw it differently. He was an accountant, and every year he paid dues to professional associations in Uganda and the United Kingdom. He took professional development courses. You could do business with him and depend on certain standards. Should Robert be held any less accountable?

"The issue is," Bahati said, thoughtfully trying to see it from Robert's perspective, "Will government exploit this power to suppress the media?" A valid concern. But not to worry. Parliament would establish an independent tribunal.

Top men, reasonable men, who would hear appeals. Did Robert not trust him?

Robert laughed, incredulous; but he could see it was no longer wise to speak plainly.

Bahati laughed, too, glad for that recognition of their common ground.

"What is important, Robert, is for us not to fear to sleep because we will dream bad dreams. Eh?"

Robert looked sick.

Me, I thought we were still being civil. "I don't understand, David."

Robert did. "Honorable," he said. "Honorable." But that was all.

There was a pause between the two men, and in the space between them, as I observed the conversation instead of occupying one side, I suddenly grasped the nature of the recognition Bahati demanded. It was the same as at C Street in America; the same as Coburn in Beirut, Inhofe in Nigeria. He was asking us to trust his good intentions. He would be our night watchman.

"You see?" Bahati said, turning back to me. He waved a few fingers at Robert. "They fear to go to sleep because they fear bad dreams." As if they had a choice. God had already decided for us. That's what Bahati had learned from the Family. Not religion or law but love, trust, sleep, the killing to come like a dream.

A servant appeared, her eyes downcast, to summon Honorable and his guests to the dining room. Our meal was prepared, the table set.

5

THE WAR

STAFF SERGEANT Jeffery Humphrey woke at 7:00 AM. *Easter in Iraq,* he thought, and then put the holiday out of his mind. He and his squad of nine men, part of the 1/26 Infantry of the 1st Infantry Division, were assigned to a Special Forces compound in Samarra. Although Humphrey was a combat veteran of Kosovo and Iraq, the men to whom he was detailed, the Tenth Special Forces Group, didn't speak much to grunts like him. They called themselves the "Faith element," but they didn't talk religion, which was fine with Humphrey. Muslim hearts and minds wouldn't be won by an army proclaiming another religion.

Humphrey's first duty that Easter Sunday 2004 was to make sure the roof watch was in place: a machine gunner, a soldier with a squad automatic weapon, or SAW (a gas-powered automatic rifle on a bipod), and another man armed with a submachine gun on loan from Special Forces. Together with two Bradley fighting vehicles on the ground and snipers on another roof, they covered the perimeter of the compound, a former elementary school overlooking the Tigris River.

Early that morning a unit from the 109th National Guard Infantry dropped off their morning chow. With it came a holiday special—a video of Mel Gibson's *The Passion of the Christ* and a chaplain to sing the film's praises, a gory cinematic sermon for an Easter at war. Humphrey ducked into the chow room to check it out. "It was the part where they're killing Jesus, which is, I guess, pretty much the whole movie. Kind of turned my stomach." Humphrey considered himself a Pagan—a conviction he kept to himself after too many encounters with superiors who told him he served in the armed forces of a Christian nation—but he liked Jesus, too, and he couldn't understand why the Faith element seemed to take so much pleasure in watching their savior being tortured. He decided he'd rather burn trash.

He was returning from a run to the garbage pit when the 109th came barreling back. Their five-ton (a supersized armored pickup) was rolling on rims, its tires flat and flapping and spewing greasy black flames. "Came in on two wheels," remembers one of Humphrey's men, a machine gunner. On the ground behind it were more men from the 109th, laying down fire with their M4s. Humphrey raced toward the truck as his shooters on the roof opened up, their big guns thumping above him. When he climbed into the back, the stink was overwhelming. He reached down to grab a rifle covered in blood; his hand came up wet with brain.

The rest of that Easter was spent under siege, as insurgents held off Bravo Company at a bridge across the Tigris and ammunition ran low. "We were at 100 percent. Everybody and anybody able to fight is on the roof." But down in the day room, *The Passion* kept playing for exhausted men, fake blood flayed off a fake Jesus for hours on end. "They must have had it on repeat."

As dusk fell, the men prepared four Bradley fighting vehicles for a "run and gun" to draw fire away from the compound. Humphrey headed down from the roof for a briefing. He found his lieutenant, John D. DeGiulio, with a couple of sergeants, snickering like schoolboys. Somebody had commissioned the Special Forces interpreter, an Iraqi from Texas, to paint a legend in giant red Arabic script across the armor of one of the Bradleys.

"What's it mean?" asked Humphrey.

"Jesus killed Muhammad," one of the men said. The soldiers guffawed. JESUS KILLED MUHAMMAD was about to cruise into the Iraqi night.

The Bradley, a tracked "tank killer" armed with a cannon and missiles—to most eyes, indistinguishable from a tank— rolled out. Instead of taking the fight to the enemy, the men would invite every devout Iraqi to join the battle. Meanwhile, the interpreter took to the roof, bullhorn in hand. The sun was setting. Humphrey heard the keen of the call to prayer, the crackle of the bullhorn, the interpreter answering—in Arabic, then English for the troops. "Muhammad was a pedophile!" A Special Forces officer, "a big, tall, blond grinning type," says Humphrey, stood next to the translator. "Go on," the officer told the Iraqi. "Keep it going."

"Jesus killed Muhammad!" chanted the translator. A head emerged from a window to answer, somebody took a shot at the Iraqi who was holding the bullhorn, and the Special Forces man directed a response with an Mk 19 grenade launcher. "Boom," says Humphrey. The head and the window and the wall around it disappeared.

"Jesus killed Muhammad!" Another head, another shot; boom. "Jesus killed Muhammad!" Boom. In the distance Humphrey heard the static of AK fire and the thud of rocket-propelled grenades. He saw a rolling rattle of light that looked like a firefight on wheels. There couldn't be that many insurgents in Samarra, Humphrey thought. He heard Lt. DeGiulio reporting in from the Bradley's cabin, opening up on every doorway that popped off a round, responding to rifle fire—every Iraqi household was allowed one gun—with 25 mm shells powerful enough to smash straight through a front door and the back door behind it. Lt. DeGiulio was on a mission. "Each time I go into combat I get closer to God," he'd tell me.

Humphrey was stunned. He'd been blown off a tower in Kosovo and seen action in the drug war, but he'd never witnessed a maneuver so fundamentally stupid.

The men on the roof thought otherwise. To them the lieutenant was a hero, a kamikaze on a death mission to bring Iraqis the American news:

عيسى قتل محمد

JESUS KILLED MUHAMMAD

*　　*　　*

When Barack Obama moved into the Oval Office in 2009, he inherited a military not just drained by a two-front war in the Middle East but fighting a third battle on the home front, a subtle civil war over its own soul. On one side are the majority of military personnel, professionals who, regardless of their faith or lack thereof, simply want to get their jobs done; on the other is a small but powerful movement of spiritual warriors concentrated within the officer corps.

There's Maj. Gen. Johnny A. Weida, who, as commander of Squadron Officer College, at Maxwell-Gunter Air Force Base, created an evangelical code for subordinates: whenever Weida said "air power," they were to respond, "Rock, sir!"—a reference to Matthew 7:25. Weida took the code with him when he was promoted to commandant at the United States Air Force Academy, where he turned its ostensibly ecumenical National Day of Prayer, an event derived from the Family's Prayer Breakfast, into an explicitly Christian consecration of the academy.

There's Lt. Gen. Robert L. Van Antwerp Jr., who lent his army uniform to the Christian cause, in direct violation of the Department of Defense regulations. He did it first for a Trinity Broadcasting Network tribute to Christian soldiers, *Red, White and Blue Spectacular.* The second time was at a Billy Graham rally, televised around the world on the Armed Forces Network, at which he declared the baptisms of seven hundred soldiers under his command proof of the Lord's plan to "raise up a godly army."

There's Maj. Gen. Robert Caslen, who, in 2007, was found by a Pentagon inspector general's report to have violated military ethics by appearing in uniform in the Christian Embassy's promotional video. Caslen was promoted to commandant of West Point. Cadets say he infused the academy with religiosity, preaching his faith at mandatory events and declaring the future officers "God's children." "I feel like I'm back in church in the front pews," Steve Warner, a top-ranked senior cadet, told me. "It's like Bible school."

For his work at the Air Force Academy, Weida received a second star; Van Antwerp is army chief of engineers. And Caslen is on a fast track: in 2008, the secretary of the army, Pete Geren, also featured in the Christian Embassy video, bumped Caslen up yet again, awarding his brother in Christ one of the army's ten division commands, that of the 25th Infantry, Tropic Lightning, at Hawaii's Schofield Barracks. In his last speech at the academy, Caslen advised the next generation of officers to "draw your strength in the days ahead from your faith in God." In 2010, he was promoted again, to the command of the Combined Arms Center, responsible for doctrine development for the army.

What such men have fomented is a quiet coup within the armed forces: not of generals encroaching on civilian rule but of religious authority displacing the military's once staunchly secular code. Not a conspiracy but a cultural transformation, achieved gradually through promotions and prayer meetings, with personal faith replacing protocol according to the genuinely best intentions of commanders who conflate God with country. They see themselves not as subversives but as spiritual warriors, "ambassadors for Christ in uniform," according to Officers' Christian Fellowship (OCF), which, with fifteen thousand members active at more than 80 percent of U.S. military bases, is the biggest fundamentalist group within the military. According to Campus Crusade's Military Ministry, the wealthiest of the civilian fundamentalist organizations that "target" young officers, these men are "government paid missionaries." Both groups have roots in the Family's early days, but the military movements lack the Family's subtlety—and its constraints. In the civilian world, the Family seeks invisibility; in the officer corps of the armed forces, secular men and women keep quiet about their beliefs. "It's a fucking clown show," says a three-star general on the wrong side of the divide. He's afraid to put his name to his words lest his secular views dead-end his career.

Taken as a whole, the military is actually slightly less religious than the general population: 20 percent of the roughly 1.4 million active-duty members checked off a box that says "no religious preference," compared to the 16.1 percent of Americans who describe themselves as "unaffiliated." These ambivalent soldiers should not be confused with the actively irreligious, though—only half of 1 percent of the military accept the label "atheist" or "agnostic," a number far lower than in the general population. (Jews are even scarcer, accounting for only one service member in three hundred; Muslims are just one in four hundred.) Around 22 percent, meanwhile, identify themselves as affiliated with evangelical or Pentecostal denominations. But that number is misleading, because it leaves out those among the traditional mainline denominations—about 7 percent of the military—who describe themselves as evangelical. Among the 19 percent of military members who are Roman Catholic, a small but vocal subset tends politically to affiliate with conservative evangelicals. And 20 percent of the military describe themselves simply as "Christian," a category that encompasses both those who give God little thought and the many evangelicals who reject denominational affiliation as divisive of the body of Christ. "I don't like 'religion,'" Army Major Freddy Welborn, who goes by the MySpace handle "Ephesians 6 Warrior," told me. "That's what put my savior on the cross. The Pharisees."

Within the fundamentalist elite of the officer corps, the best-organized group is Officers' Christian Fellowship. With six magazines for military personnel of all ranks, conferences, retreats, missionary trips, three "major military education centers," and countless small groups, OCF functions most effectively as a propaganda mill, grinding down religious difference in the name of a unity founded on the principle of us (the believers) versus them (everyone else). In a lecture titled "Fighting the War on Spiritual Terrorism," offered on OCF's website as a "resource," Lt. Col. Greg E. Metzgar, of the army, explains that good Christian soldiers must always consider themselves behind enemy lines, even within the ranks; every unsaved member of the military is a potential agent of "spiritual terrorism." The strategic question then becomes, says Metzgar, "How do we train our personnel to overcome unconventional spiritual warfare in a predominantly non-permissive environment?"

OCF's answer lies in the ideas it shares with C Street. A manual by retired colonel Dick Kail, OCF director of leader development, declares the group's interest in senior officers (lieutenant colonel or commander and above) as rooted in its mission to "claim and occupy territory for Jesus Christ within the military services." It's the *how* that most clearly echoes the ethos of C Street: Col. Kail encourages officers to follow the same "concentric circles" model of authority favored by the Family. At the heart of the first ring is God; the circle around him represents struggle for his authority over the armed forces. The next ring is family. Wives are advised to "adapt yourself to your husbands." And then there is the military itself. Like the Family, OCF teaches that promotion to power is not the result of merit but God's plan. Rank itself ultimately exists for the dissemination of His orders. But the road the Christian officer must walk is paralleled by a ditch on either side. To the left is "abuse of your authority." Don't worry about that one: "when you fall into the left ditch, at least people start talking about the proper relationship between the Christian faith and the military profession." The real risk is on the right, the ditch of passive Christianity. "Those who hold senior positions in the U.S. Armed Forces will never have a neutral effect on their comrades-in-arms," advises the guide. "Will your influence be godly, or will it be tainted by the values of this darkening world?"

OCF's world has been "darkening" since it was founded, in 1943, as Officers' Christian Union. But from its first days, the organization was as much about America's growing power in the world as it was about providing spiritual solace to officers. OCF's official history, *More Than Conquerors*, makes much of the ministry's predecessor organization in the fading British Empire, conceived of following World War I as a spiritual antidote to what officers feared would be the coming peace. Peace, that is, that would make men too soft to spread the gospel by force of arms. Founding general Hayes A. Kroner, a crisply alert Georgian with a black brush mustache, had married an aristocratic Englishwoman and adopted her manners while serving in China, and at early meetings of the group that would become OCF, he and several British advisers made certain that the tea was strong. Sipping alongside them were the C Streeters of the day, a group of congressmen organized by Abram Vereide: segregationist Democrats and the isolationist Republicans who'd been opposed to war with Germany. Kroner was an "ardent supporter" of Abram's movement, according to Family documents, responsible for establishing prayer cells at West Point and Annapolis. He also brought an ulterior motive to the cause. Toward the end of the war, not long before he joined the Family's board of directors, he told a committee investigating Pearl Harbor—he'd been head of Military Intelligence on December 7, 1941—that "religious societies" and missionaries were tools of the spymaster's trade.

His successor was Lt. Gen. William K. Harrison, nationally famous as "the Bible-reading general" who negotiated the truce that ended the Korean War. Near the end of his life he declared that he had read the New Testament 280 times, achieving what one admirer described as a "mind programmed with God's Word." The Word that mattered to Harrison was Matthew 24:6, "wars and rumors of war." Until the Second Coming, war is our natural state, preached the old soldier, to be accepted and even embraced in anticipation of Jesus Christ's imminent, and most likely violent, return. In the 1980s, OCF modernized Harrison's gospel of permanent war—the Family's so-called Worldwide Spiritual Offensive, made material—as a doctrine of "Christian realism" with which to justify nuclear escalation. The "don't ask, don't tell" debates of the 1990s sidelined OCF into a losing fight with homosexuality, but the attacks of 9/11 reinvigorated the organization, nearly doubling it in size and provoking its most militant turn yet.

According to a recent OCF executive director, retired air force lieutenant general Bruce L. Fister, the "global war on terror" is "a spiritual battle of the highest magnitude." As jihad has come to connote violence, so spiritual war has moved closer to actual conflict, "continually confronting an implacable, powerful foe who hates us and eagerly seeks to destroy us," declares "The Source of Combat Readiness," an OCF scripture study prepared on the eve of the Iraq War. But another OCF Bible study, "Mission Accomplished," warns that victory abroad does not mean the war is won at home. "If Satan cannot succeed with threats from the outside, he will seek to destroy from within," asserts the study, a reference to "fellow countrymen" in biblical times and today who practice "spiritual adultery," disloyalty to Christ. "Mission Accomplished" identifies as a particular problem in biblical times the Jews responsible for taxing their fellow Jews, a two-step meant to redeem fundamentalism's tradition of anti-Semitism by drawing distinctions between good Jews (overtaxed forebears of Christianity) and bad Jews (tax collectors). Sometimes even that dubious line is not clearly drawn, as in a sermon published in 2008 in the base paper of U.S. Navy Support Facility Diego Garcia, which promises forgiveness even for "tax collectors (aka the Jewish Mafia)."

"Mission Accomplished" takes as its text Nehemiah 1–6,

the story of the "wallbuilder" who reconstructed the fortifi-
cations around Jerusalem. An outsider might take the wall
metaphor as a sign of respect for separation of church and
state. But in contemporary fundamentalist thinking, the
story stands for just the opposite, a wall within which church
and state are one. "With the wall completed the people
could live an integrated life," the study argues. "God was to
be Lord of all or not Lord at all." So it is today, "Mission
Accomplished" continues; before OCF Christians can complete *their* wall, they must bring this "Lord of all" to the
entire military. "We will need to press ahead obediently,"
the study ends, "not allowing the opposition, all of which is
spearheaded by Satan, to keep us from the mission of
reclaiming territory for Christ in the military."

Every man and woman in the military swears an oath to
defend the Constitution. To most of them, evangelicals
included, that oath is as sacred as scripture. For the fundamentalist front, though, the Constitution is itself a blueprint
for a Christian nation. "The idea of separation of church and
state?" an Air Force Academy senior named Bruce Hrabak
told me when I visited. "Dude, there's this whole idea in
America that it's in the Constitution, but it's not."* Hrabak is
broad-shouldered and has a wide smile. There is high color
in his cheeks, and he has excitable blue eyes. The Constitution, he explained, was based on the Bible. "The idea is that
God sets up a system in creation and that a lot of it
revolves around a concept of a trinity." He rattled off the

---

* It's in the first words of the First Amendment.

patterns—God, Holy Ghost, Jesus; father, mother, child—
ticking them off on his fingers as though he were keeping a
beat: *one*-two-three. "Church, family, government. Executive
branch, legislative branch, judicial." Where was the air force in
these orders? He grinned. Didn't I know angels have wings?

If the fundamentalist front were to have a seminary, it
would be the U.S. Air Force Academy, a campus of steel and
white marble wedged into the right angle formed by the Great
Plains and the Rockies. In 2005, the academy became the subject of scandal due to a culture of Christian proselytization
that led the *Princeton Review* to rank it the fourteenth most
pious school in the nation, ahead of Pat Robertson's Regent
University. Professors preached from the front of the class,
coaches instructed Division 1 athletes to win one for Christ,
Major Warren "Chappie" Watties, the 2004 Air Force Chaplain of the Year, took up a bullhorn during basic training to
warn that those not "born again will burn in the fires of hell,"
and those who still refused the savior were condemned to a
"Heathen Flight"—that is, they were marched around camp
to ponder their sins. A 2004 study conducted by scholars from
the Yale Divinity School had concluded that the academy had
adopted a command climate of evangelicalism. The air force
responded by adding a course on religious diversity. Today,
the air force touts the academy as a model of tolerance. But
after the school brought in as speakers for a mandatory assembly three Christian evangelists who proclaimed that the only
solution to terrorism was to "kill Islam," I decided to see what
had changed. Not much, several Christian cadets told me.
"Now," Hrabak said, "we're underground." He winked.

"There's a spiritual world, and oftentimes what happens

in the physical world is representative of what's happening in the spiritual," a "firstie" (senior) named Jon Butcher told me one night at New Life, a nearby megachurch that sends buses for cadets. Butcher is wiry and laconic, a sandy-haired former ski bum from Toledo who went to the academy to be closer to the slopes. "For me, it was always like a little bit of God, a little bit of drinking, a little bit of girls," Butcher said of his past. He prayed for admission to the academy, though, pledging to God that he'd change his ways if he got in. As far as he was concerned, God delivered; so Butcher did, too, quitting alcohol and committing himself to chastity. "God," he said cryptically, "is the creator of fun."

But that only took him so far. He needed direction, and he found it in Romans 13: "There is no authority except from God, and those authorities that exist have been instituted by God." It was like a blessing on the academy's hierarchical system. He turned his body and spirit over to the guidance of Christian cadets, and God rewarded him with a set of specific instructions. "God told me to join the track team." God, he realized, wanted him to spread the Gospel in the athletic world. As he approached graduation, he received new orders. "God has told me to become an infantry officer," Butcher said, explaining his plan to transfer from the air force to the army upon graduation. A pilot has only his plane to talk to, but an infantry officer, explained Butcher, has men to mold and, if overseas, natives to lead to the Lord. "Everything is a form of ministry for me," Butcher said. "There is no separation. A Christian is someone who chooses to be a slave. I'm doing what God has called me to do, to know him and to make him known."

At the academy, Butcher made God known by leading an all-male prayer group. The night I attended, two dozen cadets spoke about sex and the Orient, the girlfriends whose unchaste touch they feared and the Christ-approved lies required for missionary work in China, where foreign evangelism is illegal. Sex—not having any, that is—was as central to the mission as saving souls. Or perhaps the men's abstinence should be understood as a form of self-evangelism, since they relied on one another to stay pure, which is to say, to avoid masturbation—"every man's battle," in the language of evangelicalism. Hrabak explained this outside the meeting: "Call me at two AM. I'll give you accountability. A guy will call me, two AM: 'Oh, man, I really blew it, got on my computer.' You're like, 'Okay.' First you just love 'em about it. 'Look, dude, we need to beat this.' For lack of a better term."

Butcher said I couldn't disclose the prayer group's name; there were some, he said, who wouldn't understand its goal of making the world's most elite war college its most holy one: a seminary with courses in carpet bombing. To him, religion and war were necessarily intertwined. "How," he asked, "in the midst of pulling a trigger and watching somebody die, in that instant are you going to be confident that that's something God told you to do?" His answer was stark. "In this world, there are forces of good and evil. There's angels and there's demons, you know? And Satan hates what's holy."

Following the 2005 religion scandal, Lt. Gen. John Rosa, the academy's superintendent, confessed to a meeting of the Anti-Defamation League that his "whole organization" had religion problems. "It keeps me awake at night," he said, predicting that restoring constitutional principles to the academy would take at least six years. Then he retired. To address the problems, the air force brought in Lt. Gen. John Regni. I spent a week at the academy, but Regni agreed to speak with me only by phone. I began our conversation with what I thought was a softball, an opportunity for the general to wax constitutional about First Amendment freedoms. "How do you see the balance between the Free Exercise Clause and the Establishment Clause?" I asked.

There was a long pause. Civilians might reasonably plead ignorance, but not a general who has sworn on his life to defend these words: "Congress shall make no law respecting the establishment of religion or prohibiting the free exercise thereof."

"I have to write those things down," Regni finally answered. "What did you say those constitutional things were again?"

"The Establishment Clause and the Free Exercise Clause."

"'Establishment'?" There was another pause. Then: "I'm deferring to some of my folks here." He consulted his top chaplain at the academy, an active-duty colonel, and his public relations man, a blustering old retired colonel named Johnny Whitaker, who'd welcomed me to the academy with a bizarre bit of demographics: "We reflect society," he'd told me as cadets streamed by for an assembly. "About 80 percent Protestant." (About 50 percent of America is Protestant.) There was also, he said, "a small Jewish population." He stopped as if considering what he was about to say, then decided to forge ahead, a big man leaning in close with a voice suddenly soft. "At least, who *claim* to be Jews."

At the other end of the phone line, Whitaker and the chaplain couldn't offer the general a lifeline. "Um," said Regni, "would you be a little more specific?"

I read the First Amendment to him. Regni pondered. "Uh, okay," he said. He decided to pass.

Not long after I spoke to Regni, a general named Mike Gould succeeded him as head of the academy. A former football player there, Gould granted himself the nickname "Coach" after a brief stint in that capacity early in his career. Coach Gould enjoys public speaking, and he's famous for his 3-F mantra: Faith, Family, Fitness. At the Pentagon, a former senior officer who served under Gould told me, the general was so impressed by a special presentation Pastor Rick Warren gave to senior officers that he e-mailed his 104 subordinates, advising them to read and live by Warren's book *The Purpose-Driven Life*.

"People thought it was weird," recalls the former officer, a defense contractor, who requested anonymity for fear of losing government business. "But no one wants to show their ass to the general."

Warren's bestseller sometimes displaces scripture itself among military evangelicals. In 2008, a chaplain at Laken-heath, a U.S. Air Force–operated base in England, used a mandatory assembly under Lt. Gen. Rod Bishop as an opportunity to promote the principles of *The Purpose-Driven Life* to roughly a thousand airmen. In a PowerPoint presentation titled "Developing Purpose-Driven Airmen," Chaplain Christian Biscotti, a graduate of Regent University, contrasts "3 Levels of Purpose."

On top is "God Given." Down the scale is "Man Given," an ideology of "philanthropy" represented by Karl Marx. At the bottom of the heap there's "Self Given" purpose, supposedly championed by Darwin, despite the fact that the biologist, a devout believer, taught a science of random mutation.

The "Big Idea," the presentation continues, can be seen by contrasting the United States with the USSR, an evil empire defunct since some of the airmen in the audience were a year old. The USSR, according to the presentation, was led by a triumvirate of Stalin, Lenin, and Darwin. (Zombie Darwin, that is, since the scientist died forty years before the advent of the Soviet Union.) Evolution, from the creationist point of view of the presentation, is nearly synonymous with communism. The former suggests that God's plan is under constant revision, while the latter proposes we take up the editor's red pencil ourselves, imagining ourselves little gods, "social engineers." But even Chaplain Biscotti can't resist drawing on a little social Darwinism to make his case that "FAITH is foremost." In a diagram depicting two family trees, Biscotti contrasts the likely futures of a nonreligious family, characterized by "Hopelessness" and "Death," and a religious one. The secular family will, according to the diagram, spawn 300 convicts, 190 prostitutes, and 680 alcoholics. Purpose-driven breeding, meanwhile, will result in at least 430 ministers, 7 congressmen, and a vice president. "The Palin prophecy," one skeptical airman dubbed the scheme, which, it turns out, was borrowed from a nineteenth-century eugenics chart used to support the idea of mandatory sterilization for criminals and the "feeble-minded."

Biscotti's "Big Idea," of course, was never simply the

election of someone like Sarah Palin. Were it so, American fundamentalism would be as dead as the McCain-Palin ticket was. But Christian fundamentalism, like all fundamentalisms, thrives on defeat. It is a narcissistic faith, concerned most of all with the wrongs suffered by the righteous and the purification of their ranks. "Under the rubric of free speech and the twisted idea of separation of church and state," reads a promotion for a book called *Under Orders: A Spiritual Handbook for Military Personnel,* by air force Lt. Col. William McCoy, "there has evolved more and more an anti-Christian bias in this country." McCoy seeks to counter that alleged bias by making the case for the necessity of religion—preferably Christian—for a properly functioning military unit. Lack of belief or the wrong beliefs, he writes, will "bring havoc to what needs cohesion and team confidence."

McCoy's manifesto comes with an impressive endorsement: "*Under Orders* should be in every rucksack for those moments when Soldiers need spiritual energy," reads a blurb from General David Petraeus, the top U.S. commander in Iraq until he moved to the top spot at U.S. Central Command, a position from which he ran U.S. operations from Egypt to Pakistan; he subsequently was named the top Afghanistan war commander. When the Military Religious Freedom Foundation demanded an investigation of Petraeus's endorsement—an apparent violation of the Uniform Code of Military Justice, not to mention the Bill of Rights— Petraeus claimed that his recommendation was supposed to be private, a communication from one Christian officer to another.

"He doesn't deny that he wrote it," says Michael "Mikey"

Weinstein, president of the Military Religious Freedom Foundation. "It's just, 'Oops, I didn't mean for the public to find out.' And what about our enemies? He's promoting this unconstitutional Christian exceptionalism at precisely the same time we're fighting Islamic fundamentalists who are telling *their* soldiers that America is waging a modern-day crusade. That *is* a crusade."

"If I was the bad guys, that's the stuff I'd use as my proof, as my evidence that this is a holy war," says an air force general who requested anonymity. "Don't these guys get it? Don't they understand the perception they're creating?"

The answer, in some cases, at least, is *yes*. Petraeus's most vigorous defense came from the recently retired three-star general William "Jerry" Boykin—a founding member of the army's Delta Force and an ordained minister—during an event held at Fort Bragg to promote his own book, *Never Surrender: A Soldier's Journey to the Crossroads of Faith and Freedom*. After 9/11, Boykin went on the Prayer Breakfast circuit to boast, in uniform, that his God was "bigger" than the Islamic divine of Somali warlord Osman Atto, whom Boykin had hunted. "I knew that my God was a real God and his was an idol," he declared, displaying as proof photographs of black clouds over Mogadishu, the "demonic spirit" he said U.S. troops had been fighting: "a guy called Satan." Boykin came under congressional fire for such comments, but that didn't stop Bush from promoting him to deputy undersecretary of defense, in which capacity he sent General Geoffrey Miller, commander of the U.S. military prison at Guantánamo Bay, to "Gitmo-ize" the U.S. military prison at Abu Ghraib, in Iraq.

When I put the First Amendment question I had posed to General Regni to Boykin, he told my researcher that the real issue is "that there is less and less acceptance of the Christian faith on which our nation was founded." Exhibit A, he believes, is the Military Religious Freedom Foundation (MRFF). "Here comes a guy named Mikey Weinstein trashing Petraeus," he told a crowd of 150 at Fort Bragg's Airborne & Special Operations Museum, "because he endorsed a book that's just trying to help soldiers. And this makes clear what [Weinstein's] real agenda is, which is not to help this country win a war on terror."

"It's satanic," called out a member of the audience.

"Yes," agreed Boykin. "It's demonic."

Mikey—nobody, not even his many enemies, calls him Weinstein—likes fighting. Fifty-five years old, he's built like a pit bull: short legs, big shoulders, an oversized bald head like a cannonball, and a crinkled brow between dark, darting eyes. In 1973, as a "doolie"—a freshman at the Air Force Academy—he punched an officer who accused him of fabricating anti-Semitic threats he'd received. In 2005, after the then head of the National Association of Evangelicals, Ted Haggard, declared that people like Mikey made it hard for him to defend Jewish causes, Mikey challenged the pastor to a public boxing match, with proceeds to go to charity. (Haggard didn't take him up on it.) He relishes a rumor that he's come to be known by some at the Pentagon as the Joker, after Heath Ledger's nihilistic embodiment of Batman's nemesis. But he draws a distinction: "Don't confuse my description of chaos with advocacy of chaos."

Mikey did ten years' active duty as a JAG (a member of the Judge Advocate General's Corps) before becoming assistant general counsel in the Reagan White House. He helped defend the administration during the Iran-Contra scandal, then became general counsel for the billionaire Ross Perot. Mikey made his money with a company that tracked down deadbeat dads. Now he has become the constitutional conscience of the military, an unsubtle man determined to force its fundamentalist front to account for itself through legal assaults and media strafing. He embarked upon his crusade — a loaded term, but more accurate than any other — in 2005, with plans for a speedy victory. But his war has consumed him. He works an endless succession of eighteen-hour days, both on the road and at the foundation's headquarters: his sprawling adobe ranch house, now guarded by two oversize German shepherds, Ginger Honey Bear and Crystal Baby Blue Bear, and a five foot six former marine bomb tech called Shorty. MRFF draws on a network of lawyers, publicists, and fund-raisers, but it is at heart mainly Mikey and researcher-director Chris Rodda, author of *Liars for Jesus*, which, at 532 pages, is only the first entry in a multivolume debunking of Christian Right historical claims; the series is unfinished and potentially infinite.

Mikey's work has a similarly quixotic quality. He has won some victories, such as when he forced the Department of Defense to investigate the Christian Embassy video, or intimidated the Air Force Academy into adopting classes in religious diversity, or harassed any number of base commanders into reining in subordinates who view their authority as a license to proselytize. But every time he wins a battle or takes to the television to plead his cause, more troops learn about his foundation and seek its help. "We needed this fuse lit by Mikey to get everybody going," says Lt. Gen. Bill Lord, one of the few flag officers to acknowledge the problem. Mikey keeps his cell phone on vibrate while he's exercising on his elliptical machine; he likes to say that he'll interrupt sex to take a call from any one of the 11,400 active-duty military members he describes as the foundation's clients. For perspective, I called the Pentagon to ask how many religion-related incidents they typically deal with in a year. One spokeswoman said three. Another said there had been fifty total during a period of several years.

I interviewed more of Mikey's clients than that myself: soldiers, sailors, marines, and airmen who spoke of being forced to pray to Jesus in Iraq and at home, of combat deaths made occasions for evangelical sermons by senior officers, of Christian apocalypse video games and seminars in the "biblical" stewardship of their finances. They spoke, too, of lectures for marine recruits on creationism, and briefings for air force officers on the correlation of the global war on terror, or GWOT, to the Book of Revelation; of exorcisms designed to drive out "unclean spirits" from military bases; and of beatings of Wiccan troops winked at by the chain of command.

The most absurd case I came across was that of an atheist military policeman, Jeremy Hall, who was sent home from Iraq after the army concluded that it couldn't protect him from fundamentalist extremists — that is, his fellow soldiers who threatened to kill him lest he bring God's wrath on them all.

The saddest was that of a Muslim soldier, Eli Agee, who ignored a constant drumbeat of insults—"hajji," "terrorist"—until his eight-month-old son died and his command refused to allow the infant an Islamic burial.

But the most awful was that of a deeply disturbed young man named David Winters, who was allowed to enlist despite a history of institutionalization because the Marine Corps needed bodies. He snapped after intense anti-Semitic hazing. He'd ignored it for a while, but the spit got to him. People were always spitting on him. Spit and blood, he told me, that was what bothered him.

"Hell, yeah, the kid was *bashed,*" a Marine from Winters's platoon, 3101, Third Battalion, told me when I asked if Winters's story was true. By whom? "Everybody! All his peers and shit." Because he was Jewish? "Hell, yeah." And the marine with the swastika tattoo Winters said tortured him in the bathroom? "I had to hold that dude back once." And the noncommissioned officers (NCOs)? "All the people." How bad? "Well, it was the physical aspect that really pushed him there." Over the edge? "Definitely."

Winters was a skinny Marine, thin in the chest. The episode he remembered most was this: a drill instructor squaring his boot on the back of his head while he was doing push-ups—and smashing his face into the concrete. Winters lay there, blood in his eyes, his elbows wedged above him like chicken wings, waiting for laughter. This time there wasn't any. "Sir," he heard someone close by saying, "this recruit's bleeding." "I don't give a fuck!" snapped the drill instructor. "Keep pushing up!" Winters pushed up, his face split open and dripping and his mind cracking.

I reached him by phone at a psychiatric hospital. "I have a scar from the push-ups," he said. His voice was shy, puzzled, apologetic. "On my chin." He wanted to talk about Yom Kippur. He's observant; he reads Hebrew and he spells God "G——d," in the traditional style. On Yom Kippur, he claims—there are no witnesses—an NCO tasked with escorting him across base to services turned to him as they walked past some woods and said, "You Jewish motherfucker. I should leave you bloody, bleeding in the woods."

"At the end of boot camp, or towards the end," Winters wrote in a letter from the psychiatric hospital, "I was confused. A recruit gave me a New Testament to read and said, 'You see how bad the Jews are?'" Winters studied; he did see. *You belong to your father, the devil,* Winters read, words attributed to Jesus in the Gospel According to John. "I became pretty good friends with some other recruits," he wrote, "but this guy would tell me I am going to hell and my family, all Jews too." But there was a way he could save himself, if not his family. "I started saying I was going to convert." At home on break, he found a little fundamentalist church to pray in. He brought his family presents, a *Semper Fi* blanket for his grandmother, a marine sweatshirt for his father, Andrew. Andrew Winters, a successful architect who'd long worried about his hapless boy, was terribly proud, boasting to neighbors about his son the Jewish marine. He was wearing the sweatshirt on Christmas Day when his son proposed that they take a walk in the woods to talk about what he'd learned in the Marine Corps. He didn't tell Andrew Winters that he had a new father, Jesus, and that he had received orders, which he believed came from his drill instructor, transmitted via television waves. *Take him into the woods,* the voice in his head told him. *Leave him there.*

"They say I killed my father," he later wrote from the hospital, a maximum-security institution. "All I know is I never wanted to do anything wrong."

As night fell across the bare trees on Christmas Day 2007, Winters stabbed and hacked his father sixty-five times. He left the Jew's body there, bloody, bleeding.

What is the meaning of Winters's case? Winters hadn't converted, he'd gone crazy. His drill instructor didn't make him do it, and neither did the devil; Winters was the agent of his own tragedy. Mikey took his case not because there was any possibility he was innocent, but because his public defenders had ignored the hazing and the marines had claimed he'd been guided by Islam. Winters wanted help not because he didn't think he was guilty but because he was afraid he'd be transferred to prison. He makes a persuasive case that he belongs in an insane asylum. His story is not representative; it's not a case for reform, for new regulations. It's not data, a point on a graph charting a problem. It's a rank, blistering tumor. A veiny knot of blood and spit wrapped in pages torn from scripture. The nightmare within the fundamentalist dream: the barrel of the Jesus tank of Samarra bent and twisted round to point inward, ready, aim, fire. The fundamentalist threat to democracy isn't ultimately a problem of laws, or of amendments and clauses. It's the psychosis of self-eradication: the mythic belief that whether through the Great Commission or GWOT or a knife in the woods we can become pure, the body of Christ, singular: the roaring hallucination of one nation under one God.

Most of Mikey's clients are Christians themselves, coerced into Bible study to win promotion, bused to fundamentalist churches on the military's dime, told by commanders that women weren't made by God to be warriors, or that Mormons aren't really Christians, that Catholics aren't really Christians, that *Methodists* aren't really Christians. Mikey pulls strings, bullies their commanders, tells them they're heroes, hires lawyers for them when necessary. But as Mikey's client base grows, so do the ranks of his enemies. The picture window in his living room has been shot out twice, and last summer he woke to find a swastika and a cross scrawled on his door. Since he launched MRFF in 2005, he has accumulated an impressive collection of hate mail, grotesque amplifications of the polite disdain expressed publicly by senior officers. Some of it is earnest: "You are costing lives by dividing military personnel and undermining troops," reads one missive. "Their blood is on your hands." Much of it is juvenile: "you little bald-headed fag," read an e-mail Mikey received after an appearance on CNN, "what the fuck are you doing with an organization of this title when the purpose of your group is not to encourage religious freedom, but to DENY religious freedom? What a fuck-head cock sucker you turned out to be." Quite a bit of it is anti-Semitic. When Mikey made public a solicitation by air force general Jack Catton for campaign donations to put "more Christian men" in Congress, someone wrote: "Once again, the Oy Vey! crowd whines. This jew used to be an Air Force lawyer and got the email…just one more example of why filthy, hook-nosed jews should be purged from our society." The worst are those directed at his wife, Bonnie. He recites one over lunch as Bonnie grimaces, a phone call he received in 2007. Bonnie had driven ahead to a football game at the academy; the caller described her car, and then told Mikey: " 'We're gonna stick a shotgun up her Jewish whore's cunt and blow her clit through the top of your head.' "

The abuse has become a regular part of Mikey's routine in public appearances. There's a sense in which he likes it—not the threats, but the proof. "We've had dead animals on the porch, beer bottles, feces thrown at the house. I don't even think about it. I view it as if I was Barry Bonds about to go to bat in Dodger Stadium and people are boo-ing. You want a piece of me? Get in line, buddy, pack a lunch." Mikey thinks in terms of enemies, and he likes to know he's rattling his. "The level of antagonism toward Mikey is off the charts," a senior air force officer at the academy, who keeps his support for Mikey under wraps, told me. "Off. The. Fucking. Charts."

After Mikey called out the Air Force Academy's General Weida for his promotion of Mel Gibson's *Passion*—Weida himself performed in *The Thorn,* a megaspectacle passion play produced by New Life Church—Weida recruited the academy's rabbi to help him write two letters to Mikey in Hebrew, which Mikey doesn't read. Mikey wasn't impressed, not least because Weida had encouraged Mikey's son Casey's evangelical girlfriend (both were cadets) to bring him to Weida's passion play. Mikey's enemies rejoiced. "Weinstein is steamed because his own son went to Ted Haggard's church, became a Christian and fell in love with a Christian girl," wrote a retired air force lieutenant colonel, Hugh Morgan, in an e-mail to the executive director of the International Conference of Evangelical Chaplain Endorsers, Billy Baugham. It wasn't true—Mikey's son did fall in love with and marry a young Christian woman, but he's still Jewish, and now Mikey proudly calls that Christian woman his daughter—but Baugham passed the story along to more chaplain endorsers, followed by a later note declaring Mikey "a very angry Jewish man."

He got that part right. Mikey loathes Christian Zionism, the evangelical movement that celebrates Jews for the role they're expected to play in the Rapture. "They love us to the same extent that the Pilgrims loved the turkeys before the first Thanksgiving," Mikey says. "It's very much like, 'Places everyone!' They want all the Jews happily back in Israel and that's ground zero, stay within a circle because this will serve as an accelerant and a lubricant to bring Jesus back. And then he'll fucking kick massive ass! You'll get your chance to accept him—I mean, surrender—or be lit up like a Roman candle on the Fourth of July forever, in the lake of fire along with Einstein, Anne Frank, and Adam Sandler."

Central to Mikey's understanding of himself and his mission are two beatings he received as an eighteen-year-old doolie at the academy, apparent retaliations for notifying his superiors about a series of anti-Semitic notes he'd received. Nobody was held accountable. Mikey graduated with honors and thought he'd put it behind him; but his anger reignited in 2004, when the younger of his two sons,

Curtis, then a doolie himself, told Mikey he planned to beat the shit out of the next cadet—or officer—who called him a "fucking Jew." In 2005, when he created the Military Religious Freedom Foundation, he ornamented its board with a galaxy of brass, the dozen stars and eagles on the shoulders of each of the retired generals, admirals, and colonels he recruited meant to make clear that the foundation's enemy is not the military, and he collects and trumpets endorsements from churches to make clear that the foundation's enemy is not religion. But the head of the largest Pentecostal chaplain-endorsing agency sums Mikey up in two words, e-mailed to an active-duty army chaplain: "lawyer, Jewish." Mikey obtained a copy of the e-mail via discovery in a lawsuit MRFF has filed. The author of the e-mail says that Mikey is out to get "any and all Government entities that does anything Christian [*sic*]." In fact, Mikey defends chaplains, many of whom are his allies; his enemy, he says, is "weaponized Christianity. This country is facing a pervasive and pernicious pattern and practice of unconstitutional rape of the religious rights of our armed forces members." He calls this "soul rape."

It's a strong term that at first sounds like typical over-the-top Mikey, but it's at the root of America's First Amendment freedoms, dating from the seventeenth century and Roger Williams, the founder of Rhode Island. Williams was a devout Christian. But based on his encounters with Native American leaders, whom he deemed honest men, and his dealings with the leaders of the Massachusetts colony, who sent him into exile, he concluded that outward religion—the piety of the Puritans—was no guarantee of inner virtue.

"I feel safer down here among the Christian savages along Narragansett Bay than I do among the savage Christians of Massachusetts Bay Colony," he wrote. He knew the Native Americans he admired were not Christians in any doctrinal sense, but they taught him a nuanced concept of tolerance that would become the bedrock of American religious freedom—and, what's more, liberty of conscience. What is the distinction? Religion is a set of beliefs, ideas, rituals, or customs. Conscience is more fundamental: the faculty of searching for the beliefs, ideas, rituals, or customs that make up religion or, for that matter, the rejection of religion. What mattered most, Williams thought, was the ability to seek the good. So if the state restricted that search (through mandatory prayer, for instance, or discrimination against minority faiths), it violated the most basic freedom, that of individual conscience. Without the freedom to choose one's own beliefs, Williams concluded, no other freedom is really possible.

"In the military," Mikey told me one night in Albuquerque, "rights that we as civilians enjoy are severely abridged in order to serve a higher goal: provide good order and discipline in order to protect the whole panoply of constitutional rights for the rest of us." One of those rights is free speech. A soldier in uniform can't endorse a political candidate, advertise a product, or proselytize. That rule is for the good of the public—people don't want men with guns telling them which way to cast their vote—and for the military itself. An officer can tell a soldier what to do, but not what to believe. Conscience is its own order.

*   *   *

The evangelical transformation of the military began during the cold war, in a new American Great Awakening that has only accelerated across the decades, making the United States one of the most religious nations in the world. We are also among the most religiously diverse, but as the number of Muslims, Buddhists, Hindus, Sikhs, and adherents of hundreds of other traditions has grown, American evangelicalism has become more entrenched, tightening its hold on the institutions that conservative evangelicals consider most American — that is, Christian.

"It was Vietnam which really turned the tide," writes Anne C. Loveland, author of the only book-length study of the evangelical wave within the armed forces, *American Evangelicals and the U.S. Military, 1942–1993.* Until the Vietnam War, it was the traditionally moderate mainline Protestant denominations (Methodists, Presbyterians, Episcopalians), together with the Catholic Church, that dominated the religious life of the military. But as leading clergymen in these denominations spoke out against the war, evangelicals who saw the struggle in Vietnam as God's task rushed in. In 1966, Billy Graham used the pulpit of the Presidential Prayer Breakfast to preach a warrior Christ to lead the troops in Vietnam: "I am come to send fire on the earth!" he quoted Christ. "Think not that I am come to send peace but a sword!" Other fundamentalists took from Vietnam the lessons of guerrilla combat, to be applied to the spiritual fight through the tactic of what they called *infiltration,* filling the ranks of secular institutions with missionaries both bold and subtle. That same year, one Family organizer advised inverting the strategy of the Vietcong, who through one targeted assassination could immobilize thousands. Winning the soul "key men" in the military could mobilize many more for spiritual war.

"Evangelicals looked at the military and said, 'This is a mission field,'" explains Captain MeLinda Morton, a former missile launch commander who until 2005 was a staff chaplain at the Air Force Academy and has since studied the history of the chaplaincy. "They wanted to send their missionaries to the military, and for the military itself to become missionaries to the world."

The next turning point occurred during the Reagan administration, when regulatory revisions helped create the fundamentalist front in today's military. A longstanding rule had apportioned chaplains according to the religious demographics of the military as a whole; that is, if the census showed that 10 percent of personnel were Presbyterian, then 10 percent of the chaplains would be Presbyterian. However, all chaplains were required to be trained to minister to troops of any faith. In the mid-1980s the Pentagon began accrediting hundreds of new evangelical and Pentecostal "endorsing agencies," allowing graduates of fundamentalist Bible colleges trained to see those from other faiths as enemies of Christ to fill up nearly the entire allotment for Protestant chaplains. As a result, more than two-thirds of the military's 2,900 active-duty chaplains today are affiliated with evangelical or Pentecostal denominations. Morton thinks even that figure is an underrepresentation:

"In my experience," she says, "80 percent of the chaplaincy self-identifies as conservative and/or evangelical."

The most zealous among the new generation of fundamentalist chaplains didn't join to serve the military; they came to save its soul. To that end, they cultivated an ethos now echoed by personnel up and down the chain of command: faith first, family second, country third. Captain Morton began to see that hierarchy realized after 2001, as a new generation of midcareer officers who'd come up under the evangelicalized chaplaincy returned to the Air Force Academy to become air operations commanders (AOCs), in charge of cadet squadrons. They, in turn, began promoting God's will in the academy not as chaplains but as ostensibly secular officers. Captain Morton realized what was happening when female cadets began telling her they were giving up their coveted pilot slots to pursue "God's purpose." "These women were being counseled by their AOCs that what God really wanted them to do was to bear children and be someone's wife."

Morton was alarmed not just as a chaplain and as a woman but as an officer—fundamentalist AOCs were deliberately sabotaging a competitive system designed to produce the best pilots. The results will ripple outward for years, as women who passed up their wings are passed over for promotion, creating an officer corps shaped by religious orthodoxy at the expense of ability. Morton contributed her concerns to the 2004 Yale Report and submitted it to the head of chaplains at the academy, Colonel Michael Whittington, for whom she served as executive officer. He shelved it until Mikey made it public in 2005. In response to media reports, Morton's superior asked her to declare the report a mistake. "I refused," she says. "That pretty much sealed my fate." Maj. Gen. Charles Baldwin, air force chief of chaplains, announced an inquiry into the report's conclusions, but that didn't give Morton confidence. An adviser to the Joint Chiefs of Staff on ethical issues, Baldwin had instructed chaplains at the academy not to screen a clip from *Schindler's List* in a religious diversity program because he thought "it made Christians look like Nazis." He was even less pleased with the Yale Report. Morton realized her military career was over when Baldwin told a meeting of the academy's chaplains that they "were one big family that could tolerate no disloyalty in our ranks." The next day, "I was fired as Chaplain Whittington's executive officer ... [and] he refused to give me a new assignment." She went public. The air force tried to transfer her to Okinawa, but Mikey demanded an investigation, and eventually a deal was struck: the only chaplain to speak up for religious freedom was made a civilian.

In 2008, a filmmaker named Brian Hughes traveled to Bagram Air Base to make a documentary about chaplains, a tribute, of sorts, to the chaplain who had counseled him without regard for religion when Hughes was a frightened young airman during the Gulf War. Military personnel sacrifice their rights to legal and medical privacy; chaplains are the only people they can turn to with problems too sensitive to take up the chain of command, anything from corruption to a crisis of courage. When Hughes went to Bagram, he was looking for chaplains like the one who'd helped him get through his war. Instead, he found Lt. Col. Gary Hensley, division chaplain for the 101st Airborne and the chief army chaplain for Afghanistan.

In the raw footage Hughes shot, Hensley strips down to a white T-shirt under his uniform to preach an afternoon service in Bagram's main chapel. The shirt's logo is for an evangelical military ministry called Chapel Next; the "t" in "Next" is an oversized cross slashing down over a map of Afghanistan. "Got your seat belts on?" Hensley hollers. He's a lean man with thinning, slicked-back gray hair, and he carries a small paunch like a package. He seems to wrap himself around his belly as he paces the stage, his neck lunging forward and his right hand tapping the arm of his glasses to emphasize sight: he wants his soldiers to know he *sees.* He seems to want the filmmaker, Hughes, to know this, too; he pauses to stare directly into the camera. That's no accident. When he learned there would be media in the room, Hensley bumped another chaplain who was scheduled to preach. He wants to be seen. "The Word will not fail!" he shouts. "Now is the time! In the fullness of time" — Hensley leans forward, two fingers on his glasses, his voice dipping to a growl — "God. Sent. His. Son. *Whoo!*" Then, as if addressing thirty-three million Afghans and their belief that Muhammad was a prophet in the tradition of Jesus, he shouts, "There is no one else to come! There is no new revelation! There is no new religion! Jesus is it!" *Amen,* says the crowd of soldiers, many of them also now stripped down to their Chapel Next T-shirts. "If he ain't it, let's all go home!"

Hensley brings it down. "I'm from the Jesus movement,"

he says, presenting himself as a prophet born of American history: "Haight-Ashbury. Watergate. Woodstock. And out of that mess? Came Hensley, glory to God!"

Hensley has come, it seems, to plagiarize: "By virtue of the resurrection, Jesus was exalted to the right hand of the Father and is the messianic head of the New Israel." It's a direct quote, unattributed, from the British theologian C. H. Dodd. Dodd contributed to a complicated notion, developed in the 1930s, called "realized eschatology"—in essence, the idea that history and end-times revelations can be reconciled. His ideas are used by some liberal Christians to combat the apocalyptic fervor of fundamentalism, but Hensley takes the stolen text as a battle cry. "That's us!" he cries. "We are Israel. We are the new Israel!"

At this point, says Hughes, the army media liaison sitting next to him in the pews, responsible for making the army look like "democracy consultants," not an occupying force of crusaders, puts his head in his hands.

"There will come a day when there will be no more Holy Spirit!" Hensley shouts, hopping up and down on the stage, his speech no longer directed toward the pews but as if to some greater audience. "When the church shall be raptured up in the sky!" He draws the word out: "skyyyyy!" "And we shall be with hiiim! And all of us shall be with him!" He slows to an emphatic whisper, like a warning: "Glory to God, *that's* our message!" A little bit louder now. "The messianic Jesus is comin' back!" Louder. "And I expect him to come back before we go to the mess hall, you know that?" Which means, he says, that they have to get busy fast if they're going to save Afghanistan. "Special Forces guys," he muses, "they hunt men, basically. We do the same thing as Christians, we hunt people for Jesus. Hunt 'em down."

And the soldiers, many more of them now stripped down to their cross-over-Afghanistan T-shirts, say *Amen.*

For Lt. Col. Bob Young, the front lines were in the combat hospital that was part of his command at Kandahar Air Base. "It averaged we'd get two and a half Americans a day," he told me, the awful accuracy of that number lost on him. He cared about his troops, but they were not the ones he thought about most now. It was the Afghans, shot, blown up, and simply diseased, who haunted him. His recollections of their maimed bodies boiled in his head, forcing him to talk for hours at a time about what he'd seen. As he did, he dipped close to what a secular soul might call despair and then shot up into determined, ecstatic, desperate declarations of faith in the God he believed had sent him to Afghanistan, the God who would shortly send him to Kuwait for a second time.

I'd found him after the Military Religious Freedom Foundation reported on *Travel the Road,* an evangelical reality show featuring a pair of self-described "extreme missionaries" who embedded themselves within Young's command, intent on saving not just American but Afghan souls. Young liked that! He told them about his plan to pray for rain for Afghanistan. One of Young's captains saw the MRFF report and wrote to the foundation with a list of complaints about his commanding officer, complaints he and his fellow junior officers had registered with Young's superiors. I spoke to the captain. He told me, "Call Young. He'll tell you everything." I reached the colonel at home in Georgia late one evening. He said he was going to sit on his porch and look at the moon. In the background, I heard dogs barking. He talked for three hours.

"Another twenty, twenty-five of them, more than that," he said of the wounded in Kandahar, above and beyond his two and a half men, "would be Afghans." His southern voice snapped, as though he were bouncing on his toes. "Kids getting burned. Bad guys floating in on helicopters. You wouldn't know who they were." The base hospital treated seven thousand Afghans that year. Young, commander of the army's 325th Forward Support Battalion, lingered there, watching the bodies. "I want to tell you this. Triage area, guy strapped into gurney, Afghan guy. No shirt, skinny as a rail, sinewy muscle. Restraints on his ankles, his feet, dude is strapped into a wheelchair. I said, 'What's wrong with this dude?' 'Oh, man, he's crazy.' He's got a plastic shield in front of his face because he's spitting. 'Sir, he's crazy, we got the psychiatrist coming.' Psychiatrist walks in. He has this big syringe. I say, 'What's wrong with him, Doc?' He says, 'I don't know.' I say, 'I'll tell you what's wrong with him. The guy's possessed.'"

Young stared at the syringe. "'That ain't going to solve the problem,' I tell him. But the doc hits him with the syringe. Couple minutes later the general's son-in-law—the Afghan general's son-in-law, our translator—comes in. I said, 'What's wrong with this guy?' He says, 'How do you say in English? He has spirits.' I say, 'Doc, there's your second opinion!'"

On the phone, Young laughed, a harsh sound: "Ha!" Then his voice collapsed. "I'm telling you, it's real. Evil is real."

Young prayed over the possessed Afghan. "I always pray over them." But the doctors took him away and Young never did find out what happened. "Can't say I saw the demons shriek out of his body." He believed his prayers mattered, and he tried not to be bothered when God didn't show him the results. Mostly, he prayed over children. Burned, crushed, limbs amputated; their bearded fathers brought them in and stood like stones on one side of the bed, and Col. Young would take up a position across from them — he has five children of his own — and stand watch, praying in his mind, his hands rising above. "People were so appreciative," he assured me.

In the reality show, one of the missionaries, a skinny Christian hippie with a strawberry blond beard, interviews Young after a service at the base chapel. ("Wooden chapel, built by the 82nd Airborne," Young told me. "Amazing! A Christian church in Kandahar, right at the heart of where the Taliban started.") "Interestingly," Young says to the camera, "the drought has been in effect here since the Taliban took over." Young has a high mouth and a low brow overhanging dark brown eyes set between ears shaped like musical clefs; the effect is that of a satellite dish, beaming and receiving. "No weapon formed against us shall prosper," he says, recasting one of God's promises to the Israelites (Isaiah 54:17) in the first-person plural of the U.S. Army. "I would ask," he continues, shaking his Bible, "people of America, pray that God sends the rain to Kandahar, and they'll know that our God answers prayers."

I asked Young if he wanted to contextualize remarks that seemed, on their surface, to radically transcend his mission as a soldier. He did. His battalion, 450 strong, was responsible for logistics support for combat operations throughout southern Afghanistan. In practice, that meant working with warlords, two in particular, to whom he said he paid a million dollars a month each to transport army supplies. "My staff and me sit down with these guys. I ask, 'What can we do to get this country going?' I'm thinking, sweatshops. Get 'em working. 'No,' they say, 'we're agricultural people. What we really need is rain.' So I say, 'Back in America, our Native Americans used to do a rain dance.' I even did the little woo-woo-woo, you know? 'But,' I say, 'I am not going to do the rain dance. But I will ask my friends back home to pray to the God who made the heavens and the earth for rain.'" Young activated a prayer network that stretched from Hawaii to Georgia to Afghanistan, pastors and chaplains and evangelical congregations around the world. "Okay!" he said to me, preparing to disclose the results, which this one time God had let him witness. "Are you ready?"

I said I was. He told me to Google "Kandahar, rain, January 2005." The result he was looking for was an article in *Stars and Stripes*, "Rainfall May Signal Beginning of the End to Three-Year Drought in Afghanistan"—3¼ inches in just two days.

"That's some real rain," I admitted.

"That's what I'm saying, brother!" He told me to read the article aloud.

"'Afghans say "this is a sign from God," said Khoshhal Murad,'" I read.

"Y'see!" Young shouted.

" 'When the Taliban were in power,' " I continued, " 'some of its leaders grew so frustrated by the drought they randomly rounded up dozens of people, drove them into the desert and demanded they pray for rain. It didn't come.

" 'You can't force people to pray,' Murad said. 'They should have gone out in the desert themselves.' "

I was confused. What, I wondered, was the difference between the Taliban's God and Young's? Simple — theirs isn't real. "Allah is a moon god, is my understanding." Beyond that, though, he said, they weren't as far apart as you'd think. He thought America could use a lot more piety, Taliban-style. "I'll put it like this. I think there is more hope for a revival in Afghanistan than there is in L.A. They're not hostile to God."

What they lack, he said, was Jesus. "What you got is people like the Jews and the Muslims, who, according to the Bible, can't know God, fighting about God. If they knew the *humanity* of God they would—" He decided he needed a real-world example. "I made an observation, I think profound. The Christian soldier is willing to lay down his life for a Muslim, but a Muslim wants to give up his life to kill an American."

I asked him about another one of the captain's allegations, that Young had made some remarks that had led him to be relieved of command. It was true that he had been relieved of command, he admitted, but he had appealed on the grounds that his commanding officers had problems of their own — adultery and drinking, he explained — and he had won; his record today is as clean as Christ's robes. And the remarks? "All that was, I was speaking in reference to inner-city problems and whatnot. I said that the irony is that it would be better for a black to be a slave in America—I'm thinking now historically—and know Christ than to be free, now, and not know Christ."

With that cleared up, I asked him about the last of the captain's allegations, that he had given a presentation on Christianity to some Afghan warlords. Absolutely not, he said. It was a PowerPoint presentation about America. He e-mailed it to me as we spoke, and then he asked me to open it so he could share with me the same presentation he had given "Gulalli" and "Shirzai," as well as their aides and his staff. Without the sound track, that is. He had brought in the chapel band to strum some contemporary Christian music, though he had warned them not to sing explicitly about Jesus. "You know, just stuff like, 'My God Is an Awesome God.'"

Since it had been Presidents' Day, he had begun with a picture of George Washington. Washington, he explained, had been protected by God; evidence was an incident during which thirty-two bullet holes were found in Washington's cloak following a battle in the French and Indian War, though Washington himself was unscathed. The presentation continued: pictures of buffalo and the story of Jamestown, the Pilgrims. His goal, he explained, was to show the Afghans that nation building is a long and difficult journey. He included the text of the Mayflower Compact—"Having undertaken, for the glory of God, and advancement of the Christian faith"—and the story of the Boston Tea Party; a picture of Washington in prayer and the text of the Emanci-

pation Proclamation, which, he noted, ends with an invocation of Almighty God. "I did stress the fact that in America
we believe our rights come from God, not from government. Truth is truth, and there's no benefit in lying about
it." There were slides about the Wright brothers, the moon
landing, and NASCAR—Jeff Gordon, "a Christian, by the
way," had just won the Daytona 500. And then, the culmination of American history: the Twin Towers, blooming orange
the morning of September 11, 2001. Embedded in the
slideshow was a video Young titled "Forgiveness," a collage
of stills of people running, bodies falling, a Photoshopped
image of the Statue of Liberty holding her head in her
hand. Swelling behind the images was Céline Dion's Irish-
inflected ballad from *Titanic*, "My Heart Will Go On." Following the video was a slide of the Bush family, beneath the
words: "I believe that God has inspired in every heart the
desire for freedom."

At the heart of Young's religion is suffering: his own. Before
his battalion deployed for Afghanistan in 2004, he tried to
armor them with prayer. He invited several local churches
onto the base at Schofield Barracks, along with the highest-
ranking officer he could get—Lt. Gen. Van Antwerp Jr.,
who was then president of Officers' Christian Fellowship—
and his battalion. About five hundred people came, and
before them all Col. Young offered his testimony. He told
his troops that he'd been raised a Catholic, and hadn't
much cared; how he'd joined the army as a high school
dropout under President Carter and had quit when the
Democrat gutted military spending; how he'd gone to

college and had come back to the army an officer; how he'd made ranger; how he married a blue-eyed blonde and fathered two children and left them all in the care of his best friend from his enlisted days when he deployed to Korea.

The details, he allowed, were not important; biography is prelude to crisis, a life story simply a vehicle for a testimony, the heart of evangelical religion. "There are two kinds of phone calls you might get," he told his soldiers. "The first kind, you find out your wife is leaving you." It was 1993, and she'd taken his one-year-old son and his two-year-old daughter with her, and when he'd called his best friend to ask what had happened, the friend said Young's wife and kids were at the beach, and that he had to go, too; they were with him now. Young tried to think like an officer. "Military course of action development," he lectured himself. "Course of action one: kill him. Two: kill them both. Three: kill myself." Somebody, he decided, had to die. In the end, somebody did: Young, to the flesh. Raised nominally Catholic, he had never read scripture. Now, every page seemed to speak to him. I can't go on, Young thought. He opened his Bible and found Matthew 6:34. *Do not worry about tomorrow.* An eye for an eye, Young thought, then flipped the pages. *Love your enemies.* I have nothing to go home to, he thought, and then he came to Mark. *Let us go over to the other side.* They did, in a ship, and "a great windstorm arose," Young read, the murder in his mind subsiding as the story overcame him. "And then Jesus said, 'Peace! Be still!' Then the wind ceased, and there was a dead calm."

There is a modesty inherent in evangelicalism's preference for personal stories, for every soul's version of "I was lost, but now I'm found." In a Protestant church without rank or reward, that story is democratic, radically so; my testimony is as important as yours, the poor man's tale just as powerful as that of the rich one. But the marriage of evangelicalism and military rank turns public confession into projection. It is one thing for your neighbor in the pews to tell you that he was blind, and that now he sees; it is another for such vision to be described by your commanding officer.

Young has been a Christian soldier ever since that terrible phone call. Now, he receives the second type of phone call: from his second wife, telling him she is on her knees, raising her husband up in prayer. That's the call that makes you a warrior, Young told his soldiers. He knows he's armored, ready to kill or be killed.

"We are to live with anticipation and expectation of his imminent return," he told me. "He wants us to do all things for the glory of God." Young is particularly inspired by the work of the popular evangelical writer Joel C. Rosenberg, a former adviser for Benjamin Netanyahu who, shortly after September 11, 2001, published what would become his first bestselling end-times novel, *The Last Jihad;* written before the attacks of September 11, it opens with a Muslim terrorist crashing a plane into an American city. But you do not need to be a prophetic novelist to read the signs. Look, said Young: nuclear Iran, economic collapse, President Obama's decision to "unleash science" upon helpless stem cells.

There's a sense, he said, in which the military is now the only safe place to be. "In the military, homosexuality is illegal. I don't want to get into all the particulars of 'don't ask,' but you can't act on homosexual feelings. And adultery is illegal. Really, arguably, the military is the last American institution that tries to uphold Christian values. It's the easiest place in America to be a Christian."

It was close to midnight when I had to sign off my first conversation with Young. The next afternoon, worried that he would be misunderstood, he called me to emphasize his commitment to the military's General Order 1B in Iraq and Afghanistan, which forbids "proselytizing of any religion, faith, or practice." Then, for close to an hour, he regaled me with stories of faith in action under his command. "I'm gonna tell you a story about the only time I ever had an EO concern. EO NCO"—the noncommissioned officer tasked with handling equal opportunity issues—"comes up to me and says, 'Sir I got a soldier down in Bravo Company wants to see you about a complaint.' I say, 'Fine.' I told him, 'I don't know what I said or did to offend you, but tell me what's the issue.' The kid says—he happens to be a black guy, not that that matters—he says, 'Sir, I'm a Christian. I don't go to church, but I read the Bible every day. But I believe when it comes to talking about God, it's like watering a plant. You don't want to water it too little, you don't want to water it too much. Water it too much, you kill the plant. Sir, I think you talk about God too much.' I say, 'I think it's appropriate that a Christian is the one to come up and make that complaint. Last thing I want to do is kill the plants! Thank you. Thank you.' Then I said, 'Do you mind if I tell you why I love God so much?' And he didn't, so I told him the whole story I told you, about my wife leaving me and wanting to kill my best friend. But I told him, 'God is my governor.' If you're from a mechanical background you know a governor in an engine, a governor holds it back. A governor rules you and also keeps you in check. I said, 'It stops me from doing things I might want to do. You know, like going to a strip club, or killing my best friend and my wife.'

"That soldier says, 'Sir, that's awesome.'

"Okay, now, this is where Young gets stupid. I said, 'Every time I talk about God, you know why it bothers you? Because you're not going to church. And you have some grandmother back home that's praying for you to go to church.' And he said he did have a grandmother praying for him. Okay, next time I'm at chapel, there was the guy who complained, and he said 'Sir, wasn't that an awesome service.' And he gives me a big hug. That was the only formal EO problem I ever had."

There were more miracles, in Young's eyes. The soldier who complained and then became a churchgoer was, through God's grace, promoted. The NCO who brought him in to complain was mysteriously hospitalized after becoming "spiritually sick," only to recover once he allowed Young to pray over him. Of the fourteen Americans killed in Kandahar under Young's watch, at least six were "Bible-believing Christians," a disproportionately large number compared to the demographics of his command. He sounded joyous. Why was this a miracle? I asked.

"God took the ones that were ready to go!"

Not long after our last conversation, Young was promoted. Full-bird colonel, just a star shy of general.

*   *   *

In the weeks following Obama's election, Mikey says, he almost went to Washington. He met with campaign staffers, submitted plans, gathered endorsements from powerful insiders. His dream was a post in the Pentagon, from which he could prosecute the most egregious offenders. It didn't seem entirely out of the realm of possibility. He could have been pitched as another gesture of bipartisanship, since Mikey is a lifelong Republican who probably would have voted for John McCain if his sons hadn't run afoul of the Air Force Academy's burgeoning spirit of evangelism—a culture that McCain, hardly a friend to fundamentalism, showed no interest in challenging last time around. It wasn't clear that McCain could see it; his imagination of what life in the military is like seemed stuck before 1967, his ribald tales of U.S. Naval Academy shenanigans closer in spirit to the World War II era than the military that emerged from the Vietnam War.

Another Vietnam veteran now serving in the Senate, who asked that he not be named so as not to compromise his close connections to today's top officers, offers an analysis of how the breakdown of Vietnam led to a born-again military. Although the military integrated before much of the United States, he points out, it almost split along racial lines, particularly in the last days of war. If the military was to rebuild itself, the southern white men at the heart of its warrior culture had to come to an understanding of themselves based on something other than skin color. Many turned toward religion, particularly fundamentalist evangelicalism, a tradition that, despite its potent legacy of racism, reoriented itself during the post–civil rights era as a religion of "reconciliation" between the races. That faith would come to define itself in the early 1990s through the image of white men hugging black men, tears all around, at Promise Keeper rallies. "They replaced race with religion," says the senator. "The principle remains the same: an identity built on being separate from a society viewed as weak and corrupt."

For decades, the military forged a sense of solidarity out of a singular purpose: the cold war struggle between free markets and state-planned economies, the shining city upon a hill versus the evil empire. In that fight, pluralism, racial or religious, was ultimately on our side, and it meshed neatly with ideologies that might otherwise be challengers, easily subsuming both nationalism and fundamentalism so long as communism was presented as an alternative should we fail to unite. Fundamentalism thrived not so much in opposition to the liberal state as in synchronicity with it, a neat, black-and-white theological correlate to a foreign policy—a vision of America's place in the world, our purpose, you might say—embraced across the mainstream political spectrum. What's surprising, though, is what happened after the Soviet flag slid down its pole in 1991: deprived of its godless foe, fundamentalism didn't wither along with communism; it blossomed, free to focus its full energies on the domestic front. Absent communism, many fundamentalists within the military defined themselves not *against* but *for:* Christianity, that is.

Much as the ominously named mercenary company Blackwater has rechristened itself Xe—hipper, less partisan, more powerful—the evangelical movement, its fundamentalist front included, is, if anything, broadening the scope of its concerns, mellowing its rhetoric but strengthening its roots in all corners of American society. *The Purpose-Driven Life* has a pulpit within the Democratic Party, via the inaugural address. Economic malaise turns out to be good for filling church pews, if not coffers. And the Christian nationalism that infused our fight with the evil empire continues to morph into the Christian internationalism of the world's only superpower. Why? Because without a "good war" or a cold war to give it meaning, pluralism, for many Americans, is simply not enough. Nowhere is that more true than in the military, where unity of purpose is not just a feel-good political sentiment but also the very foundation for survival.

Lacking a clear purpose, a common foe, some began to see pluralism itself as the enemy. The emergence of "radical Islam" as the object of a new cold war only complicated the matter. Rather than revealing a new enemy for us all to share, the idea of a monolithic radical Islam fractured pluralism from left to right. Many liberals abandoned even their rhetorical commitments to liberty of conscience, while the very conservatives who had favored arming militant Islamists ever since Eisenhower concluded that their universal embrace of religion in the abstract may have been naive. Perhaps pluralism, or at least the cold war variety that sustained the rise of American empire in the second half of the twentieth century, was nothing but propaganda, after all.

That revelation forced fundamentalism's hand. Once part of the cold war consensus, then a faith apart, American fundamentalism turned toward conquest at home. A religion based on its vigorous assertion of narrow and exclusive

truth claims could no longer justify common cause with secularism. Adherents could not be *against* communism,
godlessness—they had to be *for*—the active advance of a
Christianity defined according to struggles not between
nations but between ideas. And that, of course, closes the
loop, leading believers into spiritual war against their own
countrymen: "the unsaved," as Brig. Gen. Donald C. Wurster
put it, in a 2007 address to air force chaplains, who "have
no realization of their unfortunate alliance with evil."

What is the nature of this evil? Some conservative evangelicals call it "postmodernism." What they mean is the idea
of diversity itself, its egalitarianism and its messy democracy.
That is, the conviction that my beliefs have as much right to
real estate in the public square as yours, that truth is always
a mediated affair.

American fundamentalism, the more zealous the better,
is an ingenious solution, a mirror image of pluralism that
comes with a built-in purpose. It is available to everybody. Its
basic rules are easily learned. It merges militancy with love,
celebrating the ferocity of spirit necessary for a warrior and
the mild amiability required to stay sane within a rigid hierarchy. It's a populist religion—anyone can talk to the top
man—on a vertical axis. "It's a *King*dom," fundamentalist
activists like to remind each other—not a democracy.

The Air Force Academy chapel is composed of seventeen
silver daggers rising above campus, veined with stained glass
that suffuses the space inside with a violet and orange glow.
But when one of the academy's public relations officers
takes me on a tour, it's empty. Very few cadets worship there

anymore. Instead, they meet in classrooms and dorm rooms, at mountain retreats and at the numerous megachurches that surround the academy.

One of the most popular such services, The Mill, takes place on Friday nights at New Life, in a giant, permanent tent that, not long after academy dinnertime, fills with fake fog and power chords and more than a thousand men and women ranging in age from their teens to their early twenties—three hundred of them cadets shuttled in from the academy. I attended one Friday night in the company of Bruce Hrabak. For all his fervor, he was an excellent guide to the academy, a sports junkie who worried that his deep love for the Cowboys and Rock Chalk Jayhawk Kansas basketball crowded Christ out of his mind. His jokey amiability and natural curiosity undermined his militant intentions: he liked to be friends with everyone. But he was at the academy, he said, according to the Christian doctrine of "predestination," or destiny chosen by God. In 2005, when it came time to pick a college, Hrabak took the question to God. "God," he said one night before bed, "where do you want me to be? God, just please open the door you want me to walk through." The next morning, God did. "I woke up and read this article, about a lawsuit against the Air Force Academy—it was Mikey. And I just knew—I knew!—God wanted me to come here to defend his name."

At The Mill, we found a few seats left close to the back, where we met Hrabak's girlfriend, Jennifer, a petite and pretty blonde whom Hrabak had picked up by inviting her on a missionary trip to evangelize Mormons in Utah. She shot him down then, but now they were together. They swayed to the beat during the worship time, hands in the air, then got intimate for the sermon, leaning so close they were almost touching.

The sermon that night was painful—the pastor's wife had recently delivered a stillborn baby, and he spoke in raw, awful terms about suffering and theodicy, going over the age-old question of why a loving God permits bad things to happen to good people. It's one of the central dilemmas of the Christian faith, and its persistence, its resistance to answers, has helped make Christianity the forge of much of the world's great art and philosophy. By the end of this hour-long service, though, everything turned out for the best; even the dead baby had been shoehorned into God's inscrutable plan, a rhetorical illustration of the brutal sensibility hidden within a variation of the faith that insists on both optimism and an omnipotent, interventionist God.

Over dinner Hrabak had told me he believed that all pain, that which he endures and that which he inflicts, has a purpose. He felt this truth was of special solace for soldiers. I asked what he meant. "Well, you're pulling a trigger, you know?" He thought about that fact a lot. He pictured the dead. In his classes, he watched videos of air strikes. He imagined suffering. He was not as afraid of dying—he believes his salvation is assured—as he was of killing unjustly. He was afraid of sin. His double identity—as a spiritual warrior and as an officer of the deadliest force in the history of the world—was his redemption. His faith in the air force followed along after his faith in Christ in an orbit of self-fulfilling prophecy, each faith confirming the other. It was a closed circuit of certainty in which the juice, the electricity, was the blood of the lamb—the price he believed Jesus had paid for his, Hrabak's own, freedom. In turn, Hrabak was willing to pay that price, too, but not just for democracy. "You're laying down your life for others," he said. "Well, there has to be some true truth to put yourself in harm's way for." *True* truth; truth that requires an amplifier.

But what would he do if he ever received an order that contradicted that truth?

Hrabak looked shocked. He giggled, then composed himself and took a big bite of pizza, speaking confidently through his food. "Impossible, dude. I mean, I guess it *could* happen. But I highly doubt it."

What if he was ordered to bomb a building in which terrorists were hiding, even though there were civilians in the way?

He shook his head. "Who are you to question why God builds up nations just to destroy them, so that those who are in grace can see that they're in grace?" he asked. A smile lit up half his face, an expression that might be taken for sarcastic if Hrabak wasn't a man committed to being in earnest at all times. What he'd just said, he thought, might be something like a Word of Knowledge, a gift of wisdom from God. It blew his mind. He had to repeat it, his voice picking up a speed and enthusiasm that bordered on joy. "He"—the Lord—"builds up an entire nation"—Iraq or Vietnam, Afghanistan or Pakistan, who are you to question why?—"just to destroy them! To show somebody else"—America, maybe, or a young man guided to college by God—"that they're in grace."

6

THE NOW

WHAT IF Mark Sanford hadn't gotten caught? What if C Street's man had emerged from the woods untouched, or, at least, untainted by scandal, his secrets safe with the Coes?

Maybe, instead of a confession, this: on June 24, 2009, Mark Sanford calls a press conference in Columbia to address questions about his absence during the previous several days. There have been rumors, of course, but Jenny Sanford has dispatched them like the help that lingers too long after bringing tea. She knew *exactly* where her husband was, she told reporters: He was hiking the Appalachian Trail. A vacation without the family? Not at all. He'd been asked to write a book, and he was *thinking*. She knew this because he called every night to share the ideas he'd come up with during the day; they're that kind of couple.

"I won't begin in any particular spot," Sanford says. He

opens the press conference with Jenny, the couple's four boys, and his spiritual adviser, Cubby Culbertson, by his side. "Let me just start with: I love the Appalachian Trail." What follows is a twenty-minute speech that rambles with purpose, an account of hiking the trail as extended metaphor for the governor's vision of what conservatism could be. "Speech" isn't really the right word; it's more like a story. There's a black bear who'd rustled through Sanford's backpack; a nice young couple who'd restocked him with food; a wise old man he'd met at the foot of a thundering waterfall who'd reminded him that creation cuts its own path through the world. There are detours, off the trail and away from the straight line of time, up a mountaintop and through memory, back to his early mornings on his farm, in his tractor, beneath the morning-pink sky, listening to country music and scooping the earth; *building.*

The nation is watching as Sanford spins his tale. Folksy, yet pointed. The bear is a reminder that even God's creation has its dangers; the young couple who helped the governor an example of the best kind of charity, face to face; the wise old man at the waterfall—well, in the years to come, after everybody has read the memoir that will propel Sanford to the presidency, *On the Trail,* there will be disagreement over who that magical old man was. Some will say he was just a wise old man reminding the governor of natural law, the impossibility of social engineering, the truth of the invisible hand. But there will be many others who'll insist he was the Holy Spirit, setting Sanford on his special path. Sanford will never offer his opinion, just that wry expression and toothy smile we'll all come to love.

What changed in Mark Sanford? What transformed him from an able, even charming Republican politician to this gentle prophet, calling the nation back to the virtues of risk, generosity, contemplation, and enterprise? That's the first question from the press, of course.

Sanford apologizes for keeping everybody in the dark for a few days. "Leadership's about listening," he says. "But as much as I love talkin' to, and listenin' to, and just, just bein' with y'all, a leader, sometimes he's got to get away from the voice of the crowd just so he can separate out what he wants from what God wants." The governor settles in on the theme; it's clear there's something important he needs to say here. "You know, it's easy to mistake your own will for God's will. When you're surrounded by noise, people, you get into listening to yourself. And if you aren't careful, you start thinking the self has all the answers. That's something I've learned. But it doesn't. The self is the world, it's— desires, pride. And the biggest self of self is indeed self. But leaders must be called to higher things. You know, I'll tell you why I went out into the woods, there, the wilderness. It was because I want to listen to God, to what he has to say." Then Sanford reaches over and claps a hand on the shoulder of Cubby Culbertson. "I want to thank this man," Sanford says. "He's, he's a—a spiritual giant, I'd call him." The truth is, Sanford says, that he and Jenny had gone through a rough patch in their marriage, which was strained by political pressures, but Cubby and a group of guys up in Washington—"believe it or not, a Christian Bible study"— had kept them "moving forward."

"Moving forward"—that, he says, is what being on the

trail was all about. Moving forward without leaving anyone behind. "Not just 'no child,'" Sanford says, his broad, bony hands spreading out to encompass the whole room. "All of us. What I know now is that we all have to move forward together, to get on that trail and just—"

Sanford pauses. Never a Bible thumper, he's probably worrying that what he's about to say will be misconstrued. It won't. There's no presumption in his words. History, his supporters will say, would provide the evidence of his anointing. But this early summer day in Columbia, Sanford just smiles, his big eyes looking out from TV screens all over the land, and speaks the truth of his power: "Just let God show us the way."

What if we had? What if Sanford hadn't confessed, and C Street had continued to cover for him? Imagine the book he might have written. It might even have been a good book, had he poured the passion of his tractor letters into it. And then how far would it really have been to the White House? He might have gotten there by 2012, or 2016, with Obama having been crippled by Afghanistan or drowned in oil or defeated by some other bad turn, or maybe simply followed at the end of two happy terms by a Democrat who couldn't compete with Sanford's folksy charm.

Or maybe it's not Sanford but somebody else. Sam Brownback, his conservative credentials unsurpassable and yet able to appeal to centrists and even liberals with his humanitarian concern for Africa. "The Wilberforce Republican," the *Economist* has called him, after the British parliamentarian who helped lead the fight to abolish the slave trade.

Or maybe it'll be John Thune, a man in the Ensign model—tall, square-jawed, not overly burdened by deep thoughts. An amiable face for a fundamentalist politics of economic deregulation and social control. A student of Doug Coe's. Or Rep. Mike Pence, of Indiana, third-ranking Republican in the House, a former right-wing radio host with White House eyes. Or maybe it's not a C Streeter at all but one of the self-made heroes of populist fundamentalism: Mike Huckabee, from Arkansas, or even Sarah Palin. Huckabee the squirrel hunter and Palin the winking, wise-cracking moose skinner are too tacky for the C Street style; both of them are outsiders who barged their way onto the national stage, to the consternation of establishment figures. But would they govern that differently than a Sanford or a Brownback or a Thune?

The names don't really matter. The fundamentalist threat to American democracy isn't a person, a politician whose defeat would put the matter to rest once and for all. It's an idea. In its most modest shape it's the question posed by a future air force officer: "Who are we to question why God builds up nations?"—imperial narcissism so blind that the questioner believes his fatalistic acceptance of his own power is a form of humility. In its bluntest expression it's the "government by God" preached at C Street. In its most awful, it is the "God-led politics" of Uganda, the nightmare scenario of fundamentalism in power.

And yet the idea—Abraham Vereide used to capitalize that word, the Idea—is most effective and most enduring when it's pursued not as a doctrine, not with a manifesto in hand, but as a kind of continuity. Maybe *patience* is a better term, the unsung virtue of the American Right that has allowed it to endure through liberal and conservative seasons, transforming the nation not so much through grand programs as by tiny steps, one proposal leading to the next, often at the state level or even lower.

For instance, a fight by congressional conservatives to roll back democratically supported gun laws in the District of Columbia (an effort in which Brownback and Ensign were both active) went national when the Supreme Court issued a ruling that could block cities from taking guns off their streets. Meanwhile, several states have passed laws ensuring that gun owners can carry concealed weapons into churches. Sometimes the process moves in from the margins, such as the case of the 2010 Utah law that effectively criminalizes miscarriage, leaving it to prosecutors to decide whether a woman's miscarriage was "intentional." The spectrum of possibility moves rightward, so that one day a milder anti–reproductive rights initiative that once would have seemed outlandish, such as requiring women to review ultrasound images of their fetuses before getting an abortion, starts to seem like a compromise. How many steps would it take to get from a conscience clause allowing pharmacists to refuse prescriptions for birth control—possible under the Workplace Religious Freedom Act, not yet passed but supported by members of both parties—to a mainstream discussion of making contraception unavailable altogether, a goal spoken of seriously by an increasing number of fundamentalist politicians?

It's not just sex. The Idea is bigger than its many manifestations. It's a current more than an agenda, a river into which all the tributaries of the Right find their way eventually. Tea Party candidates are mocked for zany ideas like the abolition of the Department of Education, as if they were proposing to strip an amendment from the Constitution. Most of us forget, or never knew, that the Department of Education—like the Department of Energy, another target for demolition—was a creation of the Carter administration. What has been done can be undone, and it's not just Tea Partiers who want to see the federal government shrunk to the size that it can be drowned in a bathtub, as the conservative leader Grover Norquist has put it. For Norquist, that shrinkage is a secular ambition; for C Streeters like Brownback and Thune, it's a spiritual goal. Business might applaud the decommissioning of the Environmental Protection Agency or the radical rollback of worker safety laws or the end of the minimum wage for economic reasons, but political fundamentalists see deregulation as a moral crusade, one that will restore to citizens the ability to choose between right and wrong. What good is the concept of sin, they ask, if there's a safety net to catch you when you fall?

And what good is virtue if it's not freely chosen? That question leads elite fundamentalists to celebrate the outcome of *Citizens United v. Federal Election Commission,* the 2010 Supreme Court case in which the Court's conservative justices decided that the First Amendment protects the political speech of corporations, allowing them to flood money into the elections. Several months later, in *Holder v. Humanitarian Law Project,* the Court ruled that even peaceful advocacy—what David Bahati calls "promotion"—for an organization the government deems a threat can be prosecuted as terrorism itself. The ruling marks "the first time [the Supreme Court] has permitted the government to make it a crime to advocate lawful, nonviolent activity." One needn't be a spokesman for Al-Qaeda, or even just poor, confused Mark Siljander to cross the line—under this ruling, say legal scholars, former president Jimmy Carter could be prosecuted for monitoring elections in Lebanon. For that matter, it's possible that I could be prosecuted for saying it was wrong for the United States to help Sri Lanka massacre its Tamil minority, and if you repeated that notion on a blog, you could be marked a terrorist, too.

The real dream of American fundamentalism isn't just a paring down of government, a return to the days of Coolidge and Harding. It's a transformation into something new, something that has never existed before. Consider one small program that might be up for expansion in the future: Fugitive Safe Surrender. As originally implemented in 2007, the program moved the apparatus of the legal system out of the courthouse and into a local megachurch for four days. The event would be preceded by an advertising blitz advising fugitives to turn themselves in not to a police station but to the church; implicit was the promise of special consideration for those who came to the law by way of a house of the Lord. At one such event, in Akron, Ohio, which I attended, participants passed through metal detectors into a gymnasium, where, to the sound of piped-in instrumental gospel music, they were given the option of speaking first to a sheriff's deputy in light riot gear or a pastor: a man with a gun, or a man with a Bible.

For those who chose neither, the four-day church-court

would be followed by a massive sweep, with marshals rolling through America's inner cities in armored vehicles and kicking down doors like they were back in Baghdad. "Kind of a yin to the yang," explained the program's creator, U.S. Marshal Pete Elliott. "Look, if people surrendered at the police department, we wouldn't have to do this. But they don't. And why don't they? Because they don't trust people like me. So I went back to the institution in my life that I trust the most. The church! If we brought the whole justice center out and put it in a church, people will *turn* themselves in."

Fugitive Safe Surrender falls under the auspices of faith-based initiatives, a program many mistakenly believe was left behind with the Bush presidency. The real genius of Bush's faith program—rooted in decades of smaller-scale Family-led experiments with the U.S. Department of Housing and Urban Development, prisons, and education—was its creation of permanent offices throughout government with mandates to seek ways to channel secular funding into faith-based initiatives. Some of these are universally admired, while others are questionable; a few, like Fugitive Safe Surrender, seem to have simply dispensed with the First Amendment. At its strongest, this apparatus is an engine for the privatization of public funds into religious hands; at its weakest, it's a patronage machine.

Either way, it's been institutionalized.

As has its parallel movement in the military. We've already gone far beyond the problem of a few rogue officers. And as the line moves, so do those who'd rather be out in front of it. If Gen. Petraeus, with his endorsement of Christian command manuals, and Gen. Caslen, with his "aroma of Jesus Christ," are at the center, who else is out there on the front lines of the fundamentalist advance along with Col. Young? Are there senior commanders who share the newly mainstream idea of "religious freedom" as a mission statement for invasion? It's a vision that extends not just to Iraq but to the Sudan, the Philippines, Syria, and Venezuela, all nations targeted for liberation from radical Islam in the imaginations of leading conservatives like some of the politicians named above. How many little wars might the United States be fighting by 2016 or 2020?

"We could never afford it," say the skeptics. That's the good news: we're too poor to fulfill fundamentalism's imperial ambitions. Instead, fundamentalism will have to settle for fighting a war of attrition at home, wearing down one of the movement's most hated enemies, secular education, school by school. The "liberal" side of the dream is represented by Dennis Bakke, a friend of the Family, a former energy tycoon, and current leader of the for-profit charter school movement, who suggests that churches subsidize the salaries of missionary teachers in public schools. The more radical vision is the end of public schooling altogether.

Suppose it could be done—not all at once but gradually, through budget crises (not hard to imagine) that lead schools into public-private partnerships with whoever's ready with funding. That is, churches, with pledges of strict separation, of course. Then again, the Bush-era decision to allow recipients of federal money to discriminate based on religion still stands, its revocation one of Obama's broken promises. And bus route by bus route, teacher by teacher,

America's experiment with public education—little more than a century old in its modern form—winds down to an end.

"The end." That's the fear secular critics of fundamentalism all too often focus on, as if fundamentalist politicians spend their days studying the numerology of Hebrew words instead of chipping away at banking regulations and thinking of ways to privatize Social Security, more strategies for untying the invisible hand of God's economy. The political elites who implement the ideas of American fundamentalism are most often postmillennialists, not premillennialists, which is a theologically wonky way of saying they're in no rush for the Rapture. They want to bring their God into this world, not usher in the next. Premillennialists, considered crass by the sophisticated fundamentalists of the Family, believe Christ will come back soon and rule for a thousand years. Postmillennialists insist that we need at least a thousand years of God-led government before we prove ourselves worthy of his return. Premillennialists are apocalyptic; postmillennialists are political, their faith not in what is to come but in what is, the "powers that be" of Romans 13 rather than the prophecy of Revelation.

Apocalypse? This? *Then one of the four beasts gave unto the seven angels seven golden vials full of the wrath of God, who liveth forever and ever. And the temple was filled with smoke from the glory of God and from his power, and no man was able to enter the temple until the seven plagues of the seven angels were fulfilled.* Please. C Streeters, the Brownbacks and the Ensigns, the Wamps and the Pickerings, interchangeable placeholders—theirs is the power and the bureaucracy. Fundamentalism is a subtler religion than we realize; the end is just a metaphor for tomorrow, and today there's still time for business as usual. *Patience*, not apocalypse, is the watchword of American fundamentalism. Not waiting for the Kingdom, but building it slowly, brick by brick, a foundation strong enough to endure any electoral tides.

When Obama entered the White House, editorialists and newsweeklies and talking heads on television declared the age of culture war over. This resolution of hostilities came after some of the conflict's nastiest battles during the 2008 campaign. Then again, pundits had decided in 2006 that the Democratic victories of that year were proof that the culture wars had come to an end. That message of Mission Accomplished was announced in 1996, too, when Bill Clinton was reelected—just two years after the sweeping victories of Christian Right–backed Republicans, which in turn came two years after the press declared the culture wars over in 1992.

It's an American tradition, declaring conflict a thing of the past. But the conflict continues because fundamentalism continues; because the Right didn't wither up and blow away on January 20, 2009; because the disarray of the Republican Party no more equals the end of American conservatism than it did in 1964, when Lyndon Johnson's crushing defeat of Barry Goldwater laid the foundation for the decades of much harder Right politics that would follow LBJ's departure. Beyond conservatism, the dream of fundamentalism's elite, a new "social order," as Doug Coe describes it, is an enduring one, the age-old dream of all-encompassing authority, Our Father not just in heaven but presiding over all of our daily affairs, from our government to our economy to our armed forces. That this dream can never be fully realized in a democracy, even one as flawed as ours, makes it no less dangerous.

The threat isn't theocracy, an idea nearly every fundamentalist denounces as the province of mullahs and the Middle Ages, but the conflation of democracy with authoritarianism. Not the jackbooted kind or even the iron fist within the velvet glove, but rather the "Father knows best" variety, trickle-down paternalism, the authority of the Father-God descending down upon us through his chosen, our servant leaders, men and even the occasional women who are to society as fundamentalists believe fathers should be to their families, both loving and stern.

If "trickle-down," in the context of paternalism, evokes the wrong kind of flow, consider the old bit of Reaganspeak a clue to the repurposing of language that is the real art of fundamentalism: *democracy* redefined as rule by a class of the anointed; *religion* reduced to the (mistaken) beliefs of other people; *law* a euphemism for scripture, and *scripture* itself not just malleable but liquid, easily poured into any vessel, a Sanford or a Palin, a Thune or a Pickering— fuel for the long march toward *freedom*, which is just another word for no questions asked. "Starve doubts, feed freedom," as Abram Vereide put it shortly before he died.

Fundamentalists don't want to do away with the Constitution; they just want to abolish its ambiguities. How? By finding certainties between its lines. There is nothing literalist or originalist about the fundamentalist approach to the Constitution; the right way to read it, they believe, is the way they study scripture, alert not just to reason but also to magic. They read it like Daniel the Israelite, taken into bondage in Babylon, interpreting the king's dreams. Fundamentalists see themselves as being in bondage to secularism, liberalism. To them secularism is an unimaginative regime that looks at the words of the Constitution and sees only ink, not a divinely inspired, "God-breathed" document in the manner of 2 Timothy 3:16 ("All scripture is God-breathed"). The very term *constitution* is derived, so the thinking goes, from the biblical *covenant.* Which means, of course, that it belongs to the faithful. If they are like Daniel, the captive interpreting the king's dream, they are also like his captor, King Nebuchadnezzar. They are both victim and oppressor, the prophet and the power, interpreting their own dream as evidence of the Father's intentions.

This book, *C Street,* isn't about a piece of real estate in Washington. It's not about the Family, or Officers' Christian Fellowship, or even the murderous potential of American culture wars waged by proxy overseas. It's about the Idea, as Abram put it, the monolithic vision of fundamentalism always threatening to subsume the many lowercased ideas that constitute democracy. In Uganda we see the Idea verging on murder, in the military we see it gathering force, at C Street we encounter its enduring corruption. Let's briefly consider a more complicated example, one preferred by the C Streeters themselves: William Wilberforce, a politician who was never troubled by questions about his personal failings.

That was because he had none, or at least none that bothered his evangelical admirers. He was as much of a saint in his personal life as he was in Parliament, where, in 1807, after two decades of effort, he led to victory the legislative fight to abolish the slave trade. Responding to a reporter's questions about the Family, John Hart, director of communications for Sen. Coburn, declared Wilberforce's prayer group, the Clapham Fellowship, "a model for 'The Family.' Ignoring the prominence of Wilberforce to a group like 'The Family' would be like writing a story about the Catholic Church but leaving out the Pope."

In fact, there's very little mention of Wilberforce in the 592 boxes of the Family's papers stored at the Billy Graham Center Archives. His influence is a late addition, part of the proliferation of Wilberforce-themed entities and initiatives within conservative evangelicalism since the movement's recognition that it had been, for the most part, on the wrong side of the struggle of another "saint," Martin Luther King Jr. Wilberforce, a long-dead upper-class white man — and an evangelical Christian — is the movement's redemption. MLK? Just a late entry in a struggle practically invented by Wilberforce, goes the thinking.

Eric Metaxas, the bestselling author of a conservative biography of Wilberforce called *Amazing Grace* (unrelated, says Metaxas, to the 2006 Hollywood hagiography of the same title), told me that, without Wilberforce, there'd be no concept of social justice in Western civilization—that nobody had seriously dreamed of freeing the slaves before God gave the notion to "the nightingale of the House of Commons," as Wilberforce was known for his beautiful singing voice.

Leaving aside the millions of slaves to whom the idea may have occurred, Metaxas and Wilberforce's contemporary admirers—Sen. Brownback told me he wept when he first read another Wilberforce biography, and Rep. Frank Wolf says he keeps a life-size poster of Wilberforce on his office door—mostly ignore the deep and often radical abolitionist tradition, both religious and secular, to which Wilberforce was a late arrival. That's not all they leave aside. When I asked Metaxas about Wilberforce's opposition to the first successful slave revolt in history, the Haitian Revolution, he said that wasn't part of his story. When I asked about Wilberforce's opposition to the rights of working people, he said that part hadn't interested him.

"That part" was one of Wilberforce's guiding passions: he was for the abolition of slavery, but ardently and explicitly opposed to "democratical principles." Chuck Colson, the Watergate felon born again through the intervention of the Family as a Christian Right leader, told me that it was for this that he most admired Wilberforce: "There were very few that stood against the Enlightenment," he says, but Wilberforce was one of the boldest. Throughout Wilberforce's life, writes Adam Hochschild in his history of British abolitionism, *Bury the Chains*, he supported "all the era's repressive measures, arguing in favor of a law that provided three-month jail terms for anything remotely resembling labor organizing, which he thought 'a general disease in our society.' " Freedom of speech or even of belief did not interest him. His Society for Carrying into Effect His Majesty's Proclamation Against Vice and Immorality arranged to have a British publisher of Tom Paine's jailed because of Paine's atheism. His support for the so-called Gagging Acts of 1795 was crucial to their passage. "Went to Pitt's," he wrote in his diary, of a visit to his friend William Pitt the Younger, the prime minister, "to look over the Sedition Bill—altered it much for the better by enlarging." The result was a law that banned meetings of more than fifty people, joined by a law that made criticism of the government punishable by seven years in prison. The laws were intended to squash "mad-headed professors of equality and liberty," as Wilberforce put it, and they worked, setting the abolition movement back by years.

The story preferred by Wilberforce's admirers today is the same as the simple one told in the song "Amazing Grace," written by a mentor of Wilberforce's, a repentant slave trader named John Newton, and *Amazing Grace* the movie, bankrolled by a fundamentalist billionaire with a dream of Christianizing pop culture. The feckless son of a wealthy merchant, a twenty-one-year-old Wilberforce bought his seat in Parliament in 1780 at the cost of roughly eight pounds per vote. "The first year that I was in Parliament," he'd recollect, "I did nothing.... My own distinction was my darling object." He sought it through socializing. He was an ardent gambler, a nimble flatterer, charming but chaste and thus welcomed into the salons of the day by both women and men. The revolutionary novelist Madame de

Staël, no friend to Wilberforce's conservatism, called him "the wittiest man in England." He had the build of an elf and the hair of an owl. Masculinity framed the face of a pudgy boy: dark brows above, a cleft chin below, and in between, flushed lips, chubby cheeks, and a friendly squash for a nose. His fingers were long, his legs were short, and his shortsighted eyes were kindly, if wincing. His stomach was given to grumbling, but his voice — that's almost the whole story right there. Untrained but lovely, in song or in speech it was one of the greatest weapons in the arsenal of abolition. He could and did speak against slavery for three hours, and even his opponents would listen. The biographer Boswell, witness to one of Wilberforce's first campaign speeches, delivered outdoors in a hailstorm, reported that the little man's words pummeled back the wind and made a space in which a country crowd stood rapt for an hour. "I saw what seemed a mere shrimp mount upon the table; but as I listened, he grew, and grew, until the shrimp became a whale."

Not long after his twenty-fifth birthday came the beginning of what his traditionally Anglican mother would call his "perversion": his conversion from a proper Protestant into a zealous evangelical Christian. The catalyst was a long carriage ride in the company of his former school headmaster. The two whiled away the hours reading an earnest treatise on religion that made a great impression. Thereafter, a new note began creeping into Wilberforce's diary, until then dedicated to observations such as "jolly good party." Now there were sterner points made: there'd been too much laughter at a christening, he'd note, or a distasteful dance at the opera. A second trip with the headmaster, to a Swiss spa, led to an immersion in the New Testament, followed by a rejection of theater and novels. (His Clapham Fellowship would later attempt to save Shakespeare by editing out all that was unwholesome.) His diary soon proved insufficient for the depth of his sentiments, and it was paralleled by a more secret journal, a ledger of rhetorical self-flagellation: "shame"; "pride"; "my dangerous state"; "blindness"; "hatred"; "miserable"; "blind"; "naked"; "vain"; "punishment"; "fear"; "callous"; "wretched"; "tremble"; "coldness"; "darkness."

His salvation was, well, his salvation. The conservative evangelicalism of his day, like ours, emphasized personal transformation and the value of setting an example for Christian living. But in practice it all too often took as its proof-texts acts of control, the imposition of one's alleged grace on others. Saving someone else allowed the believer to avoid what John of the Cross called "the dark night of the soul." For a brief moment in an otherwise unbothered life, Wilberforce had contemplated doubt and had encountered faith not as a matter of certainty but as a great and sometimes troubling mystery. That didn't feel good. So he turned his new obsession with sin and its amelioration outward.

In 1786 he carried a bill to relieve the suffering of women convicted of murdering their husbands by replacing the punishment of burning with hanging. But the noose, too, chafed him; not its rub but its inefficiency. It killed, but it did not prevent. Wilberforce went to the root cause, proposing a society in favor of "the ancient censorship," with himself "the guardian of the religion and morals of the people." It's this Wilberforce, the champion of what he called the Reformation of Manners, a program for not just a God-led government but also a God-led society at every level, who would become the model for modern fundamentalism. A man who had found God, struggled briefly, and then concluded, with Hobbit-like satisfaction, that the Lord shared the precise concerns of his class and time, tsk-tsked over the same plays Wilberforce did, perused the same papers Wilberforce read with a sharp eye for vulgarity, and, most important, wished all to be happy in their station. For Wilberforce, the idea that God loved everyone just as they were was a mandate for preservation of the class system. Spiritual equality before God, which he believed in, did not mean the same thing as worldly equality, which he decidedly did not. *Amazing Grace*, the movie, depicts Wilberforce as having been great friends with Olaudah Equiano, a freed slave who wrote a bestselling autobiography. However, there's no evidence they ever met, or that Equiano, a brilliant abolitionist, would have accepted Wilberforce's terms had they done so. Freed slaves, Wilberforce believed, were to become "a grateful peasantry." The English poor, meanwhile, should be thankful "that their more lowly path has been allotted to them by the hand of God; that is their part...contentedly to bear its inconveniences."

And yet, for all his failings, Wilberforce did something great, something worthy of the attachment of "Amazing Grace" to his memory: he played an essential part in the abolition of the slave trade. He didn't invent social justice, and he didn't lead the abolitionist movement. He simply but crucially gave it a voice in Parliament. The abolitionists needed a front man. "He must never be morbid," wrote R.

Coupland, his 1923 biographer. "He must not pile up the horrors.... It must be impossible...to deride him in London drawing rooms as an obscure crank, a wild man from beyond the pale." He must be upper-class, but not aristocratic; not an eccentric. He could be Christian, but he must move among the swells. He must be popular. He must be witty, but not too clever. Not a prophet but a promoter.

That is what the abolitionist movement needed then, and that is all fundamentalism values now. Today's champions of Wilberforce, those who look to him for a model of the Christian politician, ignore not only the strategists and the writers and the radicals, in thought and in action, who made Wilberforce's fine speeches possible, but also the most visible evidence of the democracy from which the idea of abolition gained its power, the masses of petitions that forced Parliament's hand. In Wilberforce's time, he brought up the rear of the abolition movement, poking and prodding respectable society to catch up before Britain's slaves caught up with those of Haiti's and took their freedom rather than accepting it from their betters. For today's fundamentalists, Wilberforce, not the slaves, is the point. The most notable scene in *Amazing Grace* featuring Thomas Clarkson, the abolitionist who drew Wilberforce to the cause, depicts Wilberforce bravely rejecting Clarkson's appeal to seek allies among the French revolutionaries. Lest viewers feel the temptation themselves, an ominous cello and several screeching violins stand in for the warnings of the British arch-reactionary Edmund Burke, the most eloquent opponent of democracy in history and, like Wilberforce, a hero today of fundamentalist intellectuals. Thus abolition, a fight for freedom, is recast as a warning against freedom's excesses and even as a tribute to a different kind of obedience, to divine authority. The same natural law that forbade slavery required that the poor be poor, the corollary of which, of course, was that the privileged were made by God for the very sake of privilege. They might do great and generous things with their privilege, as Wilberforce did, or they might do stingy and cruel things with their privilege, as Wilberforce also did, but either way the principle was the same. Serve God. Accept your station. Starve doubt, feed freedom.

Feed it what, exactly? All the uncertainties of creation, the endless arguments that are the noise of democracy.

*　　*　　*

When the Republican National Convention came to New York City in 2004, my friend Ann decided she wanted to join the hundreds of thousands of New Yorkers who took to the streets in protest. Ann, like most of the marchers, wasn't an activist or even a terribly political person. Much of the dissent stemmed from anger with the decision of the Republican Party—traditionally not very friendly to urban concerns—to invade Manhattan on the last weekend of summer. Ann's position was more principled. A liberal on nearly every issue, she's a conservative at heart, her politics shaped as much by the rural hollow in which she was raised as by her subsequent life of wandering among artists and academics. She grew up in a house her father, a stubborn apostate from his family's Mennonite tradition, built by hand, with a foundation of stones young Ann and her sister hauled up from a stream. They weren't hippies, Ann would say, they were hicks, and proud of it, commonsense people from a commonsense corner of the country where Mennonites and Amish set the pace of political thinking. Of course, Ann had moved on; for instance, her Mennonite relatives would likely not approve of her kitschy Jesus paint-by-number collection. But there was an earnestness in those paintings, in their carefully filled-in shadows and their patchwork skies, which was why, when Ann decided to become a political protester for the day, she turned to her collection for a sign to carry. Something a little subtler than "Down with this" or "Up with that." She settled on a thoughtful Christ in red and white robes, the kind of calm divine she knew from Lancaster County, Pennsylvania—a fine antidote, she believed, to the hyped-up, militarized Jesus then looming over the Republican Party. She taped a necklace of twine to the back and wore her quiet Christ like a sandwich board.

Hmm. Too quiet, maybe. He had to say something. But what?

I'd admired the picture in her office before (we both worked in a university religious studies department at the time, Ann as an administrator and I as the department's token journalist), but where Ann saw the serenity of a Mennonite Jesus, I saw the *oy vey* of a Jewish carpenter. We'd discuss this, Ann and I, surrounded by people who could read scripture in its original languages, bending our minds instead toward the interpretation of a work of paint-by-number art. The answer, Ann concluded, was part Mennonite, part Jewish, common sense with a *yidishe kop:*

Ann is just over five feet tall, with short, wild red-blond hair, big blue eyes, and arched eyebrows when she's riled — which she was by her decision to get political, or religious, or religiously political, or whatever it meant to carry that sign out into a city on lockdown, with hundreds of thousands of protesters filling the street like a slow-moving river clogged with timber, police and press rolling everyone along. Ann had outfitted herself in a black blouse and black pajama pants and black sneakers, a ninja canvas for her head-in-his-hands Jesus, praised and applauded as we moved in and out of the river, a little band of us — the religious studies department, nerds, not activists — dipping in and stepping out to observe and wax academic on the ritual of crowds. Ann with her sign was a walking altar. She was short enough that most people had to bow a little to read the sign, which they did because, after all, it was Jesus. "What's this," they'd say, wondering if they'd come upon a thumper, a distributor of tracts, or a "counter-protester." "What's this — 'That's not what I meant' — Oh, I know what you mean!" Photojournalists clicked and snapped, urging her to strike a pose. Who knows how many readers of *El País* or *Le Monde* or the *Hindustan Times* briefly saw the face of dissent in America as a redheaded ninja pixie proclaiming the virtues of a paint-by-number Jesus?

But Ann wasn't really the face of dissent, she was a liberal New Yorker with a funny line, a bit of wit, and a twist that put her somewhere off to the side of the great, earnest divide between believing and unbelieving America — off to the side, where so many of us live, far from conviction of any kind. We are an uncertain nation, restless, our unsettled identities borne out by the annual polls that show Americans shifting and sliding between denominations and religions. These surveys neglect other matters of ultimate concern — there really is more than one ultimate, paradoxical as it sounds. They neglect the many affections of an enchanted nation where interventionist angels and flickering flying saucers occupy the hearts and minds of a clear majority. Not just the rubes. A majority of us — Methodists and Catholics and born-again evangelicals — believe in the supernatural or the supranatural, in invisible winged advisers on our shoulders and even wingless extraterrestrials high above. Count me even a city's worth of Americans who do not embrace either ghosts and hauntings and presences, or reincarnations or higher powers, the demon-filled world of Tibetan Buddhism or the subtle spiritualities of yoga, or sports obsession, or *Star* magazine. Legitimately religious, all. God bless our pluralistic nation.

Ann wasn't the face of dissent, she was just playing her part. But we did meet a real dissenter that day: "Sarge" Bill McDonald, a veteran of twenty years in the army. Called a preacher by his flock of winos and junkies back home in southern Illinois, and briefly brought into our circle of friends that day by Ann's Jesus sandwich board, he was a man who bucked expectations. He'd come to New York City to represent a member of his congregation back home, a poor woman who'd broken her wrist and couldn't even afford a cast. "So she's just gonna try to keep it real still for fourteen weeks," he explained. To that end he found himself marching in the crowd. He planned on voting Republican, but that didn't stop him from protesting. "What they don't need is mumbo jumbo," he said. "They" included himself and his friend with the broken bone. "'Compassionate conservatism,'" he scoffed. "Poor people need something for this!" He rubbed his belly as though he were a good-luck Buddha. "You sit there and listen for decades, or centuries, while some rich guy says, 'Hold on awhile.' Well, after a while, you get fed up, you know?"

The politics of that year are old now, but the problem remains the same, the real culture clash of American life. It's between the essence of fundamentalism—paternalism, authority, and charity—and the messy imperatives of democracy, "the din of the vox populi" once derided by Abram Vereide. It's the difference between false unity, preached from above, and real solidarity, pledged between brothers and sisters—the kinds who are always bickering. It's the

difference between the harmony of a politics with few
options and less imagination, and the cacophony of believers and unbelievers gathered together. Gathered, that is,
not by the narrow borders of "common ground"—a euphemism for the stronger faction's conventional wisdom—but
by a commitment, grudging or willing, to disagreement:
"the noise of democracy," as President James Buchanan
(1857–1861) called the American sacrament of arguing, his
failures myriad but for the high regard in which he held
dissonance.

The names on the ticket against which Sarge would protest and for which he would vote were ephemeral; the spirit
of stubborn self-contradiction that guided him was not. It
was as old as Ann's head-in-his-hands Jesus and as timeless
as the recognition with which people greeted her misunderstood Christ. Sarge was a large red-bearded man in
double-wide jeans and he had half-squatted to read Ann's
sign through square metal-framed glasses. When he took in
what it said, he raised the brim of his "Jesus Is Lord" hat and
grumbled his approval with absolute sincerity, one sidewalk
prophet recognizing another.

After Sarge mustered out of the army, and after two
decades of keeping born-again beliefs to himself (he was
born the first time around Catholic in the Bronx), he
began preaching on street corners, in St. Louis, Kansas City,
Indianapolis, as far afield as New Orleans. Or rather, not so
much preaching as receiving: the lost, the curious, and the
mocking. Like most Christians, Sarge considered them all
beloved by God in heaven; but, unusual for a man of his literally Bible-thumping beliefs (or maybe Bible-patting; he

tended one while we spoke like it was a needy puppy), that translated into equality here on earth as well. "Anyone wants to talk, I'll listen to 'em. It's the gutter punks and the skate punks a lot of the time. Also, gay men and women. I don't seek 'em out, they just come to me. That's gotta be Jesus, 'cause I know I ain't cute." He happened to be conservative on moral matters and felt the Bible backed him up, but his Word, the verse he felt he'd been given by Jesus to study and to share, was Proverbs 14:31. He flipped his Bible open and read, tracing the highlighted line with a finger. "He who oppresses the poor shows contempt for their maker, but whoever is kind to the needy honors God."

Look, he said. He waved toward a group of protesters in tight pink dresses standing near us. Across their chests were the words "Axis of Eve." "God doesn't say 'Bang! You fail.'" Sarge pointed toward one of the women, who turned and stared. "'Bang! You fail!'" He pointed to another. And another. And another. The Axis of Eve glared with perfect pink fury. Sarge smiled, oblivious and benign. "God doesn't actually say that."

That's why he liked Ann's sign. His sign, meanwhile, read: DELIGHT YOURSELF IN THE LORD JESUS AND HE WILL GIVE YOU THE DESIRES OF YOUR HEART. Delight; desire; it struck me as a fine message, even if Sarge had taken it upon himself to edit scripture, adding a *Jesus* to the Hebrew Bible's Psalm 37. That's religion in America, under constant revision. Only when it settles does it become dangerous, only when it begins to replace the uncertainty of democracy—of life—with the absolute of authority. Sarge was a fundamentalist, but he had a more equitable notion of the divine. "I'm here to give God an opportunity to be part of the democratic process," he said. "He's got as much at stake in this as anyone." He aimed to pay his God the highest compliment possible: he wanted to make him legal. That is, a citizen, a voice in the crowd, part of the noise.

Acknowledgments

My first thanks must go to Mark Sanford, John Ensign, and Chip Pickering, who ensured that my last book, *The Family*, would find a second life in paperback and lead to an opportunity to follow up with this contemporary investigation. I thought about sending them flowers; this book will have to do.

"Investigation" would be too grand a term for this book were it not for the brilliant help of a number of talented researchers and interviewers, including Paige Boncher, Samantha Fields, Andrew Grossman, Vanessa Hartmann, and Meg Murphy. Kiera Feldman and Robert Kagolo are even more deeply implicated: they were collaborators, responsible for the best reporting in this book. Monica Gallegos was also of crucial assistance. Susan Strauss provided a fine space to work in. Esther Kaplan and The Nation Institute are two of the last pillars upon which investigative journalism in America rests; praise them, and send them money. Part of chapter 5 first appeared in *Harper's* magazine, where it was much improved by Bill Wasik and Chris Beha. Sadly, I had to cut the story of an army medic named Dustin

Chalker, who was exceptionally generous with his time; his insights, however, inform the final draft.

I was fortunate to have a number of talented writers serve as readers: Kathryn Joyce, Peter Manseau, Ann Neumann, and my father, Robert Sharlet, among them. My father's insights, especially, have been essential. This is all his fault. Lori McGlinchey is too smart to waste her time writing, but generously killed some hours reading. Even more important than readers, especially when writing a book on a tight deadline, is a forgiving family: I'm grateful beyond words for the support of all the Sharlets, Tezcans, Rabigs, Bakers, and Dotis—and Fiona.

John Parsley and Geoff Shandler at Little, Brown were generous with their enthusiasm and, more important, with their patience. If you're holding this book in your hands, that probably has something to do with the work of Amanda Brown, Janet Byrne, Dev Chatillon, Heather Fain, Peggy Freudenthal, Laura Keefe, Carolyn O'Keefe, and others at Little, Brown who did their jobs well in difficult circumstances, which is always worth acknowledging. And in that spirit I want to thank Amy Baker at HarperCollins, too. I won't thank Rachel Maddow, Andy Dallos, and the rest of Rachel's staff for helping me get this story to a wider audience—that's just journalism, and for their excellence in that regard they don't need my recognition—but I'm exceptionally grateful to them for backing me up while I was in Uganda. Most of all I'm indebted to my agent and pal, Kathy Anderson, who is the sort of person who reminds me of why I wanted to be a writer.

I'm extremely grateful for the wisdom and sharp tongues

of those who helped me talk this book into being by supplying wisdom, expertise, liquor, or all three (thank you, Anthea Butler): Adam Becker, Martin Cook, Evan Derkacz, Omri Elisha, Becky Garrison, Queue Gaynor, Christina Honchell, Kristen Leslie, Victoria McKernan, Sarah Posner, Frank Schaeffer, Nathan Schneider, Rev. Osagyefo Uhuru Sekou, Meera Subramanian, Warren Throckmorton, Boo Tyson, Diane Winston, JoAnn Wypijewski, and Angela Zito. I've always thought the line drawn between journalism and activism was fuzzy, so I'm also glad for those who cross back and forth with ease in regard to the issues raised in this book, including Diana Butler Bass, Fred Clarkson, Jodi Jacobson, Rev. Kapya Kaoma, Pastor Dan Schultz, and Bruce Wilson.

I'm thankful to everyone who spoke with me, even those who may wish they hadn't. There are sources, there are subjects, and then there are the saints every writer depends on, people who throw their lives or their ideas open to you even at risk to themselves. Among those I can name are Eli Agee, Toufic Agha, Blessed Busingye, Dustin Chalker, Jeremy Hall, Jeffery Humphrey, Val Kalende, Kate Phillips, Chris Rodda, and Mikey Weinstein. A strange and special thanks goes to three subjects who knew who I was, guessed that they might not like what I'd write, and spoke to me anyway: David Bahati, Bruce Hrabak, and Col. Bob Young.

No-Prizes for those public servants from both parties who should have talked and didn't: Sen. John Ensign, Gov. Mark Sanford, and former representative Chip Pickering, of course, and also Sen. Tom Coburn, Sen. Jim Inhofe, Rep. Robert Aderholt, Rep. John Carter, Rep. Mike Doyle, Rep.

Joe Pitts, Rep. Bart Stupak, Rep. Zach Wamp: legislators like you make Uganda look like a democracy.

Fortunately, I'm married to a woman who lets me yammer on enough to make up for all our reticent leaders. Thank you, Julie, for allowing me to babble the wrong turns and dead ends of this book-writing into your ear, and for responding with the love, patience, and belief necessary to setting it on a better path. Our daughter is too young to know how many times she saved her father from insanity when dealing with some of the uglier characters in this story, but I'll always be grateful to her for banging on the door to my office and demanding that I replace the words on the screen with pictures from our latest adventure. Roxana, this book is dedicated to your grandfather, without whom I couldn't have written it; but it's for you, that someday the debates it's about may be justly forgotten.

Notes

Abbreviation used in the Notes:

BGCA   Billy Graham Center Archives

CHAPTER 1: The Confessions

"As much as I did": CQ Transcript Wire, "South Carolina Gov. Mark Sanford Holds a News Conference to Discuss Disappearance and Admits Affair," *Washington Post*, June 24, 2009, http://www.washingtonpost.com/wp-dyn/content/article/2009/06/24/AR2009062402099.html. But for the full effect, I recommend watching the video, many copies of which are available on YouTube.

the congressman's wife says: TPM Documents Collection, "Leisha Pickering's Alienation of Affection Complaint," July 14, 2009, http://www.talkingpointsmemo.com/documents/2009/07/leisha-pickerings-alienation-of-affection-complaint.php?page=1.

"singular goal": Richard Carver quoted in Lara Jakes Jordan, "Religious Group Helps Lawmakers with Rent," Associated Press, April 20, 2003.

Sen. Tom Coburn: Coburn told reporter Tom Hess of his C Street residence for a feature in James Dobson's fundamentalist *Citizen* magazine, "'There's No One I'm Afraid to Challenge,'" http://www.family.org/cforum/citizenmag/coverstory/a0012717.cfm. Coburn on abortion: "I favor the death penalty for abortionists." Richard Cohen, "Democrats, Abortion and 'Alfie,'" *Washington*

Post, December 14, 2004. Coburn's efforts in the Middle East with the Family are discussed in chapter 3.

Sen. Jim Inhofe: "The house also serves as a venue for business—Sen. James Inhofe (R-Okla.), for example, hosts a quarterly lunch with African ambassadors at C Street to discuss foreign policy issues. 'It's a great place,' Inhofe said. Inhofe said he is undeterred by the negative news surrounding the affairs of the three members with ties to the house and will continue hosting his lunches at C Street." Jessica Brady and Jackie Kucinich, "Intrigue Grows over C Street," *Roll Call*, July 20, 2009. That same week in 2009, Inhofe won a coveted seat on the Senate Foreign Relations Committee. As for climate change, Inhofe argues that global warming is "the second-largest hoax ever played on the American people, after the separation of church and state." Charles P. Pierce, "In Praise of Oklahoma," *American Prospect*, February 23, 2005, http://www.prospect.org/cs/articles?articleId=9236. Inhofe's extensive travel for the Family is discussed in chapter 3.

Sen. Jim DeMint: Jordan, "Religious Group Helps Lawmakers with Rent." On God and government: "Government is not our salvation, and in fact more and more people see government as the problem, and so I think some have been drawn in over the years to a dependency relationship with government, and as the Bible says you can't have two masters." The Brody File Blog, CBN, April 21, 2010, http://blogs.cbn.com/thebrodyfile/archive/2010/04/21/senator-demint-to-brody-file-tea-party-movement-will-bring.aspx. DeMint's *Saving Freedom: We Can Stop America's Slide into Socialism* (Nashville: Fidelis, 2009) is as close to a contemporary primer as one will find on the fundamentalist paradox of libertarian authoritarianism, opposition to "big government" paired with a determination to use government to enforce a particular religious perspective; DeMint's efforts, along with those of fellow C Streeter Sen. Coburn, on behalf of a 2009 coup that overthrew the democratically elected government of Honduras shed light on his concept of "freedom."

Sen. Sam Brownback: Author's interview with Sam Brownback. Pages 260–72 of my last book, *The Family* (Harper, 2008), explore Brownback's deep relationship with the Family based on extensive interviews with Brownback and his associates. The alignment between his political career and the Family is nearly complete, dating back to his college days, when he first lived in a C Street–like house for young men while interning for his predecessor, Sen. Bob Dole.

Sen. John Thune: Emily Belz, "On the House," *World,* November 21, 2009. In an interview with ChristianityToday.com, Thune said he attended not one but two weekly Bible studies for congressmen, those of Christian Embassy, a Family-related initiative I discuss later, and C Street. "Q. Is this something you do behind closed doors, a 'members only' sort of thing? A. It can be. I mean the Bible studies are, yes, sort of, members only." Collin Hansen, "Q&A: John Thune," ChristianityToday.com, February 10, 2005, http://www.christianitytoday.com/ct/2005/februaryweb-only/42.0a.html.

Sen. Chuck Grassley: On pp. 280–82 of *The Family* I discuss Grassley's participation in the Family's disastrous attempt to trade access to American power for the submission of Somali dictator Siad Barre to Christ, documented in folders 18–24, box 254, collection 459, BGCA. Grassley's work with the organization in Uganda was more recently confirmed in an interview with Bob Hunter, designated by the Family as a spokesman for its controversial relationship with that East African nation. On December 11, 2009, a spokesman for Grassley told MSNBC's *The Rachel Maddow Show* that the senator had never had any relationship at all with the organization.

Sen. Mike Enzi: Author's interviews with Sam Brownback and Mark Pryor. "Youth Corps Update November 2004" (Jen Thomson, December 20, 2004), a document provided to me by a whistleblower in the organization, notes that Enzi and a Family employee traveled in South Africa, where they visited several of the Family's associates.

Rep. Frank Wolf: Author's interview with Wolf. Wolf's extensive travel for the Family is discussed in chapter 3.

Rep. Zach Wamp: " 'C Street is one of the most misinterpreted, miscommunicated things I've ever seen in my life,' Wamp said. 'My experience is nothing like all these things I've read. I hated that two people, out of the 17 that lived in the house, have raised all this suspicion.' " Liz Engel, "Zach Wamp Speaks on Health Care, Education in Stop Here," *Cookville (TN) Herald Citizen,* September 3, 2009. Earlier that year, Wamp, who moved into the house in 1997, declined to comment on discussions that had been held about

Sen. Ensign's affair and cover-up: "I don't want to go into details about what he said or I said or they said. That's almost like this Michael Jackson ordeal." Michael Collins, "Wamp, Housemates Linked to Scandals," *Knoxville News Sentinel,* July 10, 2009. In an interview with a Christian student journalist, Wamp seemed to suggest scripture as a license to dispense with public accountability altogether: "The principle of [the Fellowship] is based on 1 John 1:7. 'If we walk in the light with each other, you know, He will cleanse us from our sin, and we will have fellowship with one another.'" Sara Horn, "Faith & Power," *Unionite,* fall 2000, http://www.uu.edu/Unionite/fall00/faithandpower.html.

Rep. Joe Pitts: Pitts was a frequent guest at the Family's Arlington head-quarters when I lived across the road at its house for younger men in 2002, an experience I recount in the first chapter of *The Family.* He is well represented in the Family's archives, going back thirty-four years, when he received a "Briefing Introductory Letter," dated March 5, 1976, folder 1, box 362, collection 459, BGCA. In 2009, Pitts used semantics to separate himself from the scandal-plagued C Street House: "I am not involved in any way.... I have not lived there." Louis Jacobson, "Divisive Amendment to Health Care Bill Caps Pitts' Anti-Abortion Career," PoliticsPA, December 14, 2009, http://www.politicspa.com/divisive-amendment-to-health-care-bill-caps-pitts%E2%80%99-anti-abortion-career/3654/. Pitts's statement is technically correct, but money has flowed both ways between the congressman and the Family, which has paid for his overseas travel (see chapter 3) and received donations from him in turn. In a video interview with fundamentalist activist Rev. Rob Schenck, Pitts describes the movement as "a leadership led by God.... First of all, pray for kings." Rob Schenck, "Rob Speaks with Congressman Joe Pitts," Faith and Action, February 5, 2009, http://www.faithandaction.org/2009/02/05/rob-speaks-with-congressman-joe-pitts/.

Rep. Mike McIntyre: Author's interview with Sam McCullough of C Street's sister ministry, Christian Embassy. McIntyre later acknowledged his attendance at a weekly C Street meeting: "McIntyre Has Ties to Christian Group," *News & Observer,* July 28, 2009, http://projects.newsobserver.com/under_the_dome/mcintyre_has_ties_to_secretive_christian_group.

Rep. Heath Shuler: Emily Belz, "The C Street House," *World,* June 26, 2009, http://www.worldmag.com/webextra/15584.

Rep. Bart Stupak: "I don't know what you're talking about, [the] Family and all this other stuff," Stupak told Michigan reporters, when asked about his residence in the house following the 2009 scandals. Ed Brayton, "Stupak Denies Knowledge of Connections to Mysterious 'C Street' House He Lives In," *Michigan Messenger,* July 23, 2009, http://michiganmessenger.com/23484/stupak-denies-knowledge-of-connections-to-mysterious-c-street-house.

"God's leadership": In a letter to Pitts dated September 2, 1980, in which Family organizer Fred Heyn pledged to support Pitts's anti-abortion activism, Heyn wrote, "We pray for you and God's leadership in the days ahead as you work on it," folder 8, box 386, collection 459, BGCA.

"Christ ministered to a few": From a response to my March 2003 *Harper's* article, "Jesus Plus Nothing," posted on Free Republic by "Blessed," April 29, 2003: "Having been loosly [*sic*] involved with some of the Fellowship for over 10 years I can tell you this is a hit piece.... The basic message of this group is Christ ministered to a few and did not set out to minister to large throngs of people. He just invited a few people to follow him and be in a relationship. What the lost world fails to realize is that true Christians don't have plans for Theocracies or Armagedan [*sic*], we believe in a soveriegn [*sic*] God that controls it all," http://209.157.64.200/focus/f-religion/902630/posts.

"tools": Author's interview with Bob Hunter.

registered as a church: A thorough description of C Street-as-church can be found in the complaint against C Street's status as a tax-exempt church filed with the Internal Revenue Service by Clergy VOICE, a group of pastors from six mainline Protestant denominations on March 29, 2010, available as a PDF download from The Wall of Separation, the blog of Americans United for Separation of Church and State: http://blog.au.org/2010/02/23/street-fight-ohio-clergy-seeks-end-of-tax-exemption-for-d-c-structure-owned-by-%E2%80%98the-family%E2%80%99/.

"I've seen pictures": I provided video of this sermon to NBC producers for an April 13, 2008, NBC *Nightly News* segment titled "The Fellowship."

"a thing called slavery": *The Ed Show,* MSNBC, June 23, 2009, http://www
.msnbc.msn.com/id/31525810/ns/msnbc_tv-the_ed_show/.

$450,000: Brian Naylor, "GOP Freshmen Weigh Medicare Reform
Against Re-Election," *Morning Edition,* NPR, September 25, 1995.

"presidential material": Donald Rothberg, "GOP Revolutionaries Run
into Reality," Associated Press, July 25, 1997.

"Mark Sanford literally likes to go his own way": Mark McKinnon, "Sanford
for President," *Daily Beast,* June 23, 2009, http://www.thedailybeast
.com/blogs-and-stories/2009-06-23/sanford-crazy-like-a-fox/.

a reporter for the Columbia State: Gina Smith, interview by research
assistant Paige Boncher.

"lay out that larger story": CQ Transcript Wire, "South Carolina Gov.
Mark Sanford Holds a News Conference to Discuss Disappearance and Admits Affair."

"spiritual weaponry": Cubby Culbertson, "Am I Truly a Christian?"
Cubby's Talks, http://www.ciu.edu/seminary/resources/articles/
ztemp/am_i_a_christian.php.

"Never underestimate the influence": Cubby Culbertson, "Is the Old Testament Law Still Valid?" *Cubby's Talks,* http://www.ciu.edu/
resources/displaypdf.php?359. Yes and no, is Cubby's answer. Feel
free to eat pork and wear wool with linen, he argues; what matters
is obedience not to rules but to the mystically perceived word of
God, a subject on which he approaches fire and brimstone: "Lawlessness is Satan's vomit costumed to resemble Bathsheba's beauty.
Lawlessness is treasonous unholiness seducing man to dine upon
a disordered love."

"The ostrich": Culbertson, "Am I Truly a Christian?"

"heart connection": Jenny Sanford, *Staying True* (New York: Ballantine,
2010), 187.

"We sort of don't talk": Lisa Getter, "Showing Faith in Discretion," *Los
Angeles Times,* September 27, 2002.

"The C Street residents have all agreed": Collins, "Wamp, Housemates
Linked to Scandals."

Not in 1952: Associated Press, "Wiley Trip Declared in U.S. Interest,"
Washington Post, May 21, 1952.

No questions at all: Andrew Kopkind, "The Power of Prayer," *New Republic,* March 6, 1965.

In 1975 Playboy: Robert Sherrill, "Elmer Gantry for President," *Playboy,* March 1975.

The New York Times *noted that President Ford:* Paul Wilkes, "Prayer: The Search for a Spiritual Life in Washington and Elsewhere: A Country on Its Knees?" *New York Times,* December 22, 1974. The other members of the group were Defense Secretary Melvin Laird and Republican congressmen John Rhodes of Arizona and Al Quie of Minnesota.

"almost an underground network": "The God Network in Washington," *Time,* August 26, 1974, http://www.time.com/time/magazine/article/0,9171,944968,00.html.

Dan Rather challenged: Charles W. Colson, *Born Again* (Grand Rapids, MI: Chosen, 2008), 179.

"A veritable underground": Ibid., 148.

"is only one-tenth": Nick Thimmesch, "Politicians and the Underground Prayer Movement," *Los Angeles Times,* January 13, 1974.

"But it's working precisely because it's private": Ronald Reagan, "Remarks at the Annual National Prayer Breakfast," January 31, 1985, http://www.reagan.utexas.edu/archives/speeches/1985/13185a.htm.

"Bible Beltway": Alessandra Stanley and Richard N. Ostling, "Inside the Bible Beltway," *Time,* February 6, 1989.

"vow of silence": Getter, "Showing Faith in Discretion."

"a secretive religious organization": Jordan, "Religious Group Helps Lawmakers with Rent."

He uses Hitler, his defenders declare: David Kuo quoted on NBC *Nightly News,* April 3, 2008.

the Washington Post *would have none of it:* Editorial, "Unfair Tactics," *Washington Post,* October 28, 2004. Michael Laris, "Wolf Deflects 'Extremist' Label Portrayed in Ad; Congressional Race Marked by Nasty Attacks," *Washington Post,* October 28, 2004.

"Hitler, Goebbels": Coe, quoted an NBC *Nightly News,* April 3, 2008.

"What I find interesting": Zachary Roth, "Sanford: King David Didn't Resign, So Why Should I?" *Talking Points Memo,* June 26, 2009, http://tpmmuckraker.talkingpointsmemo.com/2009/06/sanford_king_david_didnt_resign_so_i_wont_either.php.

"God appoints": John C. Maxwell, *The Maxwell Leadership Bible* (Nashville: Thomas Nelson, 2008), 1360.

"substitution": Bruce Alger, "God in Our Government," August 30, 1962, box 373, collection 459, BGCA.

"tan lines": "Exclusive: Read E-mails Between Sanford, Woman," *Columbia (SC) State,* June 25, 2009, http://www.thestate.com/2009/06/25/839350/exclusive-read-e-mails-between.html.

Coe lessons seem like gentle musing: To men, that is. Some former female students of the younger Coe's teachings recall a harsher tone. Kate Phillips, an alumna of Potomac Point—a house for young women across from the Cedars—cites an unsettling coed counseling session in which Coe warned the young men from getting involved with women who had been abused, on the premise that they would want more of the same. Author's interview with Kate Phillips.

Modern Viking: My account of Abram's early work with what would become the Family is shaped by his own reminiscences in letters and notes for a biography, stored in collection 459, BGCA, and the two full-length English-language biographies (there is a third, by an evangelical admirer, in Norwegian) written about Abram: *Modern Viking: The Story of Abraham Vereide, Pioneer in Christian Leadership* (Grand Rapids, MI: Zondervan, 1961), written by a revivalist named Norman Grubb mainly for private distribution to Abram's followers; and *Abraham, Abraham,* by Abram's son, Warren Vereide, and Claudia Minden Weisz, a privately published book with no publication date included. I received my copy from a former member of the Family, Clifford Gosney.

New Order: Chuck Taylor, "Ralph B. Potts, Political Reformer, Attorney and Promoter of the Arts," *Seattle Times,* April 19, 1991.

"It is the age of minority control": Finding the Better Way, periodicals, collection 459, BGCA.

"the Better Way": Ibid.; Warren Throckmorton, "Doug Coe's Vision for the Fellowship," ChristianityToday.com, May 13, 2010, http://www.christianitytoday.com/ct/2010/mayweb-only/29–42.0.html.

"Hitler's leading banker": "Over Twenty Years of the Simon Wiesenthal Center," archived at http://www.kintera.org/site/pp.asp?c=fwLYKnN8LzH&b=242620. For more on the role of Abs and the Nazi regime (which he did not formally join), see Harold James, *The Nazi Dictatorship and the Deutsche Bank* (New York: Cambridge University Press, 2004). James is ambivalent on Abs, a powerful figure in Hitler's financial establishment whose commitment, however, seems to have been to money itself, not to the particulars of National Socialism ("Should it be the historian's role to condemn him for this?," 226)—an apt illustration of Doug Coe's maxim "We work with power where we can."

Worldwide Spiritual Offensive: Abraham Vereide to Ed Allen, February 11, 1955. Folder 30, box 200, collection 459, BGCA.

Haiti: Traveling on Fellowship behalf: *Christian Leadership,* December 1959, periodicals, collection 459, BGCA. "Capehart and Carlson Meet Duvalier; U.S. Senators Pledge Assistance to Haiti, *New Pittsburgh Courier,* December 5, 1959.

"One of the worst mass murders": R. E. Elson, *Suharto: A Political Biography* (New York: Cambridge University Press, 2002), 125.

"spiritual revolution": Abraham Vereide to Frank McLaughlin, February 14, 1968. Folder 1, box 168, collection 459, BGCA.

delegations of congressmen and oil executives: Sen B. Everett Jordan, "Personal and Confidential Memo" to members of Congress on Fellowship assets around the globe, April 1969, folder 2, box 363, collection 459, BGCA. Jordan to members of the U.S. Senate and House of Representatives involved with the presidential and congressional Prayer Breakfasts, October 1970. "Mr. Howard Hardesty, Executive Vice President of Continental Oil company, recently traveled to Indonesia where he met for a day with men in the leadership groups there. He also had dinner with President Suharto and Members of the Indonesian Cabinet. The sense of spiritual relationship which was formed caused Mr. Hardesty to comment, 'This is one of the greatest days of my life,'" folder 8, box 548, collection 459, BGCA.

"cells": National Committee for Christian Leadership Newsletter, April 1948, periodicals, collection 459, BGCA.

"work behind the scenes": Doug Coe to Dick Barram, July 1, 1962, folder 5, box 168, collection 459, BGCA.

"It is important to note": "ICL Budget, Fiscal Year 1965" notes that the group's relatively small budget "just serves to pave the way for men to give to many efforts for Christ in reaching leaders throughout the world," pointing to $320,000 in expenses covered by other funders as an example, folder 5, box 580, collection 459, BGCA.

"in all cases": Coe to Dick Barram, July 1, 1962.

"Men who are picked by God!": "Leadership Development Notice," August 5, 1966, folder 6, box 204, collection 459, BGCA.

"a great and thrilling experience": Doug Barram to Doug Coe, June 12, 1962, folder 5, box 168, collection 459, BGCA.

"The Fellowship...recognizes": Abraham Vereide, 1966, folder 2, box 563, collection 459, BGCA.

seventy nations: David Lawrence, "Prayer Breakfasts Are a Memorial," *Washington Star,* May 19, 1969.

"In this way we convert ourselves": Quoted in Clifton J. Robinson to Elgin Groseclose, December 1, 1972, folder 6, box 383, collection 459, BGCA.

"cannot afford": Letter to Abraham Vereide and Marian Aymar Johnson, October 15, 1950, folder 5, box 202, collection 459, BGCA.

"Though the background": Notes on 1966 reorganization document, folder 2, box 563, collection 459, BGCA.

"The purpose of the changes": Ibid.

"Christian Mafia": D. Michael Lindsay, "Is the National Prayer Breakfast Surrounded by a 'Christian Mafia'? Religious Publicity and Secrecy Within the Corridors of Power," *Journal of the American Academy of Religion* 74, no. 2 (June 2006): 390–419.

"religious work": Maxine Chesire, "'Tregaron': A Spiritual Home for Sen. Hughes?" *Washington Post*, April 27, 1974.

"We've asked the Lord": Ibid.

Harold McClure... donated the use of a private plane: Support for Tregaron: Harold McClure and Billy E. Loflin to Sen. Joe Tydings, November 2, 1973, no box number, collection 459, BGCA. Private plane: Sen. B. Everett Jordan memo to members of Congress involved in the Family, circa 1971, folder 2, box 362, collection 459, BGCA.

"Tregaron, if handled properly": "The Vision for Tregaron," October 1, 1973, folder 2, box 362, collection 459, BGCA.

"front men": Merwin Silverthorn, circa 1973, folder 2, box 362, collection 459, BGCA.

"infection of secularism": Rev. Richard Halverson, "Endorsement," July 18, 1994. Halverson, a longtime Family leader, wrote: "At a time when secularism has infected not only society but the church as well, the C. S. Lewis Institute is a strategic instrument in calling America back to the faith of our fathers," http://www.cslewisinstitute .org/about/endorsements/halverson.htm.

Potomac Point... $580,000: See http://www.arlingtonva.us/departments /realestate/reassessments/scripts/Inquiry.asp?action =view&lrsn=7673.

Tim Coe, meanwhile, sold his house... $107,000: The 2007 990 tax return form for the Wilberforce Foundation can be accessed, with free registration, at http://www2.guidestar.org/organizations/72 -0973244/wilberforce-foundation.aspx#.

Youth With a Mission: Zachary Roth, "C Street House No Longer Tax Exempt," *Talking Points Memo*, November 17, 2009, http://

tpmmuckraker.talkingpointsmemo.com/2009/11/c_street_house_no_longer_tax_exempt.php.

revoked 66 percent: Ibid.

Citizens for Responsibility and Ethics in Washington: Citizens for Responsibility and Ethics in Washington, "CREW Files Ethics Complaints Against C Street House Residents," April 1, 2010, http://www.citizensforethics.org/node/44583.

"It helps them out": Getter, "Showing Faith in Discretion."

Stupak... contributed $2,500: Jonathan Allen and Jake Sherman, "Bipartisanship, C Street Style," *Politico,* October 14, 2009, http://www.politico.com/news/stories/1009/28301.html.

"The fact that everyone": Emily Belz, "On the House."

"My roommate": Alex Isenstadt, "Will C Street Ties Sway Race?" *Politico,* October 23, 2009, http://www.politico.com/news/stories/1009/28644_Page2.html.

"I'm always third": Ben Daniel, "Dysfunction in the Fellowship Family," September 13, 2007, http://bendaniel.org/?p=110.

"The Fellowship comes first": Emily Belz, "Unmoved," *World,* December 19, 2009, http://www.worldmag.com/articles/16190.

"In order for God": Doug Coe to Michael Cassidy, October 7, 1976, folder 3, box 373, collection 459, BGCA.

CHAPTER 2: The Lovers

shepherd who led: Lynette Clemetson, "Meese's Influence Looms Large in Today's Judicial Wars," *New York Times,* August 17, 2005.

a note Abram wrote: No box number, collection 459, BGCA.

"Our prayer": A paraphrase of Psalm 72 in a 1970s Prayer Breakfast program, folder 7, box 365, collection 459, BGCA.

"We try to be nearly invisible": Curt Suplee, "The Power and the Glory in the New Senate; A Growing Congregation of Born Again Believers," *Washington Post,* December 20, 1981.

"an invisible Kingdom": Author's notes on Bible study session with Coe, 2002.

"I told Chip often": Interview with researcher Kiera Feldman.

"a good-looking boy": Author's interview.

"heaped with embarrassment": Joseph Crespino, *In Search of Another Country: Mississippi and the Conservative Counterrevolution* (Princeton, NJ: Princeton University Press, 2007), 103.

"heinous, reprehensible": Mary Jayne McKay, "Judge Pickering Denies Racism," *60 Minutes,* March 28, 2004, http://www.cbsnews.com/stories/2004/03/25/60minutes/main608667.shtml.

"drunken prank": Resolution of the Board of Directors, National Association of Criminal Defense Lawyers, May 1, 2004, http://www.criminaljustice.org/public.nsf/26cf10555dafce2b85256d97005c8fd0/b913a03ea518a88185256d97005c81c2?OpenDocument.

Sentence: Neil A. Lewis. "A Judge, a Renomination, and a Cross-Burning Case That Won't End," *New York Times,* May 28, 2003.

"Pickering has a prewar mentality": Author's interview with Scott Horton.

"our Southern way of life": Resolution of the Board of Directors, National Association of Criminal Defense Lawyers.

"He's a glowing example": Interview with Feldman.

"I don't support Chip Pickering": David Rogers and Bruce Ingersoll, "Two GOP Insurgents for House Seats in the South Cash In on Their Ties to Patrons in Washington," *Wall Street Journal,* November 1, 1996.

"pornographic-friendly": Ana Radelat, "Federal Judges Rule Pickering's Anti-Porn Law Unconstitutional," Gannett News Service, May 31, 2002.

The "M.O.": D. Michael Lindsay, "Is the National Prayer Breakfast Surrounded by a 'Christian Mafia'? Religious Publicity and Secrecy Within the Corridors of Power," *Journal of the American Academy of Religion* 74, no. 2 (June 2006): 390–419.

"male model": Melinda Hennenberger, "Putting a Christian Stamp on Congress," *New York Times,* November 6, 1997.

"There are too many people": Ibid.

According to the lawsuit Leisha would file: Leisha Jane Pickering v. Elizabeth Creekmore Byrd and John and Jane Does 1–7, available at "Leisha Pickering's Alienation of Affection Complaint," *TPM* Document Collection, http://www.talkingpointsmemo.com/documents/2009/07/leisha-pickerings-alienation-of-affection-complaint.php?page=1.

According to Leisha: Ibid.

Leisha says: Ibid.

"I can't think of a single instance": Author's interview.

"When they say 'Christ' ": Author's interview.

"I pressed my face": Jenny Sanford, *Staying True* (New York: Ballantine, 2010), 20.

"I was noticing": Ibid., 22.

"If I had to name the top ten sins": Interview by Boncher.

"I thought he was asexual": Will Folks, interview by Boncher.

"the pride I felt": Jenny Sanford, *Staying True,* 8–9.

"The tough decisions": Ibid., 40–41.

"But I never thought": Ibid., 15.

His Democratic opponent "implied": Ibid., 74.

"more libertarian than republican": Chip Felkel, interview by Boncher.

"Mark was an ideologue": Jenny Sanford, 55.

"You know what he was?": Author's interview.

"He's an old Southern blueblood": Interview by Boncher.

"the human needs we have for grace": Mark Sanford, "Atlas Hugged," *Newsweek,* October 22, 2009.

"reconciliation": The Family's concept of reconciliation as a form of compromise on the terms of the stronger party was pervasive in the early work of Family founder Abram Vereide with labor unions and management, but as a buzzword it first became prominent in a 1960 Bible study of 2 Corinthians 5:20–21, published in the January issue of *Christian Leadership,* the movement's newsletter at the time: "Now then we are ambassadors for Christ, as though God did beseech you by us: we pray you in Christ's stead, be ye reconciled to God," periodicals, collection 459, BGCA.

By the 1970s, the term "reconciliation" would come to define the movement's mission, as stated in a January 19, 1971, letter from Sen. B. Everett Jordan to President Nixon, in which Jordan describes the "men in positions of responsibility in many nations on every continent [*sic*]" as receiving indoctrination in the Family's concept of Christ and "becoming the catalyst necessary for reconciliation among men," folder 1, box 355, collection 459, BGCA.

A newsletter dated September 9, 1975, declares that Sen. Harold Hughes and Chuck Colson had held prayer sessions with federal prison officials and had concluded that prison must be "Christ-centered if reconciliation is to occur"—the beginning of what would become Colson's blueprint for federal faith-based initiatives, folder 1, box 362, collection 459, BGCA.

Notes for a report on poverty prepared for the movement's leadership ("Justice for All," July 28, 1982) argue that poverty is the result of disobedience and that it should be "reconciled" rather than eradicated, assimilated rather than opposed, folder 5, box 449, collection 459, BGCA. For a more contemporary discussion of reconciliation and conservative evangelicalism, see chapter 3.

"Self-interest by proxy": Will Wilkinson, "Jeff Sharlet on Free Will," Will Wilkinson.net, May 19, 2008, http://www.willwilkinson.net/flybottle/2008/05/19/jeff-sharlet-on-free-will/.

"I feel absolutely committed": Ralph Z. Hallow, "Sanford, Invoking Palin, Vows to Fight On," *Washington Times,* September 2, 2009.

"He'd be talking to a crowd of schoolteachers": Interview by Boncher.

"Something he'd learned": Jenny Sanford, 97.

"governed like a bug lamp": Interview by Boncher.

"Sanford did what no one thought was possible": Interview by Boncher.

"The Sanfords understood": Author's interview.

"our strategy . . . was to pay lip service": Interview by Boncher.

"Mark's balance": Jenny Sanford, 155.

"the world Mark lived in": Ibid., 98.

Galatians 5:22: Ibid., 27, 137. *Matthew 5:16:* 27. *Psalm 127:* 50. *Psalm 139:* 211.

"My heart has been pained": Ibid., 211.

"A member of the group": Ibid., 99.

"place outside of time": Ibid., 12.

"Don't know why you think you bore me": Maria Belen Chapur to Mark Sanford, "Exclusive: Read E-mails Between Sanford, Woman," *Columbia (SC) State,* June 25, 2009, http://www.thestate.com/2009/06/25/839350/exclusive-read-e-mails-between.html.

"Though I have started every day by 6": Mark Sanford to Maria Belen Chapur, July 8, 2008, "Exclusive: Read E-mails Between Sanford, Woman," *Columbia (SC) State,* June 25, 2009, http://www.thestate.com/2009/06/25/839350/exclusive-read-e-mails-between.html.

"I hate to see anybody I love fall": Allen G. Breed, "Spiritual Adviser: 'Darkness' Gripped Sanford," Associated Press, June 29, 2009, on USAToday.com, July 2, 2009, http://www.usatoday.com/news/religion/2009-07-02-culbertson-sanford_N.htm.

"the biggest self of self is indeed self": CQ Transcript Wire, "South Carolina Gov. Mark Sanford Holds a News Conference to Discuss Disappearance and Admits Affair," *Washington Post,* June 24, 2009,

http://www.washingtonpost.com/wp-dyn/content/
article/2009/06/24/AR2009062402099.html.

"The idea of the power": Author's interview.

traces "servant leader" back to its origins: Bethany Moreton, *To Serve God and Wal-Mart: The Making of Christian Free Enterprise* (Cambridge, MA: Harvard University Press, 2009), 107.

"submerge": Notes on 1966 reorganization document, folder 2, box 563, collection 459, BGCA.

"Putting aside your ego": Moreton, *To Serve God and Wal-Mart,* 110.

"the drum major instinct": James M. Washington, ed., *A Testament of Hope: The Essential Writings and Speeches of Martin Luther King Jr.* (San Francisco: HarperSanFrancisco, 1991), 259.

"soul surgery": "The History of Fellowship House," undated brochure in collection 459, BGCA. Abram borrowed the term and the concept from another evangelist with a mission to the elite, Frank Buchman, to whom the most concise and readily available introduction maybe found in "Soul Surgeon," a profile by Alva Johnson in the April 23, 1932, *New Yorker.*

"They're into living with what is": Author's interview.

"pretty intense": Breed, " 'Darkness' Gripped Sanford."

"the key": Jenny Sanford, 179.

"Sweetest": Mark Sanford to Maria Belen Chapur, July 10, 2008, "Exclusive: Read-E-mails Between Sanford, Woman."

"He had always been so good": Jenny Sanford, 175.

"His willingness": Ibid., 177.

"handful": "S.C. Governor 'Crossed Lines' with More Women," Associated Press, posted at MSNBC.com, July 1, 2009, http://www.msnbc.msn.com/id/31664990/ns/politics-more_politics/.

"Jack understood men": Jenny Sanford, 184–85.

$3.5 million beach house: Alberto Armendariz, "The Unfaithful Governor Under Pressure," *La Nacion,* June 26, 2009.

" 'Hypocrite!' they didn't quite thunder": JoAnn Wypijewski, "Triangles," *The Nation,* July 20, 2009.

"I can only imagine": Jenny Sanford, 207.

"heart connection": Ibid., 187.

"We were asked to go over and stay with the Ensigns": Transcript of Jon Ralston's interview with Doug Hampton, *Las Vegas Sun,* July 8, 2009, http://www.lasvegassun.com/news/2009/jul/08/transcript-jon-ralstons-interview-doug-hampton/.

$160,000: J. Patrick Coolican and Lisa Mascaro, "Ensign's Mistress Saw Salary Double, Son Was Paid $5,400," *Las Vegas Sun,* June 19, 2009.

"Walk alongside": Cynthia McFadden, Melinda Arons, and Lauren Sher, "Exclusive: Doug Hampton Speaks Out on Sen. Ensign's Affair with His Wife," *Nightline,* November 23, 2009, http://abc-news.go.com/Nightline/doug-hampton-speaks-sen-john-ensigns-affair-ethic/story?id=9140788.

"I chose to bring in some really close friends": Transcript of Jon Ralston's interview.

$8.5 million: Daniel J. Albregts, attorney for Doug Hampton, to Sen. Tom Coburn, May 21, 2009, reproduced in "Records Show Senator's Tangled History with Aides," *New York Times,* October 1, 2009, http://documents.nytimes.com/in-wake-of-affair-senator-ensign-may-have-violated-an-ethics-law-2?ref=politics#p=33.

"God never intended for us to do this": Sen. John Ensign to Cindy Hampton, February 2008," reproduced in "Records Show Senator's Tangled History with Aides."

"[They] think the consequences don't apply": McFadden, Arons, and Sher, "Doug Hampton Speaks Out."

told his friend Steve Wark: Author's interview.

CHAPTER 3: The Chosen

"the Prayboy Mansion": Ronald A. Lindsay, "What Constitutes a Church?" CenterForInquiry.net, February 25, 2010, http://www.centerforinquiry.net/blogs/entry/what_constitutes_a_church/.

"David from C Street": Sue Rochman, "Call Me Madam," *Advocate,* undated, http://www.advocate.com/article.aspx?id=22495.

"Senator X": Garry Trudeau, *Doonesbury,* August 3–12, 2009.

"supportive ministry . . . shelter if needed": 990 tax forms for the Fellowship Foundation and the Wilberforce Foundation, as well as for most of the other nonprofit organizations discussed in this chapter, may be viewed, with free registration, at http://www2.guidestar.org/.

"benevolent subversion": Richard Halverson to Clifton J. Robinson, May 22, 1963, folder 2, box 232, collection 459, BGCA.

"Yeast in the capital": John G. Turner, "Selling Jesus to Modern America: Campus Crusade for Christ, Evangelical Culture, and Conservative Politics," PhD diss., University of Notre Dame, 2005, 313.

"There are 435 congressional districts": John G. Turner, *Bill Bright and Cam-*

pus Crusade for Christ: the Renewal of Evangelicalism in Postwar America (Chapel Hill: University of North Carolina Press, 2008), 161.

"Income-redistributing": Ibid., 163.

"A clear testimony": "Arizona Shootout," *Time,* September 20, 1976.

In 2006, I reported: Jeff Sharlet, "Through a Glass, Darkly," *Harper's,* December 2006.

inspector general's report: Report H06L102270308, "Alleged Misconduct By DoD Officials Concerning Christian Embassy," United States Department of Defense, July 20, 2007, http://www.dodig.mil/fo/Foia/ERR/Xtian_Embassy_072707.pdf.

"Even a cursory look": Author's interview.

in 1987, Christian Embassy's Flag Officer Fellowship had been cofounded... Kicklighter: Anne C. Loveland, *American Evangelicals and the U.S. Military, 1942–1993* (Baton Rouge: Louisiana State University Press, 1996), 207. Writes Loveland: "A final component of the Christian Embassy ministry to the Pentagon was the Flag Officer Fellowship, founded in March, 1987, when Lieutenant General Claude Kicklighter and Major General Howard Graves asked [Christian Embassy Military Ministry Director Ron] Soderquist to help coordinate such a group. Beginning with about ten members, the fellowship met every Thursday morning from 6:15 to 7:15.... By the early 1990s the Flag Officer Fellowship had expanded to about forty members."

several trips funded by the International Foundation: Records for congressional travel sponsored by the International Foundation are available at http://www.legistorm.com/trip/list/by/sponsor/id/6999/name/International_Foundation.html.

"Two hundred national and international world leaders": "Youth Corps Vision," a document I copied during my first encounter with the Family, reported on in Jeff Sharlet, "Jesus Plus Nothing," *Harper's,* March 2003.

met with the president of Paraguay: Records for congressional travel sponsored by Christian Embassy are available at http://www.legistorm.com/trip/list/by/sponsor/id/5897/name/Christian_Embassy.html.

The Ambassadors came into being: See 990 tax forms for Ambassadors of Reconciliation at http://www2.guidestar.org/.

William Aramony: See "Charity Leader Had Warning on Misconduct," *New York Times,* March 15, 1995, and Michael Duffy, "Resignation Charity Begins at Home," *Time,* June 24, 2001.

$7,612: Records for congressional travel sponsored by the Ambassa-
dors of Reconciliation Foundation are available at http://www
.legistorm.com/trip/list/by/sponsor/id/5064/name/Ambassa-
dors_of_Reconciliation_Foundation.html.

"part of the U.S. Congress Leadership Breakfast Group": Zarook Marikkar's
description of Sri Lanka's Parliamentary Leadership Group is
available at http://www.grassroots.lk/members.htm. (Accessed
June 1, 2009.)

Beginning in 2004, the first year Marikkar led: "National Day Celebrations
in Washington, DC, Represent Ethnic and Religious Harmony,"
Sri Lanka Embassy in the United States, circa February 2004,
http://www.slembassyusa.org/press_releases/winter_2003/
national_day_cele_04_20feb04.html. Other members of the delegation included Sri Lankan Supreme Court Justice Shiranee
Thilakawardana, Hon. Susil Premajayantha, member of Parliament, and Harim Peiris, the president's spokesman.

the money flowed: For U.S. foreign assistance (both military and otherwise)
to Sri Lanka in 2000–2008, see table 2. Direct U.S. Assistance to
Sri Lanka, FY2000–FY2008, in a 2009 congressional report titled "Sri
Lanka: Background and U.S. Relations," available at http://fpc
.state.gov/documents/organization/138746.pdf. The figure of
about $10 million in U.S. military aid to Sri Lanka in 2000–2003 is a
compiled number. In making this compilation, I used the categories
of financing under the rubric of military aid as defined by the Fed-
eration of American Scientists (see http://www.fas.org/asmp/pro
files/aid/aidindex.htm). As pertaining to Sri Lanka's military aid in
2000–2003, I tallied these categories of funding: International Military Education and Training (IMET); Non-Proliferation; Anti-
terrorism; Demining, and Related Programs (NADR); and
Economic Support Fund (ESF). Additionally, in 2006 Sri Lanka
began receiving military aid from the Defense Department— $10.8
million that year. See table 2. Section 1206 Funding: FY2006–FY2009
Allocations, in a 2010 congressional report titled "Security Assistance Reform: 'Section 1206' Background and Issues for Congress,"
available at http://fpc.state.gov/documents/organization/138746
.pdf. A description of the Foreign Military Financing program, an
initiative that stipulates that recipients use the funds to purchase
American weapons and training, is available at http://www.dsca
.mil/home/foreign_military_financing%20_program.htm.

Jeff Sessions ... Mike Pence: "3 Ministers, Top Officials Attend 2008 US Congress National Prayer Breakfast," *Bottom Line,* March 12, 2008, http://www.thebottomline.lk/2008/03/12/B35.htm. Marikkar's delegation was even more power-packed this time, including officials from the ministries of foreign affairs, media and information, and education.

"Intentionally and repeatedly ... humanitarian operations": "War Crimes in Sri Lanka: Asia Report No. 91," International Crisis Group, May 17, 2010. The full report can be downloaded at http://www.crisis group.org/en/publication-type/media-releases/2010/asia/war -crimes-in-sri-lanka.aspx.

"force, fraud, or allurement": "U.S. Congress Pressures Sri Lanka on Anti-Conversion Law," The Becket Fund for Religious Liberty, February 5, 2009, http://www.becketfund.org/index.php/article/946 .html. The Becket Fund tends to take conservative positions on issues, in keeping with the conservative wings of Roman Catholicism and evangelicalism, decrying "exaggerated concern for 'separation of church and state.'"

"universal inevitable": Abraham Vereide to the board of the International Council for Christian Leadership, August 1964, folder 2, box 362, collection 459, BGCA.

"a small band": Tom Coburn, *Breach of Trust: How Washington Turns Outsiders into Insiders* (Nashville: WND Books, 2003), 214.

Psalm 15: Tom Hess, "There's No One I'm Afraid to Challenge," http:// www.family.org/cforum/citizenmag/coverstory/a0012717.cfm.

"attractive young congressional staffers": Ibid.

"greatest threat": "Transcript for November 6," *Meet the Press,* November 6, 2005, http://www.msnbc.msn.com/id/9898884/.

"natural battleground": Misbah Ahdab, interview by Feldman.

$6,500: Records for congressional travel sponsored by the International Foundation are available at http://www.legistorm.com/trip/list/ by/sponsor/id/6999/name/International_Foundation.html.

"Coburn could not have demonstrated": John Esposito, interview by Feldman.

$410 million: Donna Miles, "Gates, Lebanese Defense Minister Explore Expanding Bilateral Relationship," Armed Forces Press Service, April 8, 2009, http://www.defense.gov/news/newsarticle.aspx ?id=53846.

traveling with Rep. Mike Doyle, Tim Coe: Author's interview with Toufic Agha, who supplied photographs.

"Jesus for the world": Paul Hellyer, *Light at the End of the Tunnel: A Survival Plan for the Human Species* (Bloomington, IL: AuthorHouse, 2010), 143. Hellyer, a former Canadian minister of defense, has traveled extensively with the Family.

"carrier" for an "infectious agent": Mark Siljander, *A Deadly Misunderstanding: A Congressman's Quest to Bridge the Muslim-Christian Divide* (New York: HarperOne, 2008), 207.

$11,000: Congressional travel records for Coburn's federally funded trip to Lebanon in 2009 are available at http://thomas.loc.gov/ cgi-bin/query/C?r111:./temp/~r111xqt8ki.

"reckless indifference": Peter Bouckaert and Nadim Houry, "Why They Died: Civilian Casualties in Lebanon During the 2006 War," Human Rights Watch, September 2007.

Fatfat told a colleague: Author's interview with Toufic Agha.

"I had to convince them": Rick Stouffer and Bobby Kerlik, "Carnegie Man Rebuilding Sports in Iraq," *Pittsburgh Tribune-Review,* January 9, 2006.

"dougcoeleb": Toufic Agha, interview by Feldman.

$200,000: U.S. Embassy in Beirut, "U.S. Ambassador Celebrates Department of State Student Scholarships," December 6, 2007, http://lebanon.usembassy.gov/latest_embassy_news/press -releases/pr120607/.

a set-aside arranged by Rep. Frank Wolf: Daniel Scandling, Wolf's press secretary, e-mail message to Feldman, May 20, 2010.

"The expression Trible used to say": Author's interview.

"kinship": Maury O'Connell, interview by Feldman.

"They wanted to know": Abir Mariam, interview by Feldman.

"Madam Doria": "Ahmed," interview by Feldman.

the Twitter feed of . . . Clyde Lear: Clyde Lear's Twitter feed can be found at http://www.twitter.com/clydelear. It is now a friends-only feed, but it was publicly available in April of 2009. At the time, Toufic Agha saved a copy and shared it with me.

Rami Majzoub . . . listed as the center's contact person: Agha provided me with copies of the DCL's 2008 USAID application, which he said was denied. He said DCL staff told him that the 2007 application had been approved, however, and that funds from the grant were used to purchase, among other items, the Jeep Montero in which Fatfat ferried Americans back and forth to the land he hoped to develop. A spokeswoman for USAID, on the other hand, denies any funding going to DCL—or having any records of their applications, despite the apparent evidence.

"Reconciliation": The PowerPoint presentation is available at http:// www.bridgestocommonground.org/tools.html.

"operating under the name": The most recent 990 tax form on file, that of 2008, identifies the organization as "Bridges to Common Ground (formerly International Peace Organization)," headquartered in the law offices of William Aramony, but the organization's partially completed website muddies the question: http://www .bridgestocommonground.org/about.html.

an ideologue so zealous…prayer in schools: "True Believer," *Time,* May 4, 1981.

boldest voice: Douglas L. Koopman, *Hostile Takeover: The House Republican Party, 1980–1995* (Lanham, MD: Rowman & Littlefield), 104.

seeking a God-fearing woman: "W/M Congressman Seeks Wife," *Mother Jones,* December 1981.

His greatest success: R. Jeffrey Smith, "Siljander Pleads Guilty in Islamic American Relief Agency Lobbying Case," *Washington Post,* July 8, 2010.

"break the back of Satan": Sara Diamond, *Spiritual Warfare: The Politics of the Christian Right* (Cambridge, MA: South End Press, 1989), 71.

Global Strategies Inc.: While Global Strategies has indeed served an impressive list of clients, its unique achievement may come under the heading "Innovations": "One of the first to innovate restaurant salad bars and nonsmoking sections in the 1970s." That would be when Siljander was in his twenties. See http://www.gsi .cc/services.html?id=9.

"list of references": Global Strategies Inc., http://www.gsi.cc/about .html?id=2.

"As the humiliating final days": Siljander, *A Deadly Misunderstanding,* 15.

"three visiting spirits": Ibid., 26.

"Love doesn't mean": First to Know, Trinity Broadcasting Network, October 26, 2009. This interview can be viewed, in two parts, at http:// www.youtube.com/watch?v=prLMft0lsow&feature=related.

Justice Department indicted: Case No. 07–00087–01/07-CR-W-NKL, *United States of America v. Islamic American Relief Agency (IARA), Mubarak Hamed, Ali Mohamed Bagegni, Ahmad Mustafa, Khalid al-Sudanee, Abdel Azim El-Siddig, and Mark Deli Siljander.*

"charitable donations": Ibid., 26.

the very term "convert": Siljander, *A Deadly Misunderstanding,* 32–33.

"They make every effort": Ibid., p. 216.

"Anything can happen": Monday Associates Meeting, January 23, 1995, Burnett Thompson presiding. Author's copy.

"Jesus... is mentioned": Siljander, *A Deadly Misunderstanding,* 40.

"Being an ex-congressman": Ibid., 35. "I often traveled as an 'emissary' of the bipartisan House Prayer Breakfast Group," Siljander writes, which may explain his claim, on his Global Strategies website, of extensive "semi-official" travel.

He met with leaders: Ibid., 49–57. Siljander writes that he traveled on the personal plane of Algerian president Abdelaziz Bouteflika to visit the Sahrawi people of Western Sahara, who've been fighting for independence from an aggressive and far more powerful Morocco for decades. Siljander explains that he's there to talk about Jesus in the Koran, and then says, "Look, I have a suggestion. Why don't you stop fighting the Moroccans?" (53).

In Beirut: Ibid., 204.

With Coe... al-Bashir: Ibid., 59–70. "I have also stayed in contact with al-Bashir himself," writes Siljander, "visiting with him numerous times since then, both in other locations around the world and in Khartoum" (68).

"He's my prayer partner": First to Know, October 6, 2009.

"They realize it got away": Mindy Belz, "Dead Ends in Darfur," *World,* November 25, 2006.

"If Jesus were to have adopted": Warnock's blog, Amicus Dei, is no longer online, but his comments, made in the context of a review of *The Family,* are excerpted on another Christian blog: "Evangelical Leader of 'The Family' More Frightening than Jim Jones of Peoples Temple," undated, http://mysteryworshipers.wordpress .com/2010/02/21/the-family-a-cult-more-deadly-than-christian -zionism-2/.

"I told the Colonel": Siljander, *A Deadly Misunderstanding,* 87. Siljander's adventures in Libya and Benin are chronicled in chapter 8, "My Apology," 83–98.

Benin's President Kérékou'... Global Strategies: Global Strategies "as an entity does not lobby, but after careful analysis of client requirements, refers client to appropriate professional lobbying team." The list of nations for whom it has "advised lobbying teams" includes Taiwan,

Nigeria, Cyprus, Bangladesh, South Korea, Republic of Congo, Benin, Eritrea, and Liberia, http://www.gsi.cc/services.html?id=3.

Kérékou' stole an election... Titan: "US Company Admits Benin Bribery," BBC News, March 2, 2005, http://news.bbc.co.uk/2/hi/business/4310331.stm.

Hamed admitted: Case No. 07–00087–02-W-NKL, *United States of America v. Mubarak Hamed,* plea agreement, June 25, 2010.

El-Siddig pled: Case No. 07–00087–06-W-NKL, *United States of America v. Abdel Azim El-Siddig,* plea agreement, July 9, 2010.

"spiritual Muslim": Siljander, *A Deadly Misunderstanding,* 180.

"I'm guilty of two things": Chris Casteel, "Tulsa Republican Claims a Senate Record for Visiting Continent; Inhofe's Trips to Africa Called 'A Jesus Thing,'" *Oklahoman,* December 21, 2008.

"I'm trying to get": Ibid.

"3 Gs": Linda Killian, *The Freshmen: What Happened to the Republican Revolution?* (Boulder, CO: Westview Press, 1998), xii.

"I'm really proud": "Verbatim," *Washington Post,* June 8, 2006.

"a Jesus thing": Casteel, "Tulsa Republican."

He credits the Family: Rev. Rob Schenck, "Senator Takes Love of Jesus to Africa," February 25, 2009, http://www.youtube.com/watch?v=89tb3rBDvoU.

"I assumed I was a Christian": "Senator Jim Inhofe: Flying High at 72," *Community Spirit,* July 2007.

"You can't help who you are": Bob Hunter, interview by Terry Gross, "A Different Perspective on 'The Family' and Uganda," *Fresh Air,* WHYY Philadelphia, National Public Radio, December 22, 2009.

"There was a moment": Siljander, *A Deadly Misunderstanding,* 92.

"Democracy advocates": Cece Modupé Fadopé, "Nigeria," Foreign Policy in Focus, January 1, 1997, http://www.fpif.org/reports/nigeria.

CHAPTER 4: The Kingdom

Anti-Homosexuality Bill: The text of the bill is available in a report titled *Uganda's Anti-Homosexuality Bill: The Great Divide,* compiled by the Ugandan Civil Society Coalition on Human Rights and Constitutional Law (Kampala, 2010, 2d ed.). Some opponents of homosexuality, however, in Uganda and in the United States, insist that the text as presented by human rights organizations is an inflammatory fake. A download of the September 25, 2009, edition of the bill printed in the *Uganda Gazette,* a legislative news service, is available on the blog of Warren Throckmorton, a self-described conservative evangelical scholar who is critical of the bill: "Uganda's Anti-Homosexuality Bill—Full Text with Commentary," December 18, 2009, http://wthrockmorton.com/2009/12/18/ugandas-anti-homosexuality-bill-full-text-with-commentary/.

Bahati, the secretary of the Family's Ugandan branch, calls his bill traditional: Author's interviews with Bahati. I first spoke with David Bahati when he called in to Voice of America's *Straight Talk Africa* (the title of which is misleading in this context; it's an excellent all-Africa politics program), on which I was a guest on January 13, 2010. Bahati wanted to dispute my assertion that the Family had "thrown him under the bus." I pledged to report his side of the story if he'd share it with me. I was able to win his trust by doing just that in some initial reporting for broadcast media. Bahati concluded that although I don't share his views on homosexuality—and, as he told me, would be arrested in Uganda for "promotion" of homosexuality under his proposed law—I was worth talking to because my previous reporting on the Family would allow me to understand the context of his position. I conducted three lengthy phone interviews before traveling to Uganda in April 2010 at Bahati's invitation, where I interviewed him extensively on three occasions. We subsequently spoke several times by phone.

Both the disease . . . : Author's interview with James Nsaba Buturo, minister of ethics and integrity. There are a number of valuable studies of African perceptions of homosexuality. Two that I found useful for their insights into the perspective expressed by Buturo are Marc Epprecht, *Heterosexual Africa?: The History of an Idea from the Age of Exploration to the Age of AIDS* (Athens: Ohio University Press, 2008), and Neville Hoad, *African Intimacies: Race, Homosexuality, and Globalization* (Minneapolis: University of Minnesota Press, 2007). Also helpful in understanding the status of sexuality issues in East Africa is Helen Epstein, *The Invisible Cure: Why We Are Losing the Fight Against AIDS in Africa* (New York: Farrar, Straus and Giroux, 2007). Also valuable, and available online, is Kapya Kaoma, *Globalizing the Culture Wars: U.S. Conservatives, African Churches, & Homophobia* (Political Research Associates, 2009), http://www.publiceye.org/publications/globalizing-the-culture-wars/. In "Ethnohomophobia," *Anglican Theological Review* 82, no. 3 (summer 2000): 551–63, Willis Jenkins explains the logic by which many Ugandan church leaders come to view homosexuality as a form of "cultural imperialism." Sylvia Tamale, dean of Law at Makerere University, provides helpful context in "Law, Sexuality, and Politics in Uganda: Challenges for Women's Human Rights NGOs," in *Human Rights NGOs in East Africa: Political and Normative Tensions*, edited by Makau Mutua (Philadelphia: University of Pennsylvania Press, 2009). "A persistent argument against homosexuality from politicians, religious leaders, scholars, and the media," writes Tamale, "is that homosexuality is 'un-African.'" And yet, she notes, anthropologists and historians have noted the practice of homosexuality in at least fifty-five precolonial African cultures. "In Uganda, for example, among the Langi of northern Uganda, *mudoko dako* 'males' were treated as women and could marry men. Homosexuality was acknowledged among the Iteso, Bahima, Banyoro, and Baganda.... Ironically, it is the dominant [and "un-African"] Judeo-Christian and Arabic religions that most African anti-homosexuality proponents rely on to buttress their attacks on the practice as a foreign import" (58).

"It's hard for me to kill": Author's interview. See also Jo Sadgrove, "'Keeping Up Appearances': Sex and Religion Amongst University Students in Uganda," *Journal of Religion in Africa* 37 (2007): 116–44. Sadgrove notes that, under the influence of religious movements, Uganda's once-successful anti-AIDS program, ABC—which stands for abstinence, be faithful, and condoms—has come to be interpreted as meaning "Abstinence the Best Choice" or "Abstinence, Be Faithful, Christ!'"

A Family leader takes credit: Author's interview with Bob Hunter.

Uganda . . . ranked 130th: Transparency International, *Corruption Perceptions Index 2009*, http://www.transparency.org/policy_research/surveys_indices/cpi/2009/cpi_2009_table.

"Corruption is not just an element": Andrew Mwenda, "Museveni's Dance with the Donors," Andrew Mwenda's Blog, March 2, 2010, http://andrewmwendasblog.blogspot.com/2010/03/musevenis-dance-with-donors.html. Mwenda is not just a blogger but also a founding editor of the *Independent*, Uganda's leading politics magazine. All too often Americans dismiss "corruption" as a natural way of life in developing nations such as Uganda without recognizing

the role played by the West in its perpetuation. "What is intrigu-ing is that this system has always been partly financed by donors," notes Mwenda. "Their apparent inability to either recognise what is happening, or, when they do, to do something about it should trouble every Ugandan. Donors are mostly western: they have a general belief in a couple of broad principles such as decentrali-sation of democracy and strengthening of institutions.

"However, many donors know that the system in Uganda manipulates these principles to produce a highly personalised and corruption-ridden system of rule. How come that even in the face of this, they remain silent? The answer to this vexing question lies in how donors often structure their relations with governments especially ones that have initially been reform-oriented.

"In Uganda's case, donors were anxious to produce a success story in an otherwise distressful African continent. Museveni's Uganda initially offered the promise of success. On the other hand, Museveni's success at building this vast neo-patrimonial sys-tem was also predicated upon his ability to retain access to large and systematic foreign aid inflows to the treasury.

"These factors led to the development of mutual dependence between donors and Museveni. Donors need Uganda to remain successful to show the fruits of their engagement; Museveni needs them for legitimacy and for money to service his patronage— until he gets oil." Quoted with author's permission.

the government holds a National Prayer Breakfast: Author's interviews with organizers David Bahati and James Nsaba Buturo.

Sen. Jim Inhofe, and former Attorney General John Ashcroft, and Pastor Rick Warren: Ibid.

"I'm no homophobic guy": quoted in John Cloud, "The Problem for Gays with Rick Warren—and Obama," *Time,* December 18, 2008, http://www.time.com/time/politics/article/0,8599, 1867664,00.html

equates homosexuality with incest: "Rick Warren Interview: On Gay Mar-riage and Divorce," Beliefnet, http://www.beliefnet.com/Video/ Beliefnet-Interviews/Rick-Warren/Rick-Warren-Interview-On-Gay-Marriage-And-Divorce.aspx

gay life had almost flourished in Kampala: I spoke to a number of mem-bers of the Uganda LGBT community who described this brief moment of political and personal possibilities. Especially helpful were interviews with activists Val Kalende and "Long Jones."

Victor Mukasa and Yvonne Oyoo v. Attorney General: For details on this case and Mukasa's personal story and activism, see "Trial by Fire," *New Internationalist,* May 2007; Juliet Victor Mukasa, "ILGA Panel at 2nd UNCHR Session," *World,* October 23, 2006, http://ilga.org/ilga/en/article/908; Victor Mukasa, "Victor Mukasa at the UN Speaking on Grave Human Rights Violations Against LGBT People," International Gay & Lesbian Human Rights Commission, December 12, 2009, http://www.iglhrc.org/cgi-bin/iowa/article/pressroom/multimediaarchives/1073.html; Katherine Roubos and Val Kalende, "Lesbians Want Protection," (Ugandan) *Saturday Monitor,* September 25, 2007.

"I can't say this in America": Kapya Kaoma quoted in Kathryn Joyce, "The Anti-Gay Highway," *Religion Dispatches,* November 8, 2009, http://www.religiondispatches.org/archive/politics/2046/.

"from the ashes of Nazi Germany": Scott Lively and Kevin Abrams, *The Pink Swastika: Homosexuality in the Nazi Party.* There are four editions of this book, with an unclear publishing history, but the first edition appeared in 1994, and the fourth, from which I've quoted (275), is available in its entirety as a free download at the anti-gay website Defend the Family, http://www.defendthefamily.com/pfrc/books/pinkswastika/.

"monster" to "super-macho": Jim Burroway, "BTB Videos: Scott Lively Delivers His 'Nuclear Bomb' to Uganda," *Box Turtle Bulletin,* January 6, 2010, http://www.boxturtlebulletin.com/2010/01/06/19081.

"in Africa," observes Rev. Kapya Kaoma: Kaoma, *Globalizing the Culture Wars,* 6.

at least $90,000: Warren Throckmorton, "Uganda's Anti-Homosexuality Bill: Prologue," WarrenThrockmorton.com, June 30, 2010. In a 2007 op-ed, Ssempa declared that his church had never received any PEPFAR funding, a point he has used to win nationalist support in Uganda and conservative evangelical support in the United States ("Homosexuality Is Against Our Culture," *New Vision,* September 4, 2007). But Throckmorton, a conservative evangelical scholar who has been at the forefront of the fight against the Anti-Homosexuality Bill, proved otherwise, beginning with a September 30, 2005, letter from Bruce Baltas, agreement officer for USAID, to Anita Smith, president and CEO of the Children's AIDS Fund, in which one of Ssempa's projects, Campus Alliance to Wipe Out AIDS, is identified as being funded, http:// wthrockmorton.com/wp-content/uploads/2010/06/Uganda PEPFARPrevention_Grant.pdf. The following year, an article sympathetic to Ssempa in a Christian conservative magazine identified a different 2004 grant of $40,000 (Mindy Belz, "Taking Pride in Purity," *World*, November 18, 2006). Finally, Throckmorton located a 2007 PEPFAR document (http://www.pepfar.gov/docu ments/organization/103943.pdf) identifying another $50,000 in funding; notable, too, is the fact that the documentation for this grant says that Ssempa's Campus Alliance is not a new grantee, raising the possibility of more funding yet to be discovered.

"You are my brother": Max Blumenthal, "Rick Warren's Africa Problem," *Daily Beast,* January 7, 2009, http://www.thedailybeast.com/blogs -and-stories/2009-01-07/the-truth-about-rick-warren-in-africa/ full/.

iPods. Also, laptops and cell phones: As absurd as Bahati's notion sounds, it reflects, through a distorted lens, a different reality documented by Sadgrove in " 'Keeping Up Appearances,' " in which she notes that many young Ugandan women, especially middle-class ones, engage in a process of "de-toothing" older and more affluent men, trading sex or simply companionship for gifts. "The most common gift at the outset is mobile phone credit" (123).

British import: Alok Gupta, "This Alien Legacy: The Origins of 'Sodomy' Laws in British Colonialism," Human Rights Watch, 2008.

five hundred thousand homosexuals: Joshua Mmali, "Uganda Fear over Gay Death-Penalty Plans," BBC News, December 22, 2009, http:// news.bbc.co.uk/2/hi/8412962.stm.

According to the Los Angeles Times: William Lobdell, "Ex-Worker Accusing TBN Pastor Says He Had Sex to Keep His Job," *Los Angeles Times,* September 22, 2004.

September 11, 2009: Maria Burnett, "A Media Minefield: Increased Threats to Freedom of Expression in Uganda," Human Rights Watch, 2010.

"I SODOMISED CATHOLIC PRIEST" : Red Pepper, June 16, 2009.

Pastor Tom brought them four gospels, a Ugandan reporter was told: Author's interview.

"I know of no one": Bob Hunter to Terry Gross, circa November 2009.

"the world's Christian capital": Unknown author to Abraham Vereide, December 25, 1945, folder 4, box 168, collection 459, BGCA.

the Family called in media allies: Cal Thomas: Author's interview with Bob Hunter.

one of Rick Warren's top PR men: Emily Belz, "Unmoved," *World,* December 19, 2009.

Tony Hall proposed: Author's interview with Hunter.

Coe held the line: Belz.

Doug Coe made a bet: I first heard this story from Coe himself in 2002, but it can also be found across the Internet in even more distorted versions that fail to acknowledge basic facts of Ugandan history, as if Africa were little more than a setting for a fable. Among them, there's "Doug Coe Testimony," http://www.skywriting.net/inspirational/messages/testimony.html; "A Story About Doug Coe, Founder of the Fellowship, and Moving Mountains," http://the oxfordchristian.blogspot.com/2010/04/story-about-doug-coe-founder-of.html; and, perhaps most egregious, http://www.epm.org/resources/2010/Feb/16/uganda-bet-and-prayer/, on Eternal Perspective Ministries, the website of author Randy Alcorn, where, on February 16, 2010, blogger Doug Nichols identified the heartwarming and almost totally false tale as an antidote to "troubles within the nation."

He submitted two memos: Bob Hunter, "A Trip to East Africa — Fall 1986" and "Re: Organizing the Invisible," circa 1986, folder 1, box 166, collection 459, BGCA.

Grassley was by then an old Family hand: "The people in Somalia are really looking forward to seeing you again," a Family organizer wrote Grassley, on May 23, 1984, planning a trip for the senator. "The main purpose here is fellowship with our friend [President] Siad Barre....Another important point would be meeting with President arap Moi of Kenya. This can be of great importance as far as relations to Ethiopia are concerned....Efforts of reconciliation have a very practical aspect in this part of the world and a very political as well [*sic*]," folder 21, box 254, collection 459, BGCA.

NPR's "Fresh Air": "The Secret Political Reach of 'The Family,'" November 24, 2009.

He attributes his changes of position: Warren Throckmorton, interview with Tony Hall. Hall's liberal reputation is based largely on his advocacy for the hungry, but that's problematic. In 2001, President Bush appointed Hall ambassador to the United Nations for food issues, a position he used on behalf of biotech giant Monsanto, urging the overthrow of African trade barriers to genetically modified products. An NGO called Food First criticizes Hall's work as "'poor washing'—an attempt to confer legitimacy and prevent debate over a policy by making the spurious claim that the poor will benefit from it." "Pretending to Help the Poor," Food First, December 9, 2003. http://www.foodfirst.org/media/display.phpid384.

"The Pentagon has the list": "Siad Barre's Somalia and the USA: Very Confidential," undated, folder 21, box 254, collection 459, BGCA. Decker is proud of the fact that he never uttered an unkind word about any of his friends, such as the late Mobutu of Zaire, for whom the term "kleptocrat" was invented, and Sudan's Omar al-Bashir, indicted by the International Criminal Court in 2010 for genocide ("hunger and rape are his weapons," said the prosecutor). But only Barre can claim to have murdered a country. He got his guns, but instead of fighting Cubans, he waged war on his own country, until he was driven out, refuge arranged with another Family friend, Kenyan dictator Daniel arap Moi. Wolfgang Kohrt, "God's Ambassador," *Atlantic Times,* April 2005, http://www.atlantic-times.com/archive_detail.php?recordID=171. Howard French, "Mobutu Sese Seko, 66, Longtime Dictator of Zaire," *New York Times,* September 8, 1997. Stephen Robinson, "Dictator Called to Account: Omar al-Bashir," *National,* February 5, 2010, http://www.thenational.ae/apps/pbcs.dll/article?AID=/20100206/WEEKENDER/702059799/1306.

Museveni let it languish: Andrew Rice, *The Teeth May Smile but the Heart Does Not Forget: Murder and Memory in Uganda* (New York: Metropolitan Books, 2009), 13.

Orombi wants the gays out: "In April 2009, Archbishop Henry Luke Orombi said, 'I am appalled to learn that the rumours we have heard for a long time about homosexual recruiting in our schools and amongst our youth are true. I am even more concerned that the practice is more widespread than we originally thought. It is the duty of the church and the government to be watchmen on the wall and to warn and protect our people from harmful and deceitful agendas.'" Rev. Canon Aaron Mwesigye, Provincial Secretary, Church of

Uganda, "The Church of Uganda and the 'Anti-Homosexuality Bill,'" November 6, 2009, available at Thinking Anglicans, http://www.thinkinganglicans.org.uk/archives/004049.html.

"It is in the interest": Author's interview.

CHAPTER 5: The War

Easter in Iraq: Author's interviews with Jeffery Humphrey and Specialist David Downing, another soldier present for the events described. Downing on "Jesus Killed Muhammad": "I seen something written on the side of the Bradley, I don't know what it said, me and my buddies was talking and joking around with the interpreter, and the interpreter said what it meant was 'Jesus killed Muhammad,' he was trying to piss off the insurgents a little more."

"Each time I go into combat": Author's interview.

"Rock, sir!": "Report of Americans United for Separation of Church and State on Religious Coercion and Endorsement of Religion at the United States Air Force Academy," reproduced as Appendix B of Michael L. Weinstein and Davin Seay, *With God on Our Side: One Man's War Against an Evangelical Coup in America's Military* (New York: Thomas Dunne Books, 2006), 222.

Red, White and Blue: Video available via the Military Religious Freedom Foundation, http://www.militaryreligiousfreedom.org/Media_video/carman/index.html.

seven hundred soldiers: Chuck Borough, Trip Around the Sun Blog, http://www.triparoundthesun.com/SunTrip54.htm. Borough amiably describes a Billy Graham revival, "Mission San Diego," on May 9, 2003, at which Van Antwerp said more than seven hundred soldiers in his division had been baptized while in Iraq. In Graham's *Decision* magazine, Bob Paulson, Amanda Knoke, and Brian Peterson write, "The second evening of the Mission had a military emphasis and featured the testimony of Maj. Gen. Robert L. Van Antwerp. Billy Graham announced that the evening's program would be broadcast on the American Forces Radio and Television Service, which reaches military servicemen and women in countries throughout the world as well as on ships at sea," July 1, 2003, http://www.billygraham.org/articlepage.asp?ArticleID=336.

was found by a Pentagon inspector general's report: Report H06L102270308,

"Alleged Misconduct by DOD Officials Concerning Christian Embassy," July 20, 2007.

"God's children": Author's interviews with five cadets, only one of whom, Steve Warner, felt comfortable putting his name to his words. That reluctance was the most disturbing part of their reports— that men and woman willing to put their lives on the line for their country were scared that they wouldn't get a chance to do so if they were known to be critical of religious coercion.

"draw your strength": Neela Banerjee, "Religion and Its Role Are in Dispute at the Service Academies," *New York Times,* June 25, 2008, http://www.nytimes.com/2008/06/25/us/25academies.html.

"ambassadors for Christ": Ret. Lt. Col. Ward Graham, of the air force, "On Alert," OCFUSA.org, the website of Officers' Christian Fellowship, http://www.ocfusa.org/articles/alert/.

fifteen thousand members: Command, a magazine of Officers' Christian Fellowship, July 2008, 3.

"government paid missionaries": A Campus Crusade promotional video in which air force officers are described thus can be seen at http://www.militaryreligiousfreedom.org/video/USAF.mov. Campus Crusade has since updated its promotional materials.

"It's a fucking clown show": Author's interview.

Taken as a whole: These statistics are based on Department of Defense records of "Religion of Active Duty Personnel (no Coast Guard)," September 30, 2008.

"I don't like 'religion'": Author's interview.

"How do we train our personnel": Lt. Col. Greg E. Metzgar, of the army, "Fighting the War on Spiritual Terrorism—Part Two." Accessed at OCFUSA.org in 2007, "Part Two" may now be viewed only at a cached Google page: http://webcache.googleusercontent.com/search?q=cache:JdXGrfBiKpIJ:www.ocfusa.org/articles/metzgar_spiritual_terrorism2.php+%22unconventional+spiritual+warfare+in+a+predominantly%22&cd=1&hl=en&ct=clnk&gl=us&client=firefox-a.

"claim and occupy territory": Retired Colonel Dick Kail, "Professional Perspectives for Senior Officers," Officers' Christian Fellowship, 1992, 3.

"adapt yourself to your husbands": Ibid., 7. Kail writes that this directive is taken from an "amplified" version of "Epheslans [*sic*]."

"abuse of your authority": Ibid., 9. Some "amplification" of my own: It's

worth noting that Kail is veering close to the line of constitutional authority here, since he's declaring that officers face a choice between "godly influence," according to their personal and sectarian perspective, and "the values of this darkening world"—that is, the rule of law and civilian authority in a nation defined by First Amendment freedom of religion.

OCF's official history: Robert W. Spoede, *More than Conquerors: A History of the Officers' Christian Fellowship of the U.S.A., 1943 to 1983* (OCF Books, 1993).

"ardent supporter": National Committee for Christian Leadership Newsletter, February 1948, periodicals, collection 459, BGCA.

"religious societies": "Joint Committee Exhibit No. 147, Part I of Pearl Harbor Investigation Conducted by Colonel Carter W. Clarke, Pursuant to Oral Instructions of the Chief of Staff, U. S. Army," September 20, 1944. The entire report to which this exhibit is attached has been posted online at http://www.ibiblio.org/pha/pha/clarke/clarke.html.

"mind programmed with God's Word": "General Harrison: A Man of 'The Word,'" Military Christian Fellowship (Canada), http://www.mcf-canada.ca/joomla/index.php?option=com_content&view=article&id=175%3Ageneral-harrison-a-man-of-the-word-&catid=67%3Amilitary-stories-of-faith&Itemid=53.

"wars and rumors of war": Anne C. Loveland, *American Evangelicals and the U.S. Military, 1942–1993* (Baton Rouge: Louisiana State University Press, 1996), 51. Loveland quotes Harrison writing in defense of the bombing of North Vietnam for *Christianity Today* in 1966, noting that he concluded with "a theme he had been sounding since the late 1950s: 'The whole problem of the war in Viet Nam is complicated by the sincere but erroneous idea that mankind can in some way bring peace to the world....Wars will continue until man's rebellion runs its full course, terminating in the wars of the great tribulation at the end of this age. Only the second coming of the Lord Jesus Christ, as so often foretold in the Bible, will end the rebellion and bring an age of peace and prosperity (Matt. 24; Isa. 2:1–5).'" The irony of Harrison's holy war rhetoric is that he justifies it in part with the promise of a future built around one of the great pacifist verses of scripture from Isaiah, "They shall beat their swords into plowshares."

"Christian realism": Ibid., 266.

"*spiritual battle of the highest magnitude*": Ret. Lt. General Bruce L. Fister of the air force, "October 2005 Minutes," OCF Council.

"*continually confronting*": Ret. Col. Don Martin of the army, "Combat Readiness: Finding the True Source," Officers' Christian Fellowship, undated at http://www.ocfusa.org/articles/source-combat-readiness/.

"*Mission Accomplished*": "Mission Accomplished: Bible Study: Nehemiah 1–6," Officers' Christian Fellowship, undated.

"*tax collectors (aka the Jewish mafia)*": "Chaplain: Journey to the Outer Limits," *Tropical Times*, March 6, 2008.

"*born again will burn*": Chaplain Capt. MeLinda Morton, "Memorandum for Ch Col Michael Whittington," July 30, 2004. Capt. Morton's report summarized the findings of "After Action Report: BCT II Chaplain Practicum Training: Special Program in Pastoral Care, with the Resources, Supervision and Selected Students of Yale Divinity School." Morton's memo, as well as a later version of the so-called Yale Report, can be downloaded at Brian McGrath Davis, "Air Force Academy Addresses 'Challenges to Pluralism,'" The Pluralism Project at Harvard University, http://pluralism.org/research/reports/davis/afareport.php. The Yale Practicum, led by Dr. Kristen Leslie, was not initially a response to allegations of religious coercion but rather a study of pastoral care following media reports in 2003 that, in the ten years previous, there had been 142 alleged incidents of rape or sexual assault at the academy, none of which had resulted in an investigation.

"*kill Islam*": On February 6, 2008, the academy hosted as speakers for its Annual Academy Assembly an act billing itself as "The 3 Ex-Terrorists": "They don't sing. But they speak the truth," declares their slogan. As their name suggests, the three claim to have been terrorists for Islam, responsible for the murder of hundreds, before they converted to Christianity and found successful careers on the evangelical lecture circuit. "You want to know if I think we should kill Muslims," declared the lead speaker, a Palestinian convert called Walid Shoebat, who's popular on the Christian apocalypse circuit, lecturing on behalf of *Left Behind* author Tim LaHaye's rapture rallies. "I would never say that, that would be a stupid thing to say. We have to kill Islam." E-mail to Mikey Weinstein, from a member of the academy's faculty who prefers to remain anonymous, April 3, 2008.

"It keeps me awake at night": Weinstein and Seay, *With God on Our Side,* 115–16.

"Developing Purpose-Driven Airmen": Captain Christian Biscotti, "A New Approach to Suicide Prevention: Developing Purpose-Driven Airmen," presented at a Third Air Force Commander's Call, Lt. Gen. Rod Bishop, Commander. Ostensibly part of a suicide prevention program, "Developing Purpose-Driven Airmen" doesn't actually address suicide. Rather, it purports to use Warren's evangelical principles to make troops "combat ready and effective," offering as an example the late Arizona Cardinals football star and U.S. Army Ranger Pat Tillman. Tillman, as it happens, was an atheist. The army, meanwhile, relies on Pittsburgh Steelers legend Terry Bradshaw, who offers his Christian testimony in a disturbing video incorporated into another "suicide prevention" program emphasizing "the importance of faith." Bradshaw dabs invisible sweat from his massive, dimpled chin and discusses a bout of depression resistant to therapy, drugs, and "books on human behavior." The off-screen interviewer leads him to an answer, asking if his faith helped. "Oh, yeah. Well, I'm a Christian, for one thing." In the military, he continues, "who do you talk to? I'm sitting here thinking, 'Who do these young people talk to?' Your sergeant? That's a tough deal. I talked to a preacher.... My preacher was the first man I turned to." "Suicide Awareness for Leaders, 2007" and "Suicide Awareness for Soldiers, 2008."

"Under the rubric of free speech...": Dr. Bill McCoy's Amazon Blog, http://www.amazon.com/gp/blog/post/PLNK2R98UC5LSSFMQ, accessed August 17, 2008; following an article by Chris Rodda, senior research director for the Military Religious Freedom Foundation ("Petraeus Endorses 'Spiritual Handbook,' Betrays 21% of Our Troops," *Huffington Post,* August 17, 2008, http://www.huffington post.com/chris-rodda/petraeus-endorses-spiritu_b_119242.html), these comments were removed from Col. McCoy's blog.

"bring havoc": William McCoy, *Under Orders: A Spiritual Handbook for Military Personnel,* 2nd ed. (Keizer, OR: Edein Publishing, 2007), 147.

"Under Orders should be in every rucksack": General Petraeus quoted in back matter, McCoy, *Under Orders.*

"If I was the bad guys": Author's interview.

"I knew that my God": Richard T. Cooper, "General Casts War in Religious Terms," *Los Angeles Times,* October 16, 2003.

"demonic spirit": Rebecca Leung, "The Holy Warrior; General Called a Religious Fanatic Finally Speaks Out," *60 Minutes*, September 15, 2004, http://www.cbsnews.com/stories/2004/09/15/60II/main643650.shtml.

"Gitmo-ize": Sidney Blumenthal, *How Bush Rules: Chronicles of a Radical Regime* (Princeton, NJ: Princeton University Press, 2006), 66.

"there is less and less acceptance": Interview by research assistant Vanessa Hartmann.

"Here comes a guy": Chuck Fager, e-mail message to Mikey Weinstein, August 25, 2009.

"defend Jewish causes": "I find it difficult to defend Jewish causes around the world and, at the same time, have men like yourself trying to use increased government regulation to limit freedom here at home." Ted Haggard to Mikey Weinstein, quoted in Weinstein and Seay, *With God on Our Side*, 91.

"We needed this fuse lit": Author's interview.

Jeremy Hall: Author's interview with Jeremy Hall. Hall joined the army in 2004. "I figured if I go to Iraq, I'm doing God's work, because it's heathen country." Deployed to Iraq for the first time in 2006, Hall began to question his assumptions, then his faith. Sent for a second tour in 2007, he formed a chapter of an organization called the Military Association of Atheists and Freethinkers. He was thrilled when an officer, Maj. Freddy Welborn, showed up at its first meeting,. When I reached Welborn, he told me, "I asked the young man, 'What are your goals?' And he said, you won't believe this, 'To take God out of country, to take God off the money.' I said, 'How can you do that? I thought you took an oath to defend the Constitution. How can you recruit kids to come to this, and do this with you, to do unconstitutional things? It's wartime!'" Author's interview with Maj. Freddy Welborn.

The crux of the matter for Hall was what he and another enlisted man say was Welborn's warning: don't bother reenlisting. Hall, a soldier with a perfect record, contacted the Military Religious Freedom Foundation, which helped him go public. That made things worse. Soon he was getting death threats. Another soldier, whom I was able to interview on background, was assigned as a bodyguard. His commanders moved him to the sergeants' barracks, but the threats kept coming, and the army sent Hall home a month early. Before his troubles, Hall had loved the army;

he'd planned on making it a career. "I was a shiner," he recalled. But despite near-perfect ratings, he couldn't even get himself considered for promotion. One sergeant told him that a soldier who can't pray with his troops can't lead them.

Eli Agee: Author's interview.

"Sir, . . . this recruit's bleeding": David Winters's letter to Mikey Weinstein, June 4, 2009.

"Weinstein is steamed": Ret. Lt. Col. Hugh Morgan, e-mail message to Billy Baugham, November 2, 2005.

"a very angry Jewish man": Billy Baugham, e-mail message to Chaplaincy of Full Gospel Churches et al., April 3, 2006. The Chaplaincy of Full Gospel Churches claims to be the endorsing agency for more than 270 military chaplains and chaplain candidates and to represent 15 million "Spirit-filled believers." Chaplaincy of Full Gospel Churches, "About the CFGC!" Chaplaincy of Full Gospel Churches, http://www.chaplaincyfullgospel.org/about.aspx.

"lawyer, Jewish": Ret. Col. Jim Ammerman, e-mail message to Chaplain Maj. Randy Wren of the army, May 26, 2006.

"I feel safer": Quoted in Martha C. Nussbaum, *Liberty of Conscience: In Defense of America's Tradition of Religious Equality* (New York: Perseus, 2007), 47. These comments are drawn from my review, in *The Nation*, of Nussbaum's important book, a "careful reconstruction of Williams as a thinker at least as important to the tradition of liberty of conscience—the term she prefers to religion—as Locke and all the founders who followed. 'We should not focus only on the eighteenth-century arguments of the framers,' she writes, 'ignoring this prior, and distinctly American, tradition, quintessentially embodied in Williams's *The Bloudy Tenent of Persecution*,' a 1644 text that was remarkable for the empathy it extended to persecutors and persecuted alike and its call for government to refrain from enforcing orthodoxy. Recognition of good-faith differences of conviction, he believed, revealed a surer path to civil peace and liberty of conscience. The two values, so often seen as pitted against each other, were in Williams's account intertwined." Sharlet, "Beyond Belief," *The Nation*, June 9, 2008.

"I am come to send fire": "LBJ, Billy Graham Eloquent at Breakfasts," *Washington Post*, February 18, 1966.

"This is a mission field": Author's interview.

"I refused": Weinstein and Seay, *With God on Our Side*, 102–3.

"it made Christians look like Nazis": Ibid., 82.

"I was fired": Ibid., 112.

"'Afghans say "this is a sign from God"'": Kevin Dougherty, "Rainfall May Signal Beginning of the End to Three-Year Drought in Afghanistan," *Stars and Stripes,* January 16, 2005, http://www.stripes.com/news/rainfall-may-signal-beginning-of-the-end-to-three-year -drought-in-afghanistan-1.28144.

"the unsaved": Brig. Gen. Donald C. Wurster, "Centurions in the Conflict," Officers' Christian Fellowship, http://www.ocfusa.org/articles/centurions-conflict/.

CHAPTER 6: The Now

"The Wilberforce Republican": "The Wilberforce Republican: Sam Brownback Is Redefining the Christian Right," *Economist,* March 11, 2006.

A fight…to roll back…gun laws: John Ensign, "Gun Rights on the Line," *Washington Post,* March 13, 2009.

concealed weapons into churches: Brian Montopoli, "Guns in Church? Jindal Signs Louisiana Bill into Law," CBS News, July 8, 2010, http://www.cbsnews.com/8301-503544_162-20009977-503544.html; "Bill Would Allow Concealed Guns in Church," *Arkansas News,* January 27, 2009.

2010 Utah law: Carl Wimmer, House Bill 12, Criminal Homicide and Abortion Amendments, 2010, available at http://le.utah.gov/~2010/bills/hbillenr/hb0012.htm. See also Pamela M. Prah, "States Try New Tactics to Restrict Abortion," *Stateline,* July 15, 2010, http://www.stateline.org/live/details/story?contentId=498491.

it can be drowned in a bathtub: Thomas Frank, *The Wrecking Crew: How Conservatives Rule* (New York: Henry Holt and Company, 2008), 45.

"the first time…nonviolent activity": "Supreme Court Ruling Criminalizes Speech in Material Sport Law Case," *Center for Constitutional Rights,* June 21, 2010, http://ccrjustice.org/newsroom/press-releases/supreme-court-ruling-criminalizes-speech -material-support-law-case.

"Kind of a yin to the yang": Author's interview.

Dennis Bakke: See D. Michael Lindsay, "Is the National Prayer Breakfast Surrounded by a 'Christian Mafia'? Religious Publicity and Secrecy

Within the Corridors of Power," *Journal of the American Academy of Religion* 14, no. 2 (June 2006): 390–419. Bakke is also a friend of Uganda, or, at least, its ruling elite. I wrote about Bakke's involvement with what became one of the biggest corruption scandals of the Museveni regime—a project he describes as "God's work"—in *The Family: The Secret Fundamentalism at the Heart of American Power* (New York: Harper, 2008), 23. On Bakke's educational theories, see his book *Joy at Work: A Revolutionary Approach to Fun on the Job* (PVG, 2005), distributed free in at least one of the publicly funded charter schools run by Bakke's Imagine Schools, the biggest commercial manager of such institutions in the United States. "The movement to keep God out of the schools, government, and companies is contrary to the biblical mandate to steward all parts of the Creation, including the public institutions we call secular," writes Bakke (252). Proposing the churches subsidize teachers in public schools, he says, instructors "would be marked by the church as God's ambassadors to the children in the neighborhood schools." For perspectives on Imagine School's less than transparent approach, see also Stephanie Strom, "For School Company, Issues of Money and Control," *New York Times*, April 23, 2010, and Greg Richmond, "Who's in Charge at Charter Schools?," *Education Week*, July 14, 2010. Richmond, the president of the National Association of Charter School Authorizers, argues that companies like Imagine give charter schools a bad name, taking advantage of and sometimes even getting ahead of laws that turn "the concept of accountability on its head." Bakke, writes Richmond, "urged his staff to get undated letters of resignation from all board members and to remove members who didn't behave to Imagine's liking. 'It is our school, our money, and our risk, not theirs.'...He's wrong. It is a public school, it is the public's money, and the risk is being borne by thousands of parents and students who enroll at an Imagine school."

"Starve doubts": Vereide quoted in an obituary in *News in the Campus Work*, June 6, 1969 (no. 3), box 475, collection 459, BGCA.

"the nightingale of the House of Commons": R. Coupland, *Wilberforce: A Narrative* (Oxford: Oxford University Press, 1923), 4.

"There were very few that stood against the Enlightenment": Author's interview.

"all the era's repressive measures": Adam Hochschild, *Bury the Chains: Prophets and Rebels in the Fight to Free an Empire's Slaves* (Boston: Houghton Mifflin, 2005), 252.

"Went to Pitt's": Ibid., 246.

"mad-headed professors of equality and liberty": Coupland, *Wilberforce*, 179.

"The first year that I was in Parliament": Ibid., 91.

"the wittiest man in England": Eric Metaxas, *Amazing Grace: William Wilberforce and the Heroic Campaign to End Slavery* (New York: HarperOne, 2007), 28.

"I saw what seemed a mere shrimp": Coupland, *Wilberforce*, 4.

"perversion": Ibid., 33.

save Shakespeare: Hochschild, *Bury the Chains*, 251.

"shame": Coupland, *Wilberforce*, 366–68.

"the ancient censorship": Ibid., 54.

"grateful peasantry": Hochschild, *Bury the Chains*, 314.

"that their more lowly path": Ibid.

"He must never be morbid": Coupland, *Wilberforce*, 89.

Index